the **200**

MOST FREQUENTLY ASKED

LEGAL

QUESTIONS

for **EDUCATORS**

*This book is dedicated to my wife, Lorene, and my children,
Kimberly, Jarvis, and Nathalie. They have and continue to be my inspiration
and my greatest fans. To each of them, I am eternally grateful.*

the 200

MOST FREQUENTLY ASKED

LEGAL
QUESTIONS
for EDUCATORS

NATHAN L. ESSEX

CORWIN
A SAGE Company

For information:

Corwin
A SAGE Company
2455 Teller Road
Thousand Oaks, California 91320
(800) 233-9936
Fax: (800) 417-2466
www.corwinpress.com

SAGE India Pvt. Ltd.
B 1/I 1 Mohan Cooperative
  Industrial Area
Mathura Road, New Delhi 110 044
India

SAGE Ltd.
1 Oliver's Yard
55 City Road
London EC1Y 1SP
United Kingdom

SAGE Asia-Pacific Pte. Ltd.
33 Pekin Street #02-01
Far East Square
Singapore 048763

Printed in the United States of America

Library of Congress Cataloging-in-Publication Data

Essex, Nathan L.
The 200 most frequently asked legal questions for educators/Nathan L. Essex.
    p. cm.
Includes index.
ISBN 978-1-4129-6576-7 (cloth : alk. paper)
ISBN 978-1-4129-6577-4 (pbk. : alk. paper)
    1. Educational law and legislation—United States. 2. School management and organization—Law and legislation—United States. I. Title. II. Title: Two hundred most frequently asked legal questions for educators. III. Title: Most frequently asked legal questions for educators.

KF4119.85.E849 2010
344.73'071—dc22   2009007518

This book is printed on acid-free paper.

09   10   11   12   13   10   9   8   7   6   5   4   3   2   1

Acquisitions Editor:	Arnis Burvikovs
Associate Editor:	Desirée A. Bartlett
Production and Copy Editor:	Jane Haenel
Typesetter:	C&M Digitals (P) Ltd.
Proofreader:	Jeff Bryant
Indexer:	Molly Hall
Cover and Graphic Designer:	Scott Van Atta

Contents

Preface

Teachers face enormous legal challenges as they attempt to execute their legal duties of providing instruction, supervision, and a safe environment for students under their care. To properly fulfill these important duties, teachers must be aware of the legal forces that affect them on a daily basis. Teachers must also possess the necessary legal knowledge that will allow them to make legally sound decisions as they attempt to operate within the boundaries of the U.S. Constitution, federal and state laws, and school district policy.

The goal of this book is to provide a comprehensive set of carefully crafted legal questions and responses that will provide invaluable information to assist teachers in performing their duties effectively while minimizing their exposure to legal challenges. The information contained in this book is designed to be used by preservice teachers, inservice teachers, educators, and policymakers as a means of familiarizing them with basic aspects of law that impact them daily. Familiarity with aspects of law will lessen their anxiety and provide clarity regarding practices that are legally defensible and those that are not. In all cases, teachers and other professional educators should consult their school district policies for the specific application of law to their particular duties and responsibilities.

This text is not intended to provide legal advice but rather to present a wide range of legal topics in question-and-answer format based on the U.S. Constitution, federal statutes, and court decisions. The text is intended as a general guide regarding legal issues. While the information is deemed accurate at the time of publication, it does not constitute specific legal advice for teachers. These questions and answers are intended to provide guidance and direction for teachers and policymakers as they perform their professional duties.

One salient feature of this book is the inclusion of carefully selected tables that amplify and reinforce concepts covered in various chapters. Additionally, chapter guides are included that summarize key concepts discussed in each chapter. The text is written in a very simple and practical format free of legal jargon. It provides for easy reading and a direct response to legal questions raised throughout the book. Legal citations are provided to support various topics discussed, thereby allowing the reader to readily identify the legal source of authority related to specific topics. This text does not cover all issues regarding school law, but it does address legal issues that should be most pertinent to preservice teachers, inservice teachers, and professional educators. Finally, the text concludes with a resources section that includes selected amendments to the U.S. Constitution as well as annotated federal statutes that provide additional background information to assist teachers in understanding the relevance of the legal framework to the daily operation of their schools. A compilation of professional associations for teachers is included. A glossary of relevant terms is also provided to reinforce an understanding of concepts discussed in the text.

Although this text includes a range of legal questions and issues confronting teachers, some issues facing teachers may not have been presently addressed by the courts. However, the book does provide practical and useful information that will enable teachers to perform their important duties more effectively as they provide an optimal learning environment for students.

Acknowledgments

My sincere appreciation is expressed to my assistant, Carol Brown, for her diligence, passion, and technical expertise that enabled me to prepare this text. Her support and encouragement far exceeded my expectations.

I express gratitude to the following reviewers who provided their expertise and constructive suggestions that contributed to a more complete text:

Kermit Buckner, Professor
Department of Educational
  Leadership
East Carolina University
Greenville, NC

Paul Englesberg, Professor
Richard W. Riley College of
  Education and Leadership
Walden University
Minneapolis, MN

David Freitas, Professor of
  Education
Indiana University South Bend
South Bend, IN

Lisa Graham, Special Education
  Program Specialist
Vallejo City Unified School
  District
Vallejo, CA

Dolores M. Gribouski
Manager of Student Support
  Services and Alternative
  Programs
Worcester Public Schools
Worcester, MA

Carol S. Holzberg, Technology
  Coordinator
Greenfield Public Schools
Greenfield, MA

Sharon M. Redfern, Elementary
  Principal
Highland Park Elementary School
Lewistown, MT

Rose Reissman, Law Consultant
Law, Education, and Peace for Kids
Philadelphia, PA

About the Author

Nathan L. Essex is professor of Educational Law and Leadership at the University of Memphis and president of Southwest Tennessee Community College. He received a BS degree in English at Alabama A&M University, an MS degree in Educational Administration at Jacksonville State University, and his PhD in Administration and Planning at The University of Alabama.

He held public school teaching and administrative positions prior to completing his doctorate. Essex's interests include law, educational policy, and personnel administration. He has served as a consultant for more than 100 school districts and numerous educational agencies. He served as a policy consultant with the Alabama State Department of Education for twelve years and received numerous awards in recognition of his contributions in the field of education. He is the recipient of the Truman M. Pierce Award for Educational Leadership and outstanding contributions that advanced the direction of education in the state of Alabama; the Academic Excellence Award in recognition of professional achievement and academic excellence in the research, service, and teaching of education, Capstone College of Education Society; The University of Alabama Teaching Excellence Award; the Distinguished Service Award—*Who's Who in the State of Tennessee*; The University of Memphis Distinguished Administrator of the Year 1995–1996; "Educator on the Move," The University of Memphis; Phi Delta Kappa; the President's award for leadership and service to the community, Youth Services, Inc.; *Who's Who in Corporate Memphis, Grace* magazine; and President Bush's Community Service Award, just to name a few. Essex has published numerous articles, book chapters, and newsletters on legal issues. Many of his works appear in *The Administrator's Notebook, The Horizon, Compensation Review, The Clearinghouse, The American School Board Journal, American Management Association, Community College Review, Education and Law,* and many other professional journals. Essex has authored a law textbook titled *School Law and the Public Schools—a Practical Guide for Educational Leaders.* A fourth edition was released in January 2007. Essex has also published a textbook for public school teachers titled *Pocket Guide to School Law* and a booklet on No Child Left Behind. He is highly sought by educators at all levels to share his knowledge and expertise regarding legal and policy issues that affect educational organizations.

1

Educators and the Legal System

✦ INTRODUCTION ✦

The federal Constitution, state constitutions, and statutory laws provide the framework within which public schools operate. The Tenth Amendment to the U.S. Constitution enumerates that:

> The powers not delegated to the United States by the Constitution, nor prohibited by it to the states are reserved to the states respectively and to the people.

Consequently, the legal authority to establish and operate public schools resides with the state legislature. The legislature delegates the day-to-day operation and management of schools to local school officials. Therefore, it is important that teachers understand the legal framework that affects schools to ensure that they are operating within the boundaries of the law, particularly with respect to their prescribed duties and responsibilities. School rules and regulations must meet the requirement of legal defensibility to avoid conflicts with federal or state constitutional provisions, federal or state statutes, as well as case law. Teachers are expected to adhere to their school rules and district policies as they perform their teaching duties.

1. How Are Teachers Impacted by the U.S. Constitution, State Constitutions, and Federal and State Laws?

They all determine, to a large degree, the legal parameters within which teachers are expected to operate in their daily professional activities. Teachers must understand these parameters to ensure that their actions are legally defensible.

2. Why Is the United States Constitution So Important?

The U.S. Constitution is the primary source of law and the basic law of the land. All federal statutes, state constitutions, state laws, local ordinances, and school district policies are subordinate to the U.S. Constitution. Although the Constitution does not refer to education, school rules and regulations must conform to the basic provisions of the Constitution to ensure fundamental fairness and avoid legal challenges. Specific constitutional amendments affecting the operation of schools include the following:

- The **First Amendment** covers freedom of speech, the press, assembly, and religion. Most First Amendment conflicts in public schools center around symbolic expression, religious freedom, and verbal and written forms of expression, most notably involving students and teachers.
- The **Fourth Amendment** protects students from unreasonable searches and seizures and most often involves teachers in connection with their privacy rights.
- The **Fifth Amendment** provides protection for individuals accused of crimes from self-incrimination and most often involves school personnel who have been accused of improprieties involving school funds or equipment. This amendment essentially ensures that the government cannot deprive an individual of life, liberty, or property without due process. However, it should be noted that almost all school operations involve civil rather than criminal issues.
- The **Eighth Amendment** provides protection against cruel and unusual punishment and is generally cited by students in connection with the administration of corporal punishment. However, the courts have held that the Eighth Amendment applies to individuals who have been accused of crimes rather than students who are corporally punished.
- The **Fourteenth Amendment** ensures that students and teachers receive fundamental fairness in their dealings with public schools. The most prominent aspect of due process is the "equal protection" clause, which provides protection to students and teachers by ensuring that the requirements of substantive and procedural due process

are met. Procedural due process requires that a constitutionally valid procedure be employed in cases where a person's life, liberty, or property may be in jeopardy. Substantive due process requires that the state have a valid objective if it is contemplating depriving a person of life, liberty, or property. These aspects typically apply to student disciplinary matters and issues involving teacher dismissal.

These amendments to the U.S. Constitution impact school officials in their management of schools by requiring that their decisions and actions regarding students and school personnel are consistent with constitutional requirements.

3. What Should Teachers Know About Their State Constitution?

State constitutions serve the same purpose at the state level that the U.S. Constitution serves at the national level; however, state constitutions are subject to the requirements of the U.S. Constitution. State constitutions place restrictions on legislative bodies. Legislative authority is also subject to the requirements of federal law and the federal Constitution. State constitutions address the same subject matter as does the federal Constitution, including church-state relations (equal protection and individual freedoms), and prescribes certain acts that the legislature is required to perform, most notably establishing a system of public education. State constitutions represent the foundational law of each state. They essentially require that certain acts be fulfilled by legislatures, one of which involves the establishment of public education systems.

4. How Do State Agencies Affect Teachers?

State agencies are legal entities established by state legislatures. Their primary role is to ensure that state laws and policies are executed properly by local school districts. The state school board occupies prominence as a state agent. Its duties and responsibilities are determined by the state legislature. Certain powers are also delegated to the state school board. Most board members are elected by popular vote; however, in other cases, they are appointed by the governor.

5. What Are the Responsibilities of the State Board of Education?

The state board is generally provided the latitude to issue mandates and directives that affect teachers regarding local school operations, many of which carry legal ramifications. The state board, through delegated power, may develop policies covering a wide range of legal issues such as health and safety of students and employees and disciplinary practices that affect students. It also may determine through delegated authority by the legislature certification requirements for school personnel and exit requirements for graduating students, including testing and accreditation standards. The state board is essentially a policymaking body that provides guidance and direction for teachers and schools throughout the state. One important duty of many state boards of education involves the selection of a chief state school officer (CSSO). In some states, however, the CSSO is elected by popular vote.

Although the state legislature has the authority to prescribe curriculum offerings and student performance standards, the legislature may delegate that authority to the public schools; however, curriculum and content standards are typically adopted by the state board of education. These standards generally reflect a consensus among classroom teachers, parents, school administrators, and business and community leaders of what students must learn.

Curriculum standards describe the state's expectations for student learning and achievement in all grade levels and content areas. A curriculum framework or course of study may be provided that details specific knowledge and skills students must possess to meet subject matter standards. Students may be required to take state-mandated tests as a means of measuring achievement in certain content areas. Teachers are accountable for following the state course of study and ensuring that the required course content is taught in their classrooms. Content standards are designed to facilitate the highest level of student achievement through defining specific knowledge, skills, and competencies students should acquire at each grade level.

6. What Are the Responsibilities of the State Department of Education?

Each state has established a state department of education under the leadership of a CSSO that provides statewide regulatory authority. The state department also employs specialists in every area essential to school operations. The state department of education conducts research on school practices, develops short- and long-term plans for educational outcomes, enforces state and federal law, evaluates districts for accreditation, evaluates statewide testing programs, and monitors compliance of state-approved curriculum, among other duties. Although there are variations among the states, most state departments consist of specialists in the following areas: administration and finance, disability services, instruction, legislation and research, professional standards, and audits and management, among others. The department provides services and support to local school systems in virtually all aspects of local school district operations.

7. How Do Local Boards of Education Exert Control Over Public Schools?

Local school boards are responsible for the daily operations of schools in their district. Their primary role is to function as a policymaking body. The board acts as a corporate body. Individual board members have no power except for what is vested in the board as a corporate body. Board members are either elected by constituents in their geographical regions or appointed by the mayor with concurrence by city councils. In some states, one of the most important decisions local boards render involves the selection of a school district's superintendent. Superintendents are elected by citizens in other states. School boards are provided local discretion as long as their actions are not in conflict with state or federal law, federal and state constitutions, and applicable case law.

Courts are generally reluctant to interfere with school board decisions but will do so when a challenge arises involving constitutional or statutory issues. Local school policies are developed by the school board. These policies define the roles and responsibilities of teachers and also place certain legal restrictions on teachers consistent with federal and state constitutions, federal state statutes, and court rulings. School board meetings are open sessions that teachers, citizens, or other interested parties may attend. School boards hold executive session when sensitive issues involving personnel are discussed, at which time the meeting is closed to the general public.

As an example, a controversy arose in Pennsylvania when a local newspaper challenged the school board's authority to hold an executive session. The board had contracted a consultant to assist in the selection of a new superintendent of schools. Candidates were screened and reduced to a pool of six applicants. The board held an executive session to interview five candidates. A public meeting was held following the executive session to secure citizen input. The board subsequently held an executive session to interview three finalists and ranked them in order of preference. Following the fourth executive session, a public meeting was held during which time the board voted for its choice.

A newspaper publisher filed suit in a Pennsylvania trial court for a declaratory ruling that the board had violated the state's sunshine law (or open meeting law) by in effect voting in the executive session rather than at the public meeting. The court held that the executive session was permissible under the Sunshine Act because deliberations and discussions occurred rather than official actions. The publisher appealed to the Commonwealth of Pennsylvania. The commonwealth court observed that employment was an exception to the Sunshine Act. The court rejected the publisher's claim that votes taken in executive session constituted official action under the act. The actions taken in executive session were to reduce the field of candidates and constituted only deliberations; therefore, it was unnecessary for these meetings to be open to the public or for the school board to record votes. The commonwealth court affirmed the judgment of the trial court.[1]

School board policies carry the force of law in public schools as long as they do not conflict with federal or state constitutions, federal or state statutes, or applicable case law. Policies establish a direction and a course of action for school districts that affect teachers and students alike. Policies assign authority and indicate what actions should be taken and by whom in a given situation. They also establish controls and ensure that schools are accountable to the general public. Policies are typically broad in scope and cover a wide range of subject matter such as students' rights and responsibilities, curriculum and instruction issues, personnel employment practices, administration, fiscal management, facilities, community relations, and school organization and athletic programs, among others. Policies set parameters so that students, faculty, and staff understand expectations of the district. Courts may be called upon when school district policy is challenged to determine if a particular policy meets constitutional requirements at both the state and federal levels.

8. What Is the Role of the Local School Superintendent?

Local school superintendents are the chief executive officers who are responsible and accountable for the overall operations of the district. They provide a vision for the district and determine in consultation with senior-level staff the strategies needed to fulfill their vision. Local superintendents are delegated overall responsibility for selecting teachers, administrators, and staff members with school board approval. They also assume responsibility for the district's budget, facilities, student transportation, and curriculum. Superintendents are either appointed by the board or elected by local citizens. Whether appointed or elected, they must be knowledgeable about numerous state and federal laws and federal and state regulations, as well as local ordinances that affect the daily operation of the school since they are held accountable for ensuring that their districts are in compliance with all applicable laws, rules, and regulations. Superintendents are accountable to their boards as well as to the citizens of the community. The relationship between the school board and the superintendent is best described as a legislative/executive relationship where the board sets policy and the superintendent executes approved policy.

9. What Is the Most Significant Role Played by the Federal Government in Reforming Public Schools?

Perhaps the most sweeping legislation to date involves the No Child Left Behind (NCLB) Act of 2001, a landmark educational reform initiative designed to improve student achievement in low-performing schools and to change the culture of schools in America. With the passage of NCLB, Congress reauthorized the Elementary and Secondary Education Act (ESEA) of 1965. Raised standards and expectations for students and teachers are designed to ensure that a certain level of proficiency is reached by all students in reading and mathematics during their twelve years of schooling. While NCLB has been met with a number of challenges from various states, it continues to be supported by Congress. Reauthorization is pending by the Congress. One of the most critical issues regarding NCLB for state legislators and educational policymakers is that the funds appropriated by the federal government are not viewed as adequate to cover the expenses the law imposes on state government and local school districts. The law is thus seen by many as an unfunded mandate. (See Chapter 14 for a more comprehensive discussion of NCLB.)

10. What Primary Sources of Legal Protections Are Available to Teachers to Alleviate Unfair Treatment in Their Schools?

Federal laws protect teachers from discrimination in the operation of public schools by requiring that the actions of school officials be compliant with the intent of the law. Examples of these laws include the following:

- Civil Rights Act of 1964, Title VI
- Civil Rights Act of 1964, Title VII
- Education Amendment of 1972, Title IX
- Americans with Disabilities Act of 1990
- Age Discrimination in Employment Act of 1967
- Equal Access Act of 1964
- Family and Medical Leave Act
- Section 504 of the Rehabilitation Act of 1973, as well as Title II of the Americans with Disabilities Act of 1990

The laws are designed to protect teachers and school personnel against discriminatory acts based on race, gender, age, national origin, religion, disabilities, childbirth, and family illnesses. School officials must thus ensure that their decisions regarding teachers and other school personnel in these areas are legally defensible. Various federal agencies may be employed when teachers believe their rights have been violated. The Office of Civil Rights handles cases based on sexual discrimination, as does the Equal Education Opportunity Commission (EEOC). The EEOC also handles other forms of discrimination listed under Title VII. Teachers can bring action in federal court after other administrative remedies have been exhausted. See Resource A for a more comprehensive listing of federal statutes and penalties imposed for noncompliance. While this list is not all-inclusive, public schools must meet the provisions of these acts or face court litigation when violations occur.

11. How Does the Court System Affect Teachers in Public Schools?

Court rulings comprise an abundant source of law that influences how public schools operate. The courts, through their decision-making powers, alter numerous practices in public schools when there is evidence that the constitutional rights of students have been jeopardized. Case law defines relationships among administrators, teachers, and students through defined limits of authority, control, and personal freedoms.

The U.S. Constitution represents the leading source of law. All statutes, both federal and state as well as case law, are subordinate to the U.S. Constitution, meaning that they cannot be in conflict with federal constitutional provisions. Case law is subordinate to statutes unless there is evidence that state law conflicts with the Constitution, in which case court decisions or case law take precedence by invalidating the statutes in question.

Most cases pertaining to public schools that involve nonfederal questions are litigated in state courts. Those involving federal issues may be litigated at either the state or federal level. School policies and practices must be in conformity with both state and federal constitutional provisions. If they are not, when challenged, they will be ruled invalid. When a challenge is addressed by the courts, they apply basic principles of law to the factual circumstances to determine the constitutionality of the challenged school practice. In this way, the courts exercise considerable influence over the operation and management of schools. Court decisions set legal limits on the prerogatives teachers may exercise in relationship to students. Teachers must be knowledgeable of the legal parameters that must be met in their decisions and actions involving students. Court decisions represent one of the primary sources of law affecting school operations.

THE COURT SYSTEM

The court system affects schools by providing a source of law that determines whether school policies and practices are legally defensible. There is a dual system of courts: one system operates at the federal level, while the other system operates at the state level. Many educational cases are heard in state courts but may also be heard in federal courts when constitutional issues are involved. When conflicts arise, state courts are often called upon to interpret the state's constitution or statutes.

FEDERAL COURTS

Federal courts were established by Article II, Section I, of the U.S. Constitution. Federal jurisdiction is created by federal district congressional acts. The number of courts is determined by state population, with each state having at least one federal court. Larger states typically have three to four courts. The federal trial court of general jurisdiction is called the U.S. district court. Each state incorporates one or more districts for a total of ninety-five federal districts. These courts address cases involving federal or constitutional questions. They are limited to issues that are presented for resolution. Figure 1.1 depicts the federal court system.

In many instances, cases are appealed to a federal circuit court of appeals. There are thirteen federal circuit courts, eleven with geographic jurisdiction involving a number of states or territories. One court has national jurisdiction for the District of Columbia, and one involves three specialized federal courts. Figure 1.2 depicts the U.S. courts of appeals and district courts.

U.S. SUPREME COURT

The U.S. Supreme Court was established by the Constitution and presides over the basic law of the land. As stated previously, all other federal and state courts are subordinate to the U.S. Supreme Court. The nine justices who comprise the Supreme Court are required to consider appeals on a limited basis and may elect to accept an appeal from a lower court if four justices agree to accept the case. Four concurring justices must also vote to

Figure 1.1   Abbreviated U.S. Court System

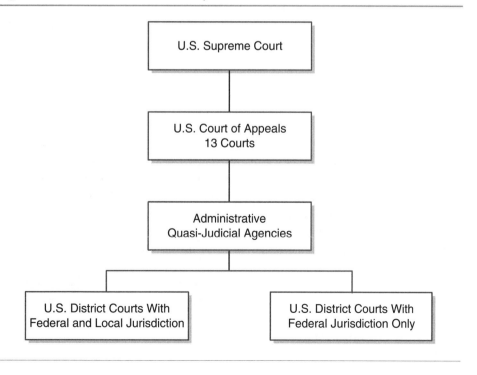

Figure 1.2 Geographic Boundaries of U.S. Courts of Appeals and U.S. District Courts

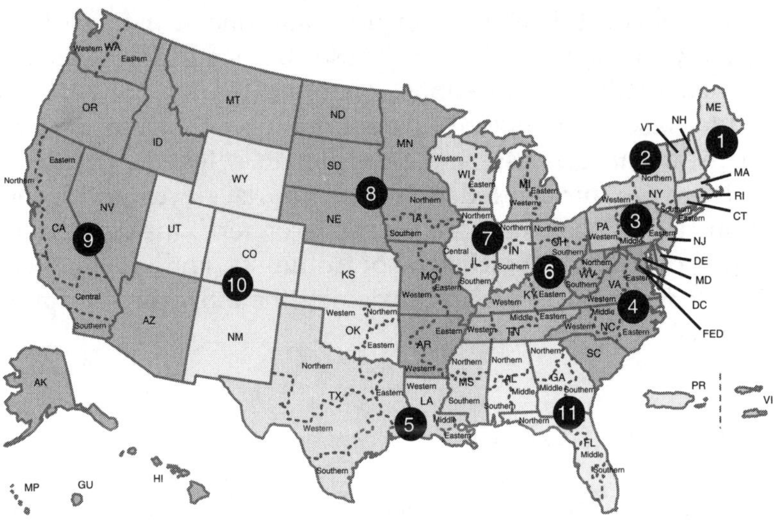

Source: www.uscourts.gov/courtlinks/

grant a review of a case brought to it by a *writ of certiorari*, which involves an original action wherein a case is removed from an inferior court to a superior court for trial. Because the Supreme Court has the discretion to accept or reject reviews from a lower court, many cases are resolved at the lower court level. The U.S. Supreme Court is the highest court in America, beyond which there is no appeal. The system of courts plays a pivotal role in influencing public school management and operational decisions, particularly as they relate to the protection of the individual rights and freedoms of teachers and students.

STATE COURTS

State courts are established in accordance with each state's constitution. The structure of state courts varies depending on the size of the state and the specific language in each state's constitution. Although the courts have broad latitude to review most types of controversies except those limited by state law, they address many of the same issues addressed by the federal courts. They determine the constitutionality of a state or federal law. Since education is a state function, many public school cases are heard by state courts. Structurally, state courts are similar to federal courts (see Figure 1.3). Most states have trial courts of general jurisdiction or special jurisdiction and appellate courts of last resort, sometimes referred to as state supreme courts. Cases can be appealed from the state supreme court to the U.S. Supreme Court.

Figure 1.3   State Judicial System

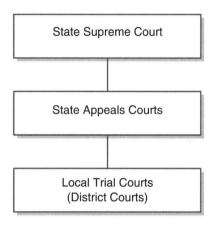

State Supreme Court → State Appeals Courts → Local Trial Courts (District Courts)

Summary Guides

1. Public schools must operate within the framework of federal and state constitutions, federal and state statutes, as well as case law to ensure legal defensibility regarding policies and practices.

2. It is essential that teachers understand the legal parameters that affect school operations.

3. State and federal courts frequently rule on the constitutionality of school practices when these practices are challenged.

4. School policies must not conflict with federal or state constitutional provisions, federal or state laws, or case law.

5. Federal laws involving various forms of discrimination as well as laws designed to improve educational outcomes occupy a pivotal role in the administration of public schools.

6. The legislature prescribes the duties and the authority of state boards of education.

7. Public schools are typically placed under the control of state boards of education.

8. The ultimate authority for public schools rests with state legislatures.

NOTE

1. *Morning Call Inc. v. Board of School Directors of the Southern Leigh School District*, 642 A. 2d 619 (Pa. Cmwlth. 1994).

2

Student Rights and Restrictions

⧈ INTRODUCTION ⧈

Students who attend public schools possess constitutional rights that are not relinquished merely as a condition of school attendance. Prior to the mid-1960s, public school teachers operating *in loco parentis* (in place of parents) exercised considerable authority over students that in many instances infringed upon their personal rights. In the *Tinker v. Des Moines* case (discussed later in this chapter), the U.S. Supreme Court held in a landmark decision that students enjoy many of the same rights as adults and that their rights do not end at the schoolhouse door. The *Tinker* ruling profoundly affected the management and operation of public schools in that it defined relationships between school personnel and students and established the limits of authority that teachers and administrators may exert over the freedom of expression rights of students under their supervision. *Tinker* also set limits for students regarding the exercise of their constitutional rights by defining conditions under which student expression may be regulated. The *Tinker* decision represented the first time the High Court held that school officials did not possess absolute authority over their students. The High Court's ruling also emphasized that student rights are not unlimited but, rather, subject to reasonable restraints by school personnel. While student constitutional rights do not rise to the level of those associated with adults, they are, however, not insignificant. One of the most highly regarded rights associated with students by the courts is freedom of expression. Teachers and school officials must be able to demonstrate that a valid or legitimate purpose exists to justify restricting the constitutional rights of students.

12. Are Students Entitled to Constitutional Protection in Public Schools?

Yes, to a degree. Students possess certain constitutional rights as long as the exercise of those rights does not infringe on the rights of others or creates substantial disruption to the educational process. During the mid-nineteenth century, students enjoyed limited rights in public schools. School officials and teachers exercised considerable control over them. When challenges occurred, they were addressed by state courts that essentially sanctioned practices by school personnel in public schools. Federal courts, for the most part, did not intervene significantly into school matters prior to the mid-1900s. The prevailing view among federal courts during this time was that education was a state function and that conflicts involving public schools were best addressed by state courts. Many parents were reluctant to challenge school practices based on the strength of *in loco parentis,* coupled with the view that school personnel would ultimately be supported by state courts.

During the mid-1900s on a number of occasions, the federal courts assumed a more active role in public school matters and began to measure school practices against the constitutional yardstick to determine their legality. This period of intervention by federal courts represented a major reformation period during which federal courts were no longer willing to allow state courts to be the final arbiter of matters involving the constitutional rights of students. The federal courts' involvement drastically altered relationships between school personnel and students based on court rulings, the most notable of which occurred in *West Virginia v. Barnette,* a case heard by the U.S. Supreme Court. The *Barnette* ruling in 1943 represented one of the few times during this era that the U.S. Supreme Court supported the constitutional rights of students in public schools.[1]

The case arose when public school students were expelled for failure to participate in a compulsory flag salute program. They, along with their parents, faced prosecution for not complying with the compulsory law. The constitutionality of the law was challenged. The court, in its ruling for the students, held that school officials cannot require students to salute and pledge allegiance to the flag. It further ruled that the First Amendment protects expression of political opinion and symbolic speech. The court concluded that passive refusal to salute the flag does not create a danger to the state that justifies impairing the students' rights to belief and expression.

A more recent landmark case challenging the daily ritual of reciting the Pledge of Allegiance arose in the Ninth Circuit Court of California in 2002 regarding the constitutionality of the inclusion of the words *under God*. This case arose when Michael R. Newdow, an atheist, filed a suit on behalf of his eight-year-old daughter, challenging the inclusion of *under God* in the pledge. A panel of the U.S. Court of Appeals for the Ninth Circuit in San Francisco ruled in a 2–1 decision that the inclusion of *under God* was an unconstitutional establishment of religion by the government.

On June 14, 2004, the U.S. Supreme Court overturned the Ninth Circuit Court's decision on technical grounds and preserved the contested phrase "one nation under God" in the Pledge of Allegiance. The Supreme Court ruled that Newdow, the plaintiff, had no legal standing to challenge the pledge since he was not the custodial parent of his daughter and could not legally represent her. This ruling failed to address whether the inclusion of the reference to God was an impermissible practice involving an unconstitutional blending of church and state. Consequently, the U.S. Supreme Court's ruling does not prevent a future lawsuit challenging the inclusion of the phrase "one nation under God" in the pledge. In fact, Newdow and three other plaintiffs who oppose the Pledge of Allegiance filed a later challenge.[2]

One of the most significant freedom of expression cases, *Tinker v. Des Moines Independent School District*, was decided by the U.S. Supreme Court in 1969.[3] *Tinker* focused on the rights of all public school students to free expression and was, in many ways, an extension of *Barnette*. In both *Barnette* and *Tinker*, the U.S. Supreme Court attempted to strike a reasonable balance between the rights of students and the interests of public schools.

The *Tinker* case is significant in that it represents the first time the U.S. Supreme Court declared that students are entitled to constitutional protection in public schools. The *Tinker* case involved an orderly and peaceful protest by students who objected to the Viet Nam War. In *Tinker*, the High Court ruled that school officials cannot restrict freedom of expression rights just because the political viewpoint expressed is displeasing to them. Perhaps the most compelling message by the U.S. Supreme Court stated:

> School officials do not possess absolute authority over their students. Students in school as well as out of school are "persons under our constitution." They possess fundamental rights which the state must respect. . . . In our system, students may not be regarded as closed circuit recipients of only that which the state chooses to communicate. They may not be confined to the expression of those sentiments that are officially approved. In the absence of a specific showing of constitutionally valid reasons to regulate their speech, students are entitled to freedom of expression of their views. Students enjoy constitutional rights similar to those of adults and those rights do not end at the school house door.[4]

It is significant to note the following in *Tinker:*

- The students' protest was orderly and did not create disruption in the school or create a clear and present danger.
- Their expression was merely symbolic.
- Students were entitled to express their political views.
- A crisis policy adopted by the principal was legally indefensible, did not follow normal policy development processes, and was not officially communicated.
- Undifferentiated fear or apprehension of disturbance was not enough to overcome the right of freedom of expression.
- Students' freedom of expression rights would have been supported even if a minor disruption had occurred.

However, in a later case, *Morse v. Frederick,* the U.S. Supreme Court limited its initial response to student expression by holding that speech that is inconsistent with the school's mission can be restricted.[5] Joseph Frederick was a student at Douglas High School in Juneau, Alaska. During an Olympic torch relay event, he held up a fourteen-foot-long banner that read "Bong Hits 4 Jesus." Even though he was standing on a public sidewalk off the school campus, high school principal Deborah Morse suspended Frederick for ten days for violating the school's policy against promoting illegal substances at a school-sanctioned event. In response to his suspension, Frederick brought suit against the school alleging that his First Amendment right to free speech had been violated.

The Ninth Circuit Court of Appeals held for Frederick by ruling that Morse had violated his right to free speech by suspending him from school. The school district appealed to the U.S. Supreme Court. In June of 2007, the U.S. Supreme Court ruled in a 5–4 decision that the school has a right to discipline students who present messages that conflict with stated antidrug policies, even when there is an absence of disruption in the school. Several points were relevant in this decision:

1. Student speech is not unlimited but subject to reasonable restriction.

2. Restricting expression that directly conflicts with clearly stated school policy is not considered an unreasonable exercise of administrative authority.

3. The impact of the message on the school's mission, not the place where it occurs, allows school officials to discipline students.

4. Free speech may be restricted based on school policies that are reasonably developed to address special circumstances in the school's environment.

5. School officials have a responsibility based on *in loco parentis* to protect the health, safety, and welfare of students under their functional custody.

6. Free speech that receives protection for adults is not necessarily protected for public school students.

13. How Do the Courts View the Interests of Students Versus the Interests of the State in Matters Involving Student Rights?

Students who attend public school have certain interests that are safeguarded by the courts. Because students enjoy a level of constitutional freedom in schools, they should expect, for example, fairness and equality of treatment. They should expect protection against unreasonable invasion of privacy, a right to be themselves within reasonable limits, and a right to due process, freedom of speech, press, and assembly. For constitutional purposes, students have a right to be treated similarly to adults.

In contrast, the state, through school districts, teachers, and administrators, has an interest in safe and peaceful schools, a right to require obedience to reasonable school rules, a right to expect prompt attendance, and a right to ban disruptive behavior among students. When a conflict arises involving infringement of students' rights or interests, the court will weigh student interests against the state's interests. If the evidence reveals that educators had a compelling state interest for restricting student rights, the courts will typically support the actions of teachers and administrators. Conversely, if evidence reveals that teachers and administrators had no legitimate interests that justify those infringements on students' rights, the courts will typically support students. The courts attempt to balance the rights of students against special interests of schools as agents of the state.

An example of the court's support for a legitimate state interest was reflected in *Ponce v. Socorro*. The U.S. Court of Appeals for the Fifth Circuit ruled that school officials did not violate a Texas high school student's free speech rights when they disciplined him for entries in his personal journal referring to mounting a "Columbine"-style attack on his school.[6] The appeals court concluded that such speech is not protected by the First Amendment because it poses a direct threat to the physical safety of the school population. E. P., a student at Montwood High School, maintained a personal journal in which he wrote a first-person account detailing his creation of a pseudo-Nazi group at Montwood and other schools in the district, as well as the group's plan to commit a Columbine-style shooting attack at Montwood or at all of the schools. School officials learned of the journal from a concerned classmate with whom E. P. had shared some of its contents. Summoned to the assistant principal's office, E. P. insisted that the journal entry was fictional. He consented to a search of his backpack, where the journal was discovered. The assistant principal determined that the entry constituted a terrorist threat in violation of the student code of conduct. He suspended E. P. for three days and recommended he be placed in the school's alternative education program. E. P.'s parents mounted an unsuccessful administrative appeal, withdrew E. P. from the school and enrolled him in a private school, and sued. They alleged violations of E. P.'s rights under the First, Fourth, and Fourteenth amendments. They sought a preliminary court order to bar the district from (1) placing E. P. in the alternative education program; (2) informing third parties that he intended to commit violence; (3) discussing the contents of the journal without his consent; and (4) retaining any reference to the infraction in his school record. The U.S. District Court granted the injunction on First Amendment grounds. Relying on *Tinker*, the court held that the evidence was insufficient to prove that the school district acted upon a reasonable belief that disruption would occur.

However, the Fifth Circuit vacated the injunction. The appeals court found that the parents had failed to show a substantial likelihood that they would succeed on the merits of their First Amendment claim.

14. Can Teachers Develop Rules for Student Conduct in Their Classrooms?

Yes, if such rules are considered to be reasonable and necessary to maintain order and proper decorum and do not unduly infringe upon student rights and freedoms. Additionally, classroom rules may not be in conflict with school or district policy. Teachers might request that their principal review their rules to ensure that they are not inconsistent with school or district policy or the mission of the school. Once approved, it would be prudent for teachers to forward classroom rules to parents so that they are aware of classroom expectations regarding student behavior. Teachers also have a responsibility to ensure that classroom rules are thoroughly discussed with students and are clearly understood. Teachers may not infringe upon the rights of students unless they are able to demonstrate that restrictions are necessary to meet a compelling school interest such as maintaining order and proper discipline and protecting students' safety. *In loco parentis* allows teachers to exercise control over student conduct. It is not a license to arbitrarily deny students their constitutional rights in public schools. Courts will generally support a fair and reasonable exercise of authority by teachers through the enforcement of reasonable rules. Whether a rule is deemed to be reasonable depends on the specific facts surrounding the enforcement of the rule if it is challenged. Courts tend to require evidence of a substantial justification of the need to enforce the rule. In such cases, the burden of proof rests with teachers to demonstrate that restrictions on student rights are justified and not based on arbitrary or capricious decisions.

15. Do Public School Students Possess Freedom of Speech and Expression Rights?

It depends. If their speech is reasonable, they are allowed to exercise it. If it infringes on the rights of others or creates material and substantial disruption, they may not. Students achieved a major victory in the *Tinker v. Des Moines* case when the U.S. Supreme Court held for students. *Tinker* did not directly address speech in its purest form but did recognize that students possess a constitutional right to express their political views without undue interference by school officials. The *Tinker* case was significant in establishing the fact that students are citizens under the Constitution. It also affirmed the comprehensive authority of state and school authorities to prescribe and control conduct in the school based on reasonable grounds and consistent with fundamental constitutional safeguards.

The standards of reasonableness suggest that student speech must not create a clear and present danger, cause material and substantial disruption to the educational process, or interfere with the requirements of appropriate discipline in the operation of the school. It also must not foster disrespect for authority or infringe upon the rights of others. Student speech may be banned if it contains vulgar or lewd content or mocks others based on race, color, ethnicity, religion, or gender.

Since *Tinker*, many conflicts have occurred in public schools between school officials and students over the exercise of student rights within the boundaries of reasonable administrative regulatory authority. Again, in cases involving student rights violations, when challenged, school officials must be able to justify that a legitimate or compelling school interest justifies the need for the restriction. Legitimate school interest generally encompasses issues involving school safety, student welfare, or an orderly school environment, among others. The courts, in their rulings, consider all facts surrounding conflicts involving student rights and attempt to render decisions that are fair and reasonable in light of the special circumstances surrounding each situation.

Conflicts involving student rights have included issues related to protests and demonstrations, student newspapers—both school sponsored and nonschool sponsored—dress and appearance, religious freedoms, searches and seizures, corporal punishment, and suspensions and expulsions. In many of these conflicts, students have alleged that school officials and teachers failed to meet the standard of reasonableness regarding their actions and thus deprived students of their constitutional freedoms. In such cases, the burden of proof rested with educators to clearly demonstrate that their actions toward students were not arbitrary or capricious but based on legitimate and defensible grounds. When school officials or teachers have failed to meet this standard, courts have supported students. When they have succeeded in meeting the standard of reasonableness, courts have supported their actions.

For example, in a recent case involving student expression, the principal of a Florida high school had an unwritten rule barring the Confederate flag from school grounds. He suspended two students for displaying Confederate flags on school grounds after they were warned against doing so. They sued the school board in a federal district court for constitutional rights violations. The court awarded summary judgment to the board, finding the principal's action justifiable because of the disruption likely to result from displaying Confederate symbols; there was evidence of racial tension in the school. The court held that school officials may limit student speech to halt disruption and to foster manners and civility. The students appealed.

The U.S. Court of Appeals, Eleventh Circuit, supported the district court's decision. The principal did not unconstitutionally restrict student speech. The district court had correctly held that it is a highly appropriate function of public school administrators to prohibit speech that is vulgar and offensive. The fact that Confederate symbols arouse particularly high emotions made it constitutionally permissible for school administrators to "closely limit the range of expression children are permitted regarding such volatile issues."[7] Since the principal and board did not violate the students' constitutional rights, the court affirmed the decision. Although this case dealt with a Confederate flag, the broader issue involves symbols that create disruption. Any type of symbol that heightens racial tension such as Nazism or KKK may be banned if there is evidence of disruption or the significant likelihood for material and substantial disruption in a highly tense school environment. Symbols of hate speech reflected in jewelry, tattoos, and other forms of expression can be legally banned by school officials.

16. Can Educators Restrict Student Dress and Appearance?

It depends on the nature of the dress and the impact it has on order and safety in schools. Within limits, students are provided a degree of latitude to dress in a manner that reflects their values, background, customs, personality, and culture. However, dress may be regulated if it creates disruption, perpetuates racial tension, is offensive, invites too much attention to the anatomy, creates unsanitary conditions, or creates other health or safety concerns.

An example of an unsuccessful school ban on offensive dress arose in Ohio.[8] An Ohio middle-school student wore a shirt declaring "Homosexuality is a sin!" "Islam is a lie!" and "Abortion is murder!" His father warned him that he might receive some opposition due to the shirt's message of intolerance. The student wore the shirt anyway, and a guidance counselor told him to remove it or turn it inside out. The student refused to do either, stating that the shirt was not inappropriate and that he had his parents' permission to wear it. The father was called to school and also argued in support of the shirt. The parents later met with the superintendent, who supported the principal's position that the student would be suspended if he wore the shirt to school again. The parents sued the school board in a federal district court for First Amendment violations.

The court rejected the board's claim that the shirt could be banned on grounds that its message was plainly offensive. It distinguished the case from *Boroff v. Van Wert City Board of Education* in which the Sixth Circuit Court of Appeals upheld the discipline of an Ohio student for wearing a Marilyn Manson T-shirt.[9] In *Boroff*, the school could prohibit the T-shirt since it contained a message promoting values patently contrary to the school's educational mission. In this case, the court found that the student's shirt was not plainly offensive. The only evidence of disruption was that a few hostile remarks were made by students outside the classroom. When no disruption occurs and there is no reasonable threat of any disruption, students have the right to express their political viewpoints. The fact that Muslims, homosexuals and those who may have had abortions might be present at school did not justify suppressing the student's message. The school's actions appeared to be based on the desire to avoid controversy resulting from the expression of political views. The court held that the board violated the student's rights and issued an order preventing school officials from barring the shirt unless imminent, substantial disruption was likely.

Dress, however, may be regulated if it contains lewd or vulgar expressions. Dress possibly related to established gangs can also be restricted. Examples might include earrings, sagging pants, sport jackets, caps, certain uniform colors involving a group of students, bandannas, words shaved into students' scalps, exposed underwear, and any other recognizable gang symbols expressed through dress.

School officials should not restrict dress that does not meet the criteria stated previously unless they are able to demonstrate a legitimate basis for doing so. Parents and students who challenge dress code restrictions tend to rely on First Amendment protection as well as equal protection guarantees of the Fourteenth Amendment. Interestingly, student dress is not viewed as significantly by the courts as other forms of free expression.

17. How Do Health and Safety Issues Affect Student Dress?

Student dress can be restricted if it poses a health or safety challenge. Under *in loco parentis*, teachers and administrators may impose reasonable restrictions on dress and appearance for those reasons.

For example, policies that address cleanliness of hair are appropriate, particularly if they curtail lice. Students can be restricted from wearing large decorative chains during vocational classes where various types of potentially dangerous equipment are used by students. Other types of loose garments may be restricted in shops and laboratories to prevent contact with the equipment and materials students are using in laboratories. Similarly, long hair can be regulated if it poses a danger to students enrolled in laboratory or vocational classes and it is foreseeable that the hair could become entangled with the equipment and thus cause serious injury to students. Failure to foresee possible danger can, in fact, result in liability for both teachers and administrators. Hair-length requirements can also be imposed when long hair presents hygienic problems. The courts have not been totally consistent in their rulings regarding hair length and style but are more inclined to support hair-length regulations when students' health, safety, and welfare are implicated.

18. Can Students Be Required to Wear School Uniforms?

Yes, students may be required to wear uniforms, especially when they are linked to school safety. School officials, in their desire to create and maintain safe schools, have implemented uniform dress-code policies for students. The intent of these dress codes is to provide easy identification of students, eliminate gang dress, promote discipline, deter theft and violence, and prevent unauthorized visitors from intruding onto campuses. Many schools also link uniform dress codes with positive learning environments. Uniform dress codes are usually more feasible when they are included as a component of an overall program to improve school safety. Parents, also often concerned with school safety, are more inclined to support uniform dress codes when they are closely connected to overall safety. School officials must be mindful as they develop uniform dress codes that students' First Amendment rights must be recognized. The Long Beach California School District was the first in the nation to require uniforms and reported a significant decline in student misbehavior one year after implementing the program.

While dress does not rise to the level of significance as other forms of First Amendment freedoms, courts have upheld a First Amendment interest in student dress. Courts have varied in their interpretation and responses to dress-code challenges. School officials have a greater opportunity to receive court support when they demonstrate that a legitimate educational interest is served by enforcing uniform dress-code policies. The *Canady v. Bossier* case supports this view.[10] In the 1998–1999 school year, a Louisiana parish school board decided to implement a mandatory school uniform policy. The school board believed the uniform policy would improve the educational process by reducing disciplinary problems. Several parents of students challenged the new dress code on First Amendment grounds. The school presented evidence that, since the adoption of the uniform policy, academic performance had increased and discipline problems declined. A district court rejected the parents' lawsuit. The parents then appealed to the Fifth Circuit Court of Appeals. In a 3–0 decision, a Fifth Circuit panel held that adjusting the school's dress code by adopting a uniform policy is a constitutional means for school officials to improve the educational process if it is not directed at censoring the expressive content of student clothing. The court noted that the school board uniform policy in this case was passed to improve the educational process by increasing test scores and reducing discipline problems. "This purpose is in no way related to the suppression of student speech," the panel wrote. "Although students are restricted from wearing clothing of their choice at school, students remain free to wear what they want after school hours."

Recent conflicts regarding mandatory uniforms have not centered around the uniforms themselves but, rather, on the accessories worn with the uniforms. For example, officials in Harrison County, Mississippi, retreated on the same day from stopping a Jewish student from wearing a Star of David necklace to class based on its policy of prohibiting students from wearing anything that could be viewed as a gang symbol. A similar conflict arose in Van Cleave, Mississippi, when a local school board banned students from wearing clothing with Christian symbols based on the school's mandatory uniform policy. In this case, two students wore T-shirts stamped with the words "Jesus Loves Me." The basis for implementing the mandatory uniform policy was safety. After an unsuccessful appeal to the school board, the parents of the two students filed a suit in a U.S. district court challenging the legality of a policy that prohibits students' free expression of religion. These legal conflicts might suggest that school leaders stop being as sensitive to the First Amendment rights of students when school uniform policies are drafted.

19. May School Officials Regulate School-Sponsored and Nonschool-Sponsored Student Newspapers?

It depends, because both newspapers are protected by the First Amendment. In fact, freedom of the press is the most highly regarded among First Amendment rights by the courts. However, under most conditions, school-sponsored student newspapers can be regulated. Traditionally, student newspapers have served as a forum for students to express their views on a variety of issues of interest to them, including statements criticizing school policies and practices. These forms of expression must not be restricted if they are not defamatory in nature or designed to create disruption.

In cases of defamation, school editors are held accountable or, in some cases, libelous for defamatory statements. However, school-sponsored newspapers can receive prior restraint, particularly when they are an integral component of the school's curriculum. School policies should address issues involving prior restraint by indicating the conditions under which newspaper material will be reviewed, the timetable involved, and by whom materials will be reviewed. The review process must not be imposed in a manner that adversely affects the production and distribution of the paper. School officials are provided greater latitude in controlling school-sponsored newspapers if it is to ensure that newspaper content is appropriate to the age and maturity of students and does not conflict with the school's mission or materially or substantially impact proper discipline in the school. Material that is considered to be indecent or vulgar can also be suppressed. It is important to recognize, however, that although limited review is permitted by the courts, broad censorship is not.

A leading school publication case was addressed by the U.S. Supreme Court in *Hazelwood v. Kuhlmeier*. The *Spectrum* was a school-sponsored, curriculum-based newspaper edited by a journalism class. The paper was published every three weeks and distributed to more than 4,500 students, school personnel, and community members. The school board allocated funds annually to support the production of the paper. Proceeds from the sale of the paper were used to supplement the production of the paper. Based on district policy, the newspaper was to be developed within the adopted curriculum. A conflict arose in the spring of 1983 when a high school principal in St. Louis prevented the *Spectrum* from publishing articles profiling three pregnant students, based on the fear that the students' identity would be revealed. The principal also suppressed materials that dealt with sexual activity and birth control based on their inappropriateness for younger students. Last, he suppressed quotes from other students regarding the reasons for their parents' divorce based on privacy considerations for the families involved and the fact that the parents did not consent or have prior knowledge that their children were providing sensitive family information to the newspaper.

Student editors challenged the principal's decisions, alleging that his actions were tantamount to prior restraint of free press in violation of the First Amendment. They claimed First and Fourteenth amendment violations based on the principal's actions. A federal district court in May 1985 ruled that the *Spectrum* was produced as a part of the school's journalism class and was curriculum based, and thus did not fall into the category of a public forum entitled to the same First Amendment protection as independent newspapers would receive. The court concluded that the principal needed only a reasonable basis to suppress the material in question. On appeal, the U.S. Court of Appeals for the Eighth Circuit reversed the district court's ruling, stating that the *Spectrum* was indeed a public forum intended for student expression and not simply a part of the school's journalism curriculum. Since the paper was considered a public forum, the principal's actions were not justified. The school district appealed to the U.S. Supreme Court. After reviewing all circumstances surrounding the case, the Supreme Court reversed the Eighth Circuit Court of Appeals' ruling and held for the school district, stating that the principal did not violate students' free speech rights by ordering that certain materials be removed from an issue of the *Spectrum*. The High Court concluded with the following statement:

> To justify a prohibition of a particular expression of opinion, school officials must be able to show that their action was caused by something more than a mere desire to avoid the discomfort and unpleasantness that always accompany an unpopular viewpoint. There must be facts that might reasonably lead school authorities to forecast substantial disruption or material interference with school activities. We cannot reject as unreasonable Principal Reynolds' conclusion that neither the pregnancy article nor the divorce was suitable for publication in the *Spectrum*. Reynolds could reasonably have concluded that students who wrote and edited the article had not sufficiently mastered those portions of the Journalism II

Curriculum that pertained to the treatment of controversial issues and personal attacks, the need to protect the privacy of individuals whose most intimate concerns are to be revealed in the newspapers and the "legal, moral and ethical restrictions imposed upon journalists within the school community" that includes adolescent subjects and readers.[11]

The following facts were pivotal to the *Hazelwood* decision:

- The newspaper was a curriculum-based newspaper associated with a journalism class.
- School officials had the authority to suppress material contained in a curriculum-based paper that is viewed as inappropriate and in conflict with the school's mission.
- Student expression in the questionable newspaper article did not conform to rules of responsible journalism.
- The curriculum-based newspaper was not intended to be used indiscriminately by student reporters or the general student body.
- School officials may, under certain conditions, be accountable for libelous content in curriculum-based school newspapers because their names and resources are linked to the production of the paper.

20. Can School Officials Exercise Control Over the Publication of Nonschool-Sponsored Newspapers?

No. Nonsponsored newspapers enjoy the same First Amendment protection as school-sponsored publications unless the school has a closed forum. A closed forum signifies that nonschool materials are not approved for distribution. However, if school officials permit nonschool-related materials to be distributed on school property, they have established a limited open forum, meaning that they are not permitted to ban distribution based on content. School officials must remain content neutral in rendering decisions regarding nonschool-sponsored publications. Typically, nonschool-sponsored or underground newspapers are published away from school facilities at the publisher's expense. These publications are subject to the same standards of responsible journalism as are school-sponsored publications. School officials are not responsible for materials published in nonschool-sponsored newspapers, including materials that are libelous, vulgar, or obscene. Those responsible for producing the newspaper are legally accountable for its content. Underground newspapers may not be broadly censored by school officials. However, time, place, and manner of distribution can be regulated by school officials. Additional restrictions may be imposed requiring that distribution areas be free of excessive papers once dissemination has been completed.

School officials should develop clearly defined and legally defensible policies governing nonschool-sponsored papers. If the policy calls for a review procedure, specific requirements must be included regarding who is authorized to review materials, the timeframe involved, the format in which materials must be submitted for review, and the types of material that might be libelous. Material that is libelous, is clearly obscene, or would lead school officials to forecast a material and substantial disruption of the educational process or violation of the rights of others may be suppressed according to a ruling in *Bystrom v. Fridley.*[12] It is important to remember that the burden of proof rests with school officials to justify the need for prior approval policies. The inclusion of these policy guides might assist students who produce nonschool-sponsored papers in understanding the parameters within which they must operate as well as the limits of liability they may incur for defamatory content.

21. Can a Faculty Advisor to a Student Newspaper Monitor Content Written for Inclusion in the Student Newspaper?

Generally speaking, **yes,** if this duty or responsibility is clearly conveyed in policy and student editors are aware of the advisor's role. An obvious distinction has to be made between monitoring the newspaper to provide advice with respect to organizational issues, grammar, syntax, and general suitability of material versus placing restrictions on what students may publish in the paper. The final decision for printed material resides with student editors who must be mindful of their obligation to adhere to responsible rules of journalism.

22. Can Faculty Advisors Be Liable for Allowing Inappropriate Content in the Student Newspaper?

Not usually. Since faculty advisors are not responsible for the content of the paper, they are not liable for what students decide to include in it. Student editors are responsible for the newspaper's content. However, the Eighth Circuit Court of Appeals upheld in *Bystrom v. Fridley High School Independent School District* a school rule that prohibited the publication of material that was pervasively indecent and vulgar even though there was a degree of objectivity contained in the newspaper's content.[13]

23. Are Controversial Slogans and Offensive Language Permitted in Public Schools Under Student Freedom of Expression Rights?

It depends on the nature of the content involved. If controversial statements are considered to be of interest to students, are free of vulgarity, obscenity, and disdain, and do not create material or substantial disruption or conflict with the school's mission, they may be allowed, particularly when they evoke healthy discourse. Statements that violate standards of common decency may be disallowed. Controversial slogans cannot mock others based on any of the protected categories such as race, religion, color, national origin, or gender. Controversial slogans containing messages in direct conflict with the school's mission may be curtailed. For example, if the school is stressing the ill effects of alcohol and tobacco use and students are wearing T-shirts containing pro-alcohol and tobacco consumption messages, school officials can ban such expressions. The same prerogatives would be available to school officials when there is evidence that certain slogans are gang related.

24. Can Students Gain First Amendment Protection When They Use Offensive Language in School?

Generally not. The courts have been fairly consistent in holding that students may not claim First Amendment privileges when they communicate offensive messages. Messages containing racial epithets that may result in racial tension can be banned by school officials. Any speech that is considered to be vulgar, lewd, sexually oriented, or racially charged may also be suppressed without offending the student's First Amendment rights. It is important to remember that student rights are not absolute but rather subject to reasonable administrative scrutiny.

Bethel School District No. 403 v. Fraser represents a leading case in this area.[14] Matthew Fraser was a student enrolled at Bethel High School in the state of Washington. He delivered a speech nominating a fellow student for elective office during an assembly program. Approximately 600 high school students attended, many of whom were fourteen years old. Students were either required to attend assembly or report to study hall. During Fraser's presentation, he used graphic sexual metaphors in his nomination speech. Fraser had discussed the content of his speech with two teachers prior to delivering it in the student assembly, both of whom advised him that the content was inappropriate and that the speech must not be delivered. He was further informed that the delivery of the speech might result in negative consequences.

During Fraser's speech, the school counselor noticed the reactions of students to the speech. Some students yelled, others simulated sexual activities referenced in the speech, while others appeared devastated and embarrassed by the speech. One teacher reported that it was necessary to forego a segment of the class to discuss the speech with students. Bethel's student policies clearly prohibited the use of obscene language in the school.

Fraser was called to the assistant principal's office the day after the assembly program and informed that his speech violated a school rule. He was provided an opportunity to explain his conduct. He indicated that he deliberately used sexual content in his speech, after which he received a three-day suspension. His name was also removed from the list of student graduation speakers. Fraser appealed the suspension through the district's grievance procedure. The hearing officer concluded that the speech was lewd and offensive to many students and faculty who attended the assembly.

A suit was filed by Fraser's father alleging a violation of First Amendment rights to freedom of speech. He also sought injunctive relief and monetary damages. The district court held for Fraser in concluding that the school's sanction violated Fraser's First Amendment rights and that the school's policy was unconstitutionally vague. The court further concluded that removal of Fraser's name from the graduation speaker's list violated his Fourteenth Amendment rights because there was no reference to such action found in school policy. The district court awarded $278 in damages and $12,750 in legal fees. The district court ruled that Fraser could not be banned from speaking at graduation. The Ninth Circuit Court of Appeals affirmed the decision of the district court. On appeal, the U.S. Supreme Court overturned the lower courts' rulings and upheld the disciplinary sanctions imposed by school officials. The High Court concluded that sexual and graphic metaphors were offensive to both teachers and students and that the school had a legitimate interest in protecting captive students from vulgar, lewd, and sexually offensive language. Last, the High Court concluded that First Amendment–protected speech for adults is not the same for children and that the impact of the speech on fellow students must be given high consideration.

The following facts were pivotal to the court's ruling:

- Fraser's conduct materially and substantially interfered with the educational process in the school.
- The speech contained use of obscenity, profane language, and sexual gestures.
- It is a highly appropriate function of school officials to protect captive students from inappropriate speech by prohibiting the use of vulgar and offensive language.
- Schools, as instruments of the state, may determine that the essential lessons of civil and mature conduct are not being conveyed when lewd, indecent, or offensive speech and conduct such as that displayed by the student are tolerated.
- Fraser's speech could be seriously damaging to a less mature audience, many of whom were fourteen years old and on the threshold of awareness of human sexuality.

25. May Teachers and Administrators Conduct Student Searches in Public Schools?

Yes, if they meet the requirements of reasonableness. *In loco parentis* allows educators to conduct reasonable searches involving students. The courts recognize, however, that students are provided Fourth Amendment protection against unreasonable search and seizure. While students enjoy a level of constitutional protection, their Fourth Amendment rights are not absolute but subject to reasonable intrusion by teachers and administrators. Student searches may be conducted when there is reasonable suspicion that the student violated a school rule or has an item in his or her possession that may prove harmful to the student or others in the school. Reasonable suspicion is established when teachers and administrators receive information considered reliable that indicates a student has a dangerous item, illegal substance, or other items that violate school rules or jeopardize safety. The person who provides the information must be known by the teacher or administrator, and the information received must be viewed as creditable. When these requirements are met, the search is considered to be legal in nature. The courts attempt to achieve a reasonable balance between students' rights to privacy protection and educators' need to provide a safe and orderly environment for students.

If approved by local district policy, teachers and administrators must consider a number of factors prior to initiating a search, such as the age and maturity of students involved, the history of their behavior in school, and the immediate need to conduct a search based on the seriousness of the problem perceived by teachers or administrators. Typically, searches are individualized, which means that teachers or administrators have reliable information that leads them to search a specific student to uncover school rule violations. Therefore, mass searches and locker raids are not legally defensible unless there is a dire emergency such as a bomb threat or evidence of weapons involving gang activities. In these cases, law enforcement officials are usually involved, and probability must be established.

Students must be informed by policy that they have no expectation of absolute privacy with respect to desks and lockers. Student automobiles registered under students' names and parked on school property may also be searched if reasonable suspicion requirements are met. Educators must be mindful that students are entitled to reasonable expectations of privacy as they assess the need to conduct a search. In all cases, students and parents must be informed through school policy that searches will be conducted based on reasonable suspicion regarding their personal possessions. A more intrusive search requires a higher degree of reasonable suspicion that approaches probable cause.

26. What Legal Standards Must Be Met in Searches Involving Educators and Those Involving Law Enforcement Officials?

Since teachers and administrators act *in loco parentis*, they are not considered governmental officials; consequently, they are not required to meet probable cause standards that law enforcement officials must meet prior to conducting a search. Probable cause standards are higher standards than those associated with reasonable suspicion requirements. Probable cause requires a search warrant prior to conducting a search. Probable cause is established when there is a reasonable belief that a crime has been committed and that the person is connected to the crime with a high degree of certainty.

The issue of reasonable suspicion versus probable cause was addressed in a landmark U.S. Supreme Court ruling involving school searches. The *New Jersey v. T. L. O.* case, in fact, represents the only instance in which the U.S. Supreme Court has addressed student searches in public schools.[15] In this case, a teacher discovered a fourteen-year-old student smoking cigarettes in a school lavatory in violation of a school rule. She escorted her to the principal's office. When the girl denied that she had been smoking and claimed that she never smoked, the assistant vice principal demanded to search her purse. After finding a pack of cigarettes, he noticed a package of rolling papers commonly associated with marijuana. His further search revealed marijuana, a pipe, plastic bags, a large amount of money, and papers implicating her in drug dealing. The state then brought delinquency charges against the student. The student moved to suppress the evidence and her subsequent confession, which she argued was tainted by an unlawful search. The Fourth Amendment does not require school officials to obtain a warrant or show probable cause before searching a student who is under their authority; rather, the constitutionality of the search depends on its reasonableness in a two-step test. First, is the search justified at its inception? Second, is the scope of the search deemed to be reasonable? In upholding the school, the court balanced the student's interest in privacy and school authorities' interest in discipline. Reasonable suspicion was all that was necessary to conduct the search, which was established when the teacher reported that the student had been smoking in the restroom.

The following facts were significant to the court's ruling:

- The search began with a view toward revealing that T. L. O. had smoked in the lavatory.
- The suspicion upon which the search for marijuana was based arose when the assistant principal observed a package of rolling papers in T. L. O.'s purse as he removed the pack of cigarettes.
- Because the search resulted in the discovery of evidence of marijuana dealing by T. L. O., the search was reasonable.
- The scope of the search was not excessive in light of the age and sex of the student and the nature of the suspected violation.
- The plaintiff's conduct created reasonable grounds for suspecting that some school rule or law had been violated.

A school search is typically conducted to determine school rule violations for disciplinary purposes and school safety. Although the intent of the search is for school purposes, the school search may reveal criminal activity, at which time local police officers will become involved. In fact, school officials have an obligation to report evidence of criminal activity to local police. Police officers are required to meet probable cause standards involving a search warrant when they act independently of the school. On the other hand, if they are merely providing assistance in a disciplinary matter, other than a search initiated by school officials, reasonable suspicion standards may be adequate. If police officers actually participate in a school search, they must meet probable cause standards accompanied by a search warrant. If it becomes necessary to involve police officers in school matters, parents or legal guardians of affected students must be contacted prior to any action taken by police. If parents cannot be contacted or are unable to be involved in the investigation, school officials must be present during the investigation and document all activities that occur.

27. Can Teachers Legally Conduct Personal Searches of Students?

Probably so. Personal searches, however, are not highly recommended and must be conducted in cases where there is a reasonably strong belief that some dangerous item is involved that may pose a threat to school safety. Personal searches must not be random searches. Students should not necessarily have a lower expectation of privacy merely because they attend public schools. They do enjoy personal protection against unreasonable search and seizure. The courts tend to be divided on personal searches, with some courts upholding them while others rule against them. Personal searches often involve strip searches, which are considered to be the most intrusive searches. While the courts have not altogether prohibited strip searches, they must be conducted very sparingly and in cases where there is significant information that warrants such an intrusion. It is becoming increasingly evident that reasonable suspicion alone may not be sufficient to justify a strip search. The more intrusive the search becomes, the closer it triggers the need for probable cause. Probable cause is based on the Fourth Amendment to the U.S. Constitution:

> The right of people to be secure in their persons, houses, papers and affects, against unreasonable searches and seizures, shall not be violated and no warrants shall issue but upon *probable cause* supported by oath of affirmation and particularly describing the places to be searched and the persons or things to be seized.

An example of one court's position regarding strip searches was expressed in *Phaneuf v. Fraikin.*[16] The U.S. Court of Appeals for the Second Circuit held that school officials violated a student's Fourth Amendment right to freedom from unreasonable search and seizure by subjecting her to a strip search after receiving a tip that she planned to bring marijuana to a class picnic. Before departing for the picnic, seniors at Plainville High School were required to have their bags checked for security reasons.

A student reported to a teacher that Kelly Phaneuf had indicated that she had some marijuana and planned to hide it in her pants during the bag check. The principal instructed the school nurse to strip-search Kelly. When the nurse expressed reluctance, the principal called Kelly's mother and requested that she come and conduct the search. Meanwhile, the principal searched Kelly's bag, finding cigarettes and a lighter, both violations of school rules, but no drugs. Kelly's mother arrived and searched Kelly but found no drugs. Kelly subsequently sued, arguing that school officials lacked the reasonable suspicion for the search required by *New Jersey v. T. L. O.*

Based on the court's decision in *T. L. O.*, the district court considered the following issues in determining the constitutional validity of the search: The first was to consider whether the search was justified at its inception—the point at which reasonable suspicion becomes significant. Second, was the search reasonable in light of the information obtained by school officials? Third, was the search reasonable and the means employed to conduct the search reasonable, and was the scope and conduct of the search reasonably related to the circumstances that gave rise to it? Last, the search must not have been excessively intrusive and must have considered the age and sex of the student. The district court concluded that the search satisfied *T. L. O.*'s two-pronged test requiring that the search be (1) reasonable at its inception and (2) reasonably related in scope to the circumstances that justified the interference in the first place.

However, the Second Circuit reversed the decision. The appeals court noted that "what may constitute reasonable suspicion for a search of a locker or even a pocket or pocketbook may fall well short of reasonableness for a nude search" and that, "as the intrusiveness of the search of a student intensifies, so too does the standard of Fourth Amendment reasonableness." The court found that the factors relied on by school officials to justify the search, whether considered individually or together, failed to meet the Fourth Amendment standard. The reliability and trustworthiness of the student tip were questionable because the principal took no steps to investigate, corroborate, or otherwise substantiate the charges. The court concluded that, "while the uncorroborated tip no doubt justified additional inquiry and investigation by school officials, it did not convince the court that it justified a step as intrusive as a strip search." The court disposed of the second factor, Kelly's past disciplinary record, finding that none of her past offenses were related to drug use. Turning to the supposedly suspicious manner of Kelly's denials, the court found that the teacher's and principal's statements were conclusory because the record was devoid of any explanation as to what they meant by "suspicious." Finally, the court found that Kelly's possession of the other contraband was minimally probative of her possible use of marijuana but was insufficient to create a heightened level of suspicion that would justify a highly intrusive search.

28. Are Canine Searches in Public Schools Permissible?

It depends on the seriousness of the situation that necessitates a canine search and the federal court district in which a challenge occurs. The courts are divided regarding the legal defensibility of canine searches. The courts that support canine searches have done so in cases where there was a high degree of individual suspicion or a perceived threat to the health and safety of students.

For example, in *Zamora v. Pomeroy*, the Tenth Circuit Court of Appeals ruled that the use of canines in an exploratory sniffing of lockers was permissible based on the fact that notice was given by school officials at the beginning of the year that lockers might be periodically opened.[17] The court's rationale was based on the view that lockers are school property and that school officials have a leading responsibility to maintain a safe environment; therefore, it is necessary for them to inspect lockers. The court noted that there might be a Fourth Amendment infringement; however, it was not considered to be significant.

The Seventh Circuit Court held in *Doe v. Renfrow* that school officials under *in loco parentis* have a right to use dogs to sniff out drugs based on the view that students have a diminished expectation of privacy in public schools.[18] Furthermore, school officials have a duty to create and maintain a safe educational environment conducive to learning.

In a contrasting decision, *Jones v. Latexo Independent School District*, a federal district court held that sniffing of students and their automobiles by dogs was too intrusive in the absence of individual suspicion and as such was not reasonable.[19] One issue that affected the court's position centered on the fact that students had no access to their automobiles during the normal school day; therefore, school officials' interest in having dogs sniff their automobiles was very minimal and unnecessary.

A different ruling occurred in *Horton v. Goose Creek Independent School District* when the district court held that the sniffing of lockers and automobiles did not constitute a search.[20] As such, no inquiry into the reasonableness of this practice was considered necessary. However, the court reiterated that school officials may not search students in the absence of reasonable cause. Further, the inspection of a student's person cannot be justified based on the school official's desire to prevent drug and alcohol abuse in the absence of individualized suspicion. Such a practice is unconstitutional.

29. Can School Officials Initiate Random Drug Testing of Students in Public Schools?

Probably not, as random drug-testing programs are difficult to justify based on the privacy protection rights of students. In two leading U.S. Supreme

Court drug-testing cases in 1989 involving railway employees and customer service employees, the High Court held that drug testing, irrespective of method, constitutes a search under the Fourth Amendment. However, the High Court upheld testing programs in both cases based on a compelling government interest in minimizing rail accidents and protecting the public against agents who carried firearms. A concern for public safety was pivotal in the High Court's decision to uphold testing programs in these two cases.

In public schools, random urine tests administered to all students for the purpose of detecting drugs would likely not withstand court scrutiny based on privacy rights and equal protection rights associated with the Fourteenth Amendment. The U.S. Supreme Court in *Vernonia v. Acton* upheld in a 6–3 decision a random urinalysis drug-testing program for student athletes.[21] This case reached the Supreme Court after the Ninth Circuit Court reversed the district court's ruling supporting the school district's random drug-testing program. School officials in Oregon had developed a policy to curtail a growing drug problem and misconduct among student athletes. There was evidence that discipline problems had increased, including the use of profanity and a view among displeased students that school officials could essentially do nothing to curtail their involvement with drugs. Student athletes were reported to be rude and disrespectful in class. Student athletes were also discovered to be leaders of the drug culture in school. Coaches had reported a sharp increase in sports-related injuries. Under the district's policy, all student athletes were required to provide a urine sample at the beginning of the season for the particular sport in which they desired to participate, followed by random tests among selected athletes. Those who tested positively were given an option to participate in counseling and weekly testing or suspension from athletics for the current year and next season.

James Acton, a seventh grader who was interested in joining a team, challenged the policy after being suspended from the team based on his parents' refusal to sign the consent form. The district court held for the school district. The Ninth Circuit Court of Appeals reversed the district court's ruling. The U.S. Supreme Court reversed the Ninth Circuit Court's ruling by holding for the school district. Supreme Justice Scalia, writing for the majority, stated that Vernonia School District's program was reasonable and constitutionally permissible for three reasons. First, student athletes have a low expectation of privacy in communal locker rooms and restrooms where students must produce their urine samples. "School sports are not for the bashful," wrote Scalia. Second, the testing program was designed to be unobtrusive, with students producing their samples in relative privacy and with samples handled confidentially by an outside laboratory. Last, the program served the district's interest in combating drug abuse. It seemed self-evident that drug use, of particular danger to athletes, is effectively addressed by making certain that athletes do not use drugs. The High Court determined that the program was reasonably calculated to curtail drug and related discipline problems, especially in light of the unobtrusiveness of the procedure, the apparent need for the program, and, last, the diminished expectation of privacy for student athletes.

In a later 2002 case, *Board of Education v. Earls*, the U.S. Supreme Court ruled 5–4 that mandatory drug testing of students in extracurricular activities was constitutional.[22] The case was brought by two students, Lindsay Earls and Daniel James, and their families against the school board of Tecumseh, Oklahoma, alleging that its policy requiring students to consent to random urinalysis testing for drug use violated the Fourth Amendment to the U.S. Constitution. The majority decision, written by Justice Clarence Thomas with a concurring opinion by Justice Stephen Breyer, held that students in extracurricular activities had a diminished expectation of privacy and that the policy furthered an important interest of the school to prevent drug use among students. This rationale was based on the precedent set by *Vernonia School District v. Acton*, which allowed drug testing for athletes.

30. Can Public Schools Control Internet Access by Students?

Yes. School officials based on policy may identify acceptable use of the Internet by students. The school should adopt filtering software to block access to visual images that are obscene, pornographic, or otherwise unsuitable. In fact, the Children's Internet Protection Act of 2000 requires schools and libraries to adopt an Internet policy and install filtering technology in order to receive E-rate funding. Schools can prescribe that computers be used solely for educational purposes, which eliminates allegations of arbitrary and capricious action. Institutional violations policy should identify sanctions for students who violate the school's Internet use policy.

31. Can Schools Disallow the Use of Cell Phones and Other Electronic Devices (PDAs) by Students?

Yes. School officials may prohibit any devices or practices that result in material or substantial disruption in the school. Students have no inherent right to use a cell phone or any other electronic device in public schools. Successful legal challenges are especially improbable in cases where there is evidence of improper use such as text-messaging answers to exams or illegal transactions involving drugs, alcohol, or other illicit purposes. However, special allowances may be granted for chronically ill students who need electronic devices for medical emergencies. School or district policy will usually provide guidance regarding cell phone use in public schools.

Allowing students to use cell phones is left to the discretion of school district officials. Cell phones can be banned by school officials based on reasonable grounds such as material and substantial disruption and even invasion of privacy regarding the use of camera cell phones. For example, students using camera phones may conceivably photograph other students in compromising situations in restrooms and locker rooms. Not only can camera cell phones create privacy evasion issues but they may also be used to gain an unfair advantage on school tests. For example, a student might photograph a test and simultaneously transmit it to classmates in a matter of seconds using a camera phone.

There is a national debate regarding cell phone use in public schools. Parents cite safety issues and the need to communicate with their children when they are required to travel long distances via public transportation to attend school. Parents also express concern regarding their ability to reach their children in the event of a shooting incident at school or other types of school or family emergencies. Teachers and administrators are concerned with disruptions, as when phones ring in the classroom or students participate in text messaging when they should be engaged in classroom activities. Mobile access might also allow students to access inappropriate content. Additionally, mobile bullying or harassment is also emerging as a challenge for teachers and administrators.

Parents are requesting that school officials seek solutions to allow cell phone use without creating disruptions, such as requiring students to turn phones off during instructional time or placing phones on silence or in a vibrate mode during the school day. Many states had, in fact, developed policies accommodating cell phone use in public schools prior to the emergence of a new generation of cell phones that feature Internet access, cameras, and text-messaging capability. The challenge currently faced by teachers and administrators is to determine how to allow students to use these new generation cell phones for legitimate purposes without infringing upon the privacy rights of other students or creating unfair advantages or classroom disruptions. How do teachers keep students focused on learning and minimize distractions and disruptions in the teaching and learning process? Increasingly, cell phones have become so commonplace that they are almost viewed as a necessity rather than a luxury by students. Parents view cell phones as essential to allowing them to keep track of their children.

Many school districts' current policies allow students to possess cell phones on school property and during afterschool functions provided that phones are concealed and remain off or in vibrate mode. Since school districts have discretionary authority to allow or disallow cell phone use, phone use by students is considered a privilege. In this sense, students who violate cell phone policies may forfeit the right to possess phones on school property. Areas of concern for school officials center around violations and the consequences of violations for activities such as

- taking and displaying inappropriate photographs;
- cheating on tests;
- sending text messages containing vulgarity, lewdness, or profanity;
- bullying other students; and
- partaking in other inappropriate activities.

As long as policies are properly developed and communicated to parents and students, the courts will likely support school districts.

In addition to cell phones, personal digital assistants (PDAs) have become popular items used by students in public schools. PDAs are handheld computers and are often referred to as palmtop computers. They may be used as a clock or calendar, to access the Internet, to videorecord, to send and receive email, and for several other applications. Based on their versatility, they might also be used as mobile phones or smart phones. Smart phones are simply mobile phones that offer many more advanced capabilities. Parents believe these devices benefit their children by allowing them to easily and conveniently access the Internet and by enhancing their organizational and study skills. School officials who oppose PDAs and smart phones believe that students' preoccupation with these electronic devices causes them to lose their focus on learning. There is thus obvious disagreement between parents and school officials regarding the use of these electronic devices in schools. Whether or not the devices are permitted depends on the discretion of school boards, who may permit their use but are not required to do so.

Technological advances continue to emerge at a rapid pace, along with added pressure from parents to allow the use of electronic devices in public schools. Officials will continue to face difficult decisions in achieving a proper balance of usage while minimizing disruptions to the teaching and learning process. (To date, there has been no reported litigation regarding the use of PDAs.)

In a recent development, the New York City Department of Education's ban on cell phones in all public schools has been upheld by the state supreme court in *Price v. New York Department of Education*.[23] An acting justice of the court upheld the ban and the department's power to impose punishment for students who violate the ban policy, including confiscation of phones. The policy allows school officials to search for illegal phones using magnetometers and roving metal detectors that are rotated among schools every day.

Plaintiffs in this case argued that the cell phone ban policy eroded the constitutional rights of parents and children to make family decisions. One attorney for the plaintiffs expressed the view that the ban policy is an intrusion into the relationship between parents and children and argued that the state must demonstrate that it has an essential interest to justify the ban. The department of education argued that anything education based is beyond the court's power to review. The court rejected the plaintiffs' argument as frivolous. The judge, however, considered the challenges to the cell phone policy and found, contrary to parents' claims, that the policy was neither arbitrary nor unconstitutional. The court concluded that the policy was rationally related to a legitimate state interest.

In a related cell phone ban case, *Laney v. Farley*,[24] the U.S. Court of Appeals for the Sixth Circuit ruled that school officials did not violate a student's due process rights by giving her a one-day, in-school suspension—without notice and an opportunity to be heard—for violating the Tennessee school district's policy banning cell phones in school. Under a Wilson County Board of Education policy, Victoria Laney, a student at West Wilson Middle School, had her cell phone confiscated when it began ringing in class and then received a one-day, in-school suspension. The due process provision of the policy requires that, "before imposing consequences, the teacher or principal shall be guided by the principle of fundamental fairness and make at least rudimentary inquiry into the incident to assure that the offense is accurately identified, that the student understands the nature of the offense, and that the student is given an opportunity to present his/her views." In addition, before an out-of-school suspension is imposed, the student "shall be given a complete due process hearing by the principal of said school and/or the Wilson County Schools Discipline Hearing Authority." Although Victoria's parents were informed that the confiscated phone would not be returned until thirty days had expired, they were not informed of her suspension until after she had served it. They sued the school district in federal district court, alleging violation of Victoria's right to due process based on the district's failure to provide Victoria with notice and an opportunity to be heard before her suspension. The district court denied the district's motion to dismiss the case, ruling that a one-day, in-school suspension implicates the procedural protections of the due process clause.

The Sixth Circuit reversed, disagreeing with the lower court's conclusion that a one-day, in-school suspension implicates a student's property interest in educational benefits or liberty interest in his or her reputation. Under Tennessee law, students serving in-school suspensions remain in the school setting and are required to complete academic requirements.

Legal Summaries of Recent Court Rulings Regarding Student Rights

• A Michigan federal district court held that a student had a right to wear a T-shirt depicting President Bush and criticizing the war in Iraq when there were no signs of disruption.[25]

• The Eighth Circuit Court of Appeals upheld an off-campus search when students were bused to an auto shop class. The teacher observed that a knife had been passed to a student by another. Even though the student surrendered the knife, a search was conducted of each student on the bus. The court upheld the search based on the view that a school liaison officer did not know whether other students might also have weapons. The fact that the search occurred off campus did not call for the stricter standard of probable cause.[26]

• The U.S. Court of Appeals for the Sixth Circuit ruled that the head varsity football coach did not violate the free speech rights of team members when the head coach dismissed them after learning that the players had circulated a petition denouncing the head coach and then refused to apologize for signing it.[27]

• A California appeals court ruled that school district officials violated a student's free speech rights under the state's education code when they publicly announced that his editorial article, which they allowed to be published, should not have been published because is was not protected speech.[28]

• The U.S. Supreme Court ruled that public school officials may restrict student speech at a school event when the speech is reasonably viewed as promoting illegal drugs.[29]

• The U.S. Court of Appeals for the Second Circuit ruled that a school district violated a student's free speech rights when they disciplined him for wearing a T-shirt critical of President Bush that featured drug- and alcohol-related images and text.[30]

• A U.S. Court of Appeals indicated that several criteria were crucial in determining whether dress code policy interfered with student rights under the Constitution.
  o If policy is viewpoint specific, courts will apply a higher standard.
  o If disputed clothing is obscene, vulgar, or worn in a manner that creates disruption, courts will allow school officials more discretion.
  o If student dress could be considered school sponsored, school officials will be allowed more discretion.[31]

Summary Guides

1. Public school students are entitled to constitutional protection when they attend school.

2. Restrictions on student rights must be justified based on a compelling interest by school officials and teachers.

3. Student rights are subject to reasonable restrictions if the exercise of those rights creates disruption or infringes upon the rights of others.

4. School-sponsored newspapers may be regulated based on reasonable grounds.

5. Time and place of distribution restrictions may be placed on nonschool-sponsored newspapers.

6. *In loco parentis* allows certified school personnel to conduct student searches if there is a reasonable basis for doing so.

7. Personal searches must be avoided except in emergencies where there is a perceived threat to health and safety.

8. Random drug tests of public school student bodies will not withstand court scrutiny.

9. To date, no state legislature or state department of education has mandated the use of student uniforms.

10. Student dress codes, including uniforms, are permitted by the courts if they meet a legitimate educational interest.

11. Cell phones and other electronic devices may or may not be permitted based on school officials' discretion.

NOTES

1. *West Virginia State Bd. of Education v. Barnette*, 319 U.S. 624, 63 S.Ct. 1178, 87 L.Ed. 1628 (1943).

2. *Newdow v. United States*, 315 F. 3d 495 (C.A. 9, 2002).

3. *Tinker v. Des Moines Independent School District*, 393 U.S. 503, at 511, 89 S.Ct. 733, 21 L.Ed. 2d 731 (1969).

4. Ibid.

5. *Morse v. Frederick*, 439 F.3d 1114 (9th Cir. 2006).

6. *Ponce v. Socorro, ISD*, 2007 U.S. App. LEXIS 26862,*;508 F.3d 765.

7. *Scott v. School Board of Alachua County*, 324 F.3d 1246 (11th Cir. 2003).

8. *Nixon v. Northern Local School District Board of Educ.*, 383 F.Supp.2d 965 (S.D. Ohio 2005).

9. *Boroff v. Van Wert City Board of Educ.*, 220 F.3d 465 (6th Cir. 2000).

10. *Canady v. Bossier Parish School Board*, 240 F.3d 437 (5th Cir. 2001).

11. *Hazelwood School District v. Kuhlmeier*, 484 U.S. 260, at 276; 108 S.Ct. 562; 98 L. Ed. 2d 592 (1987).

12. *Bystrom v. Fridley High School Independent School District No. 14*, 822 F. 2d 747 (8th Cir. 1987).

13. Ibid.

14. *Bethel School District v. Fraser*, 478 U.S. 675, 106 S.Ct. 3159, 93 L. Ed. (1986).

15. *New Jersey v. T. L. O.*, 469 U.S. 809; 105 S.Ct. 68; 83 L.Ed. 2d 19 (1984).

16. *Phaneuf v. Fraikin*, 448 F.3d 591 (2nd Cir. 2006).

17. *Zamora v. Pomeroy*, 639 F.2d 662 (10th Cir. 1981).

18. *Doe v. Renfrow*, 475 F. Supp. 1012 (N.D. Ind. 1979).

19. *Jones v. Latexo Independent School District*, 499 F. Supp. 223 (E.D. Tex. 1980).

20. *Horton v. Goose Creek Independent School District*, 690 F.2d 470 (5th Cir. 1982).

21. *Vernonia v. Acton*, 115 S.Ct. 2386, 132 L.Ed. 2d 564 (1995).

22. *Board of Education v. Earls*, 536 U.S. 822 (2002).

23. *Price v. New York Department of Education*, 109703/06 (N.Y. Sup. Ct. May 7, 2007).

24. *Laney v. Farley*, 2007 U.S. App. LEXIS 20553,*;501 F.3d 577;2007 FED App. 0344P (6th Cir.).

25. *Barber v. Dearborn Public Schools*, 286 F.Supp. 2d 847 (E.D. Mich. 2003).

26. *Shade v. City of Farmington, Minnesota*, 309 F.3d 1054 (8th Cir. 2002).

27. *Lowery v. Euverard*, 497 F.3d 594 (6th Cir. 2007).

28. *Smith v. Novato Unified School Dist.*, 59 Cal. Rptr. 3d 508, 516 (Cal. App. 2007).

29. *Morse*, op. cit.

30. *Harper v. Poway Unified School District*, 2007 U.S. App. LEXIS 9234,*;485 F.3d 1052.

31. *Castorina v. Madison County School Board*, 246 F.3d 536, U.S. Ct. App. (6th Cir. 2001).

3

Student Discipline

⚏ INTRODUCTION ⚏

Managing student behavior effectively and providing a safe environment in public schools remains a challenge for school officials and teachers. It is also one of the primary concerns among parents. Disruptive and violent behavior such as harassment, assaults, bullying, and gangs has an adverse effect on teaching, learning, and school safety. (See Figures 3.1 and 3.2 for statistics on bullying and crimes against students.)

The courts have historically presumed that schools are safe places because students are in the functional custody of certified and highly skilled professionals charged with creating and maintaining a safe school environment where teaching and learning occur. It is important that school officials, teachers, and parents work cooperatively to ensure that schools are orderly and safe. Parents' roles involve instilling proper values at home, modeling appropriate behavior to support those values, and holding children accountable for their misbehavior. School personnel should also model positive and appropriate behavior and work collectively to create a school environment characterized by openness, honesty, respect, friendliness, and tolerance for differences among students. These qualities are more evident when they are embraced by the school and translated into school values that are documented and communicated to students, parents, citizens, and community leaders to ensure that everyone understands the climate the school wishes to establish as it moves toward achieving its mission.

Figure 3.1   Percentage of Students Ages 12–18 Who Reported Selected Bullying Problems at School During the Previous Six Months, by Type of Bullying: 2005

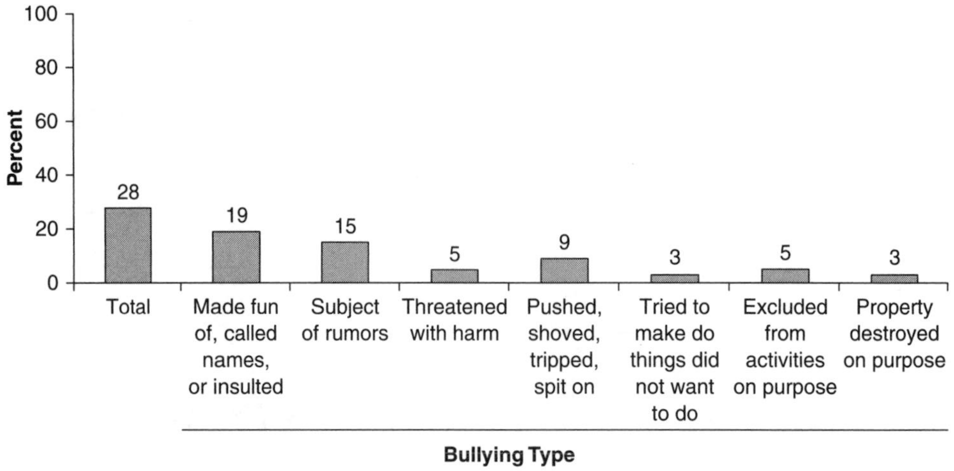

Bullying Type

Source: U.S. Department of Justice, Bureau of Justice Statistics, School Crime Supplement (SCS) to the National Crime Victimization Survey, 2005.

Note: "At school" includes the school building, on school property, on a school bus, or going to and from school. Types of bullying do not sum to total because students could have experienced more than one type of bullying. In 2005, the unit response rate for this survey did not meet NCES statistical standards; therefore, interpret the data with caution. For more information, please see Resource A. Population size for students ages 12–18 is 25,811,000 in 2005.

It would be prudent for teachers and parents to discuss school values with students to enhance their awareness of acceptable behavior as well as what is unacceptable. School discipline codes should be developed by representative teachers, parents, citizens, community leaders, and even students where appropriate, eliciting their views regarding policy content prior to their implementation. It is desirable that policies be reviewed by the school district's attorney for legality prior to their implementation. A school policy with specific consequences associated with each infraction is highly desirable with respect to legal defensibility. Student codes of conduct are generally effective when they are both rigorous and fair.

It is important that teachers feel supported as they attempt to enforce the student code of conduct. Teachers are responsible for ensuring that their classrooms are supportive, inviting, and well organized and that assignments are engaging, challenging, and activity oriented, with interesting learning experiences involving a variety of teaching strategies. School counselors' roles involve working with students by providing academic and personal counseling as well as offering conflict resolution strategies.

Bullying, harassment, assaults, and disorderly conduct/disrespect for authority, including verbal abuse, are generally prohibited by school policy. All disciplinary measures are required to meet full due process provisions. The courts have ruled consistently that a fair and reasonable exercise of administrative authority will

Figure 3.2   Rate of Student-Reported, Nonfatal Crimes Against Students Ages 12–18 per
1,000 Students, by Type of Crime and Location: 1992–2005

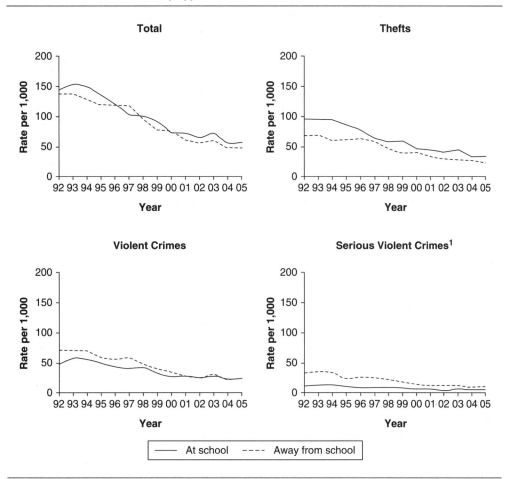

[1] Serious violent crimes are also included in violent crimes.

Source: U.S. Department of Justice, Bureau of Justice Statistics, National Crime Victimization Survey (NCVS),
1992–2005.

Note: Serious violent crimes include rape, sexual assault, robbery, and aggravated assault. Violent crimes include serious
violent crimes and simple assault. Total crimes include violent crimes and theft. "At school" includes inside the school
building, on school property, or on the way to or from school. Population sizes for students ages 12–18 are 23,740,000
in 1992; 24,558,000 in 1993; 25,327,000 in 1994; 25,715,000 in 1995; 26,151,000 in 1996; 26,548,000 in 1997;
26,806,000 in 1998; 27,013,000 in 1999; 27,169,000 in 2000; 27,380,000 in 2001; 27,367,000 in 2002; 26,386,000 in
2003; 26,372,000 in 2004; and 26,456,000 in 2005.

generally be supported. Minimizing school disruptions is more inclined to be
successful when it is viewed as a school and community issue, with all stakeholders
contributing their efforts to ensure that schools are safe and orderly. The courts
have long established the view that school officials and teachers operating in their
official capacities can exercise control over student behavior. They may discipline
students as long as they are responding in a reasonable manner.

Under *in loco parentis*, the actions of school officials and teachers are judged according to what an average and prudent parent would have done in the same or similar situation. The major challenge facing school personnel is to ensure that their actions toward students are fair and reasonable. Student policies or codes of conduct should not prohibit acts guaranteed by the U.S. Constitution. Additionally, student codes of conduct should be formulated primarily to minimize disruption to the educational process. The courts' test for determining the appropriateness of student codes of conduct requires that school officials demonstrate a substantial justification of the need for a particular policy or regulation when challenges arise regarding its enforcement. In determining whether a policy or rule is fair and reasonable, it is necessary that it be viewed in the context of its application. The enforceability of a rule depends on the particular facts surrounding the situation in which the rule is applied.

32. What Should Teachers Know About Due Process in Their Dealings With Students?

Teachers should be aware that students are entitled to due process provisions. Due process is derived from the Fourteenth Amendment, which states:

> All persons born or naturalized in the United States and subject to the jurisdiction thereof, are citizens of the United States and of the state wherein they reside. No state shall make or enforce any law which shall abridge the privileges or immunities of citizens of the United States; nor shall any state deprive any person of life, liberty or property, without due process of law; nor deny to any person within its jurisdiction the equal protection under the laws.

Since public schools are agents of the state, the Fourteenth Amendment applies to the management and operation of public schools. Due process is typically applied in cases involving student discipline where suspension, expulsion, or corporal punishment of students is involved. There are two types of due process: "procedural due process" and "substantive due process."

33. What Does Procedural Due Process Entail?

Procedural due process is defined as a legal course of proceedings set in accordance with established rules designed to enforce and protect individual rights. The essential element of due process is fundamental fairness, which means that one who is facing deprivation receives an impartial hearing and a fair, unbiased judgment. Practically speaking, any student who has been accused of serious infractions that may result in removal from the school should be provided an opportunity to present his or her side of the situation when the issue involves life, liberty, or property. It is important to reemphasize that students are entitled to due process of law when a property interest is involved, and students have a property interest in attending public schools.

A property interest was defined by the court in a leading case, *Board of Regents v. Roth,* involving teacher dismissal.[1] Property interests under the Fourteenth Amendment are characterized as follows:

- To have a property interest in a benefit, a person clearly should have more than an abstract need or desire for it.
- He or she should have more than a unilateral expectation of it.
- He or she should instead have a legitimate claim of entitlement to it.
- Operationally, students have a legitimate claim of entitlement to receive a free public school education.

The essence of due process is that it prohibits teachers and school officials from making arbitrary or capricious decisions regarding those over whom they exercise authority. For example, minimum due process generally is applied to short-term student suspension because it does not usually result in permanent or long-term separation from school. Minimal due process involves

- notification of the rule or policy violation;
- an opportunity for the accused to respond to the alleged violation;
- a fair ruling, including an explanation of the evidence used to render the final ruling; and
- no required delay between notice of hearing and the actual hearing.

Short-term suspension was defined by the courts in *Goss v. Lopez* (to be discussed later) as ten days or less. If long-term suspension is recommended by school officials, full due process must be applied.

There are several variations of procedural due process. The following minimal steps are suggested, however, to ensure that the student's due process rights are not violated in cases involving expulsions or long-term suspensions that exceed ten days:

- Notice of charges
- Right to counsel
- Right to confrontation and cross-examination of witnesses
- Privilege against self-incrimination
- Right to transcript of the proceedings
- Right to appellate review

Some districts have adopted in-school suspension policies that penalize students for violating school rules but allow them to remain in school. A more detailed procedural process is discussed later in this chapter regarding long-term suspension and expulsion.

34. What Is the Importance of Substantive Due Process in Dealing With Students?

Substantive due process is defined as a constitutional guarantee that an individual will not be deprived of life, liberty, or property for invalid reasons. It also guarantees that the means used to deprive an individual of life, liberty, or property is reasonable. Substantive due process addresses the substance of the charges brought against an individual. It requires that policies be administered fairly and equally and that they afford individuals freedom from arbitrary and capricious actions. Substantive due process can be properly characterized as a standard of reasonableness, meaning that school or district officials should act in a reasonable manner to ensure that charges meted against students are valid and not based on bias, prejudice, or personal considerations.

A case involving a substantive due process challenge was addressed by the Tenth Circuit Court of Appeals in *Butler v. Rio Rancho*.[2] Joshua Butler borrowed his brother's car and drove to his high school. Butler parked the car in the faculty parking lot without a permit. A school security guard noticed that the vehicle did not have a permit and ran a registration check. The registration check revealed that the vehicle belonged to Butler's brother.

During this time, the security guard observed the butt end of a knife protruding between the passenger seat and the center console. He contacted Butler and had him open the vehicle. The security guard found a sheathed hunting knife in the vehicle. The security guard also found a handgun, ammunition, and drug paraphernalia. Butler denied knowing that the items were in the car. The knife, gun, and ammunition belonged to Butler's brother.

The principal of the high school immediately suspended Butler. After a disciplinary meeting, a hearing officer concluded that Butler should be suspended for one year. Butler appealed the hearing officer's decision to the school board. After a hearing, the school board upheld the hearing officer's decision.

Butler's parents sued the school board and various school officials on his behalf in the U.S. District Court of New Mexico. The Butlers claimed that the school violated their son's substantive due process right to a free public education by suspending him for one year without finding that he knowingly brought a weapon or firearm to school. They also requested, and the district court granted, a preliminary injunction allowing Joshua to attend school and participate in the commencement exercises and graduation-related social events. The school appealed the court's decision, but it was dismissed because Butler had already graduated from school and received his diploma.

The school subsequently filed a motion to dismiss the Butlers' complaint, arguing that the complaint failed to state a claim and that the school was entitled to qualified immunity. The district court granted the motion on several claims but denied it on the Butlers' substantive due process claims. The school requested that the district court reconsider its ruling that the school was not entitled to qualified immunity on the Butlers' substantive due process claims. The district court denied the motion, and the school appealed. The Tenth Circuit Court of Appeals reversed the district court's ruling in favor of the school.

The appeals court stated the following:

> There is no doubt the school has a legitimate interest in providing a safe environment for students and staff. It is not unreasonable for the school to conclude that student possession of weapons on school property threatens this interest. In order to protect against this threat and further the school's interest in safety, we believe there is a rational basis for the school to suspend Mr. Butler, even for one year, when he should have known he brought a weapon onto school property. The school's decision was not arbitrary, nor does it shock the conscience. Accordingly, the decision did not violate Mr. Butler's substantive due process rights, if any. Since the Butlers failed to state a substantive due process violation, we conclude the school is entitled to qualified immunity on the Butlers' substantive due process claims.

For these reasons, the court reversed the district court's order denying the school's motion to dismiss Butler's substantive due process claims and remanded the case to the district court. The Butlers' request for costs and attorney fees was denied.

The essence of due process is that both procedural and substantive aspects should be met. One is of no value without the other. For example, a school district might be supported by the court on having met procedural safeguards but may lose a case for not having met the substantive requirements. Conversely, a district may demonstrate that a valid reason exists to deprive an individual of his or her rights but fails on procedural grounds. To succeed in matters involving the discipline of students, the school district should ensure that all procedural and substantive safeguards are met.

The following landmark U.S. Supreme Court rulings emphasize the important role the High Court plays in ensuring that the due process rights of students are preserved. In a leading case involving short-term suspension, *Goss v. Lopez*,[3] Lopez and twenty-five other students were suspended following a disturbance in the school's cafeteria over a disagreement with school officials regarding which community leader would speak during an assembly program celebrating Black History Week. Ohio law authorized public school principals to suspend students for misconduct without a hearing. Several students involved in the demonstration were suspended without the benefit of a hearing as authorized by law.

Lopez and several students brought a class-action suit against school officials, seeking a declaration that the Ohio law requiring a suspension without hearings was unconstitutional. The argument was that Lopez had had no opportunity to affirm or deny his participation in the demonstration. The district court held for the students in determining that they had been denied due process of law based on the nature of the suspensions and that the Ohio law was unconstitutional. On appeal to the U.S. Supreme Court, the High Court held that students facing temporary suspension from public school have a property and liberty interest that qualifies them for protection under the due process clause. Justice White writing for the majority stated:

> Since the state had extended the right of an education to students, it may not withdraw that right on grounds of misconduct, absent fundamentally fair procedures to determine whether misconduct has occurred. Students faced with such potential losses of liberty should be given oral or written notice of the charges against them along with the opportunity at a hearing to present their version of what happened.

The court concluded that, if a student is threatened with suspension that extends beyond ten days, more elaborate safeguards are necessary. Several points were significant in the High Court's ruling:

- The due process clause forbids arbitrary deprivations of liberty interests that Lopez and other students possessed.
- A liberty interest involves a person's good name, reputation, honor, or integrity.
- If charges are sustained and recorded, they can obviously damage students' standing with fellow students and teachers as well as interfere with later opportunities for higher education and employment opportunities.
- The claimed right of the state to determine unilaterally and without process whether improper conduct occurred collides immediately with the Constitution.
- Students facing suspension and consequent interference with a protected property interest should be provided notice and afforded a hearing.
- Students in this case were not minimally provided any type of notice or afforded any kind of hearing.

The *Gault* case has been one of the leading due process cases heard by the U.S. Supreme Court involving a juvenile. Gerald Gault was an Arizona juvenile found guilty of making an obscene phone call. The punishment for the same crime involving an adult would have been a $50.00 fine. Since Gerald was a juvenile, he was remanded by a federal court to a state reform school for a period of up to six years.

Gerald's case was appealed to the U.S. Supreme Court on grounds that his equal protection rights were being violated under the Fourteenth Amendment. The U.S. Supreme Court noted that Gault had been placed in an industrial school without the benefit of procedural due process. The High Court noted that Arizona law regarding juveniles was deficient in the following areas:

- No appeal of the conviction was permitted.
- Written statements of the charges were not presented in every juvenile proceeding.
- Privilege against self-incrimination was denied.

The High Court overturned Gault's conviction based on procedural grounds and equal protection violations. The High Court concluded that "where a substantial penalty is involved, a juvenile, like an adult, is entitled to due process of law."[4]

The *Gault* decision greatly affected disciplinary proceedings in public schools. The High Court was quite clear in holding that students are entitled to the same due process rights as are adults, meaning that school officials must ensure that students' substantive and procedural rights are met in disciplinary hearings.

35. Is *In Loco Parentis* a Viable Concept for Teachers in Their Dealings With Students?

Yes, *in loco parentis* (in place of parents) continues to prevail in public schools as a means of defining relationships between teachers and students. With *in loco parentis*, the actions of teachers are judged in relation to what an average and prudent parent would do under the same or similar circumstances. When teachers conform to this standard, their actions are generally considered to be legally defensible by the courts unless there is evidence of constitutional violations or negligence.

Although *in loco parentis* remains viable, it is limited to the standard of reasonableness. *In loco parentis* is derived from common law and literally means "in place of parent." It was never intended to grant teachers the authority that parents exercise over their children because teachers do not possess the natural affection parents hold for their children. It essentially means that teachers may exercise certain decisions regarding children who are in the functional custody of the school. Their authority over students is limited to academic matters and school functions and activities. *In loco parentis* charges teachers with the responsibility to protect the safety and interests of children under their supervision by making sound and rational decisions regarding their welfare. *In loco parentis* defines the relationship between educators and children in the public school environment. In many instances, teachers and administrators have been upheld by the courts when they have disciplined students for conduct detrimental to proper school decorum. When the discipline has been reasonable and in conformity with legally defensible school or district policy, courts have relied on *in loco parentis* as a basis to support disciplinary measures. While the courts recognize that students enjoy a level of constitutional freedom in public schools, they also recognize that their rights are not unlimited and are subject to reasonable restraints imposed by teachers and administrators. Student rights are not co-extensive with the rights of adults.

At its inception, *in loco parentis* was applied to cases involving student discipline; however, the scope of *in loco parentis* was extended in a 1968 case, *Woodman v. Litchfield Community School District*, in Illinois. The appellate court of Illinois, Fifth District, made the following statement:

> Teachers . . . shall maintain discipline in the schools. In all matters relating to discipline and conduct of the schools and the school children, they stand in the relation of parents and guardians to the pupils. This relationship shall extend to all activities connected with the school program and may be exercised at any time for the safety and supervision of the pupils in the absence of their parents or guardian.[5]

It is important to recognize that *in loco parentis* thus carries responsibility and accountability for the actions of teachers and administrators, especially in cases involving negligence. In a leading case involving liability and *in loco parentis*, an Arizona court made a distinction between parents and educators with respect to liability. A judge for the Arizona Supreme Court made the following observation:

> The relationship of a public school teacher to her pupil is in some respect *in loco parentis*. Having the right to control and supervise the pupil, there is a correlative duty to act as a reasonable and prudent parent would in like circumstances.[6]

The court clarified that the rationale of *in loco parentis* does not, however, apply in determining liability for negligent torts against the student. In most jurisdictions, the parent is not liable for negligent torts against his child, but the public school may be. The court presumed that teachers and administrators are endowed with superior skill, judgment, intelligence, and foresight. As such, they should fulfill the strong duty arising from their professional positions by exercising care commensurate with the immaturity of their charges and the importance of their trust.[7]

Historically, the courts have supported school district officials' actions in the following areas under *in loco parentis*:

- Compulsory attendance
- Curricula requirements
- Treatment of injury and illness
- Corporal punishment and discipline
- Search and seizure
- Regulation of student appearance
- Review of school-sponsored student newspapers linked to the school's curriculum
- Control over:
  - speech that presents imminent danger
  - speech that creates material and substantial disruption to the educational process
  - time and place of student protests and demonstrations
  - time and place of nonschool-sanctioned publications
  - vaccinations

36. What Legal Standards Are Required for Students Facing Suspension?

Since discipline is critical to school safety and a peaceful teaching and learning environment, student suspension is viewed as an acceptable disciplinary tool by the courts. State legislatures grant school boards the authority to impose suspensions on students who violate clearly written and legally defensible codes of conduct. In all cases, student codes should inform students of infractions that will result in school suspensions.

Short-term suspension of up to ten days or less generally involves temporary withdrawal of the privilege to attend school or school-related events. Although suspension represents a temporary separation, minimal due process is required to ensure that the student receives fundamental fairness consistent with Fourteenth Amendment provisions. The extent of the due process provisions may vary with the nature of the infraction and the length of the proposed suspension. In either case, it is important that rudimentary due process be provided to include, at a minimum, adequate notice either verbally or in writing of the specific infraction along with the nature of the evidence supporting the charge against the student. The student should be provided with an informal hearing that includes an opportunity for the student to respond to the charges brought against him or her. Last, a fair and unbiased hearing should be provided, with punishment based solely on grounds supported by the documented evidence.

Since short-term suspensions are typically viewed as nonadversarial and only involve temporary separation, there is no need for representation by legal counsel. In most jurisdictions, school-level officials are authorized to suspend students as long as due process provisions are met. Parents should be informed prior to granting permission for the student to leave the campus. If parents cannot be reached, the student can be isolated until regular school dismissal, after which time parents are notified either through written or verbal communication of the suspension unless this practice conflicts with district policy. A letter should be sent to parents that summarizes findings and the grounds supporting the findings. Terms and conditions regarding the suspension should also be spelled out. There is generally no right to appeal short-term suspensions.

Many districts have resorted to in-school suspensions where the student is punished for rules violations but permitted to remain in school and meet academic requirements. The obvious advantage of in-school suspension is that the student does not miss valuable instructional time yet receives punishment for his or her behavior. Other districts impose suspension pending a conference with parents. If parents respond promptly and issues involving the student's behavior are addressed, the student is then allowed to continue in school. Some districts have also resorted to Saturday detention programs. Many experts believe these options best serve the interests of students because there is no interruption of instruction. (See Figure 3.3 for disciplining sanctions administered by schools.)

If a student's conduct or presence creates imminent danger, school officials can suspend the student immediately and provide a due process hearing after the danger has been curtailed. Students removed from the school may, based on district policy, be allowed to complete homework and class assignments. If the student is provided the opportunity to complete homework and class assignments, parents will generally make arrangements to secure the work for their child.

Long-term suspension generally involves periods of time beyond the ten-day, short-term suspension period. Because long-term suspensions are more serious in nature, a more detailed due process procedure is required. The superintendent or district hearing officer, based on district policy, is generally the authority that will impose a long-term suspension, first ensuring that due process requirements are met.

37. What Legal Standards Are Required for Students Facing Expulsion?

Expulsion may involve permanent withdrawal or separation from the school district, including school functions and activities. In most states, only the local board of education is authorized to expel a student. Since expulsion involves a property interest regarding students, they are entitled to a full due process hearing. A written notice of intent to expel and notice of hearing should be mailed and/or hand-delivered to the parent(s) in sufficient time prior to the hearing. This letter should minimally contain the following information:

- The nature of the offenses alleged and the policies, regulations, or rules allegedly violated.
- A statement that the student is being recommended for expulsion and the restrictions to be imposed on the student during the period of expulsion.
- Definition of expulsion.
- Date, time, and place of the hearing.
- Notice of whether the board will conduct the hearing or whether a nondistrict hearing officer has been appointed and the name of the hearing officer.
- Notice of the right of the parents to indicate their objection if the board decides to hold the hearing in executive session, whether conducted by the board or the nondistrict hearing officer.
- Notice of the right of the parents to attend and/or have legal counsel attend any executive session pertaining to the proposed disciplinary action, to have access to the minutes and testimony of the executive session, and to record such session at their own expense.
- Designation of the witnesses that the superintendent may call at the hearing and a copy of all exhibits the superintendent may use at the hearing.
- Notice of the right of the parents to access any and all adverse evidence that may be presented, as well as the student's records prior to the hearing.
- Notice that upon request the parents may provide the superintendent with their list of witnesses and exhibits at a prescribed time prior to the hearing.
- Notice of the parents' responsibility to notify the district of whether they intend to attend the hearing and whether the student will be represented by counsel.
- Notice that no witness or exhibit will be used at the hearing other than those listed and exchanged, except for good cause shown or upon agreement of the parties.
- Notice of the student's right to be represented by legal counsel at his or her own expense.
- Notice of the student's right to present witnesses and cross-examine the district's witnesses and to introduce documentary evidence.
- Notice of the district's right to cross-examine the student's witnesses and to introduce documentary evidence.
- Notice of the student's right to have the district bear the burden of proof for the offense(s).
- Notice that the hearing will be recorded and that the student may request a copy of the transcript at the student's expense.
- Notice that, if the student is withdrawn from school before the scheduled hearing, the hearing may still be held and the board will record the results of the action in the student's permanent file. If parents are not satisfied with the final decision, they may pursue the matter in a court of law.

Even though grounds for expulsion vary among school districts, most expulsions involve serious violations including weapons, alcohol, drug possession, and assault and battery.

---

38. Can Students Be Disciplined for Misconduct That Occurred Off Campus and Outside the School Day?

Yes. The court in a very early case, *Burdick v. Babcock,* held that the seriousness of the offense rather than the place in which it occurs determines the right to punish perpetrators of the offense.[8] This court's position was subsequently reinforced in *O'Rourke v. Walker* when a teacher was supported for punishing a student found guilty of harassing small girls on their way home from school.[9] In yet another case, the court held that the board of education had the authority to suspend a student who was drunk and disorderly on public streets during Christmas Day.[10]

---

39. Do the Courts View Corporal Punishment as an Acceptable Form of Discipline in Public Schools?

It depends. Except in states that have banned corporal punishment, the courts have sanctioned corporal punishment as a reasonable form of discipline. However, when applied it should not be administered with malice or in an excessive manner. There is considerable disagreement over the use of corporal punishment in public schools. Many states have abolished corporal punishment as a disciplinary measure. There are pros and cons regarding the use of corporal punishment. Although a number of courts support its use, the decision to administer it in schools is left to the discretion of school boards in states where corporal punishment is allowed. (Figure 3.3 depicts corporal punishment and paddling statistics by state, and Table 3.1 details the percentage of students struck by educators.)

Corporal punishment is the infliction of physical pain on another with the intent of changing the person's behavior. Those who support corporal punishment suggest that students are more aggressive and violent because there are minimal consequences associated with misbehavior. Suspensions, for example, are viewed as a vacation for many disruptive students.

Minority groups, however, cite the disproportionate impact of corporal punishment on minorities, especially African American students. It is estimated that more than 273,000 students were corporally punished during the 2004–2005 school year, which represents a 10 percent decline from the late 1980s and early 1990s. Despite the decline, corporal punishment remains at the center of the national debate regarding its appropriateness in public schools.

A leading corporal punishment case, *Ingraham v. Wright,* arose during the 1970–1971 school year in Dade County, Florida, when corporal punishment

Figure 3.3   U.S. Corporal Punishment and Paddling by State

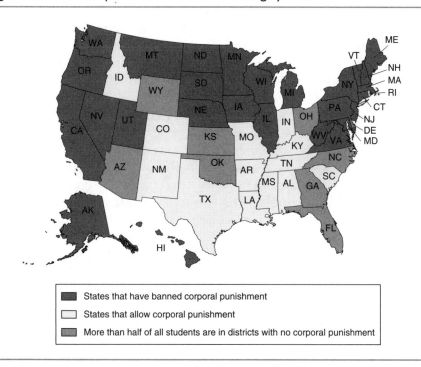

States that have banned corporal punishment

States that allow corporal punishment

More than half of all students are in districts with no corporal punishment

Source: The above data and more can be found at the U.S. Department of Education, Office for Civil Rights, Web site at http://ocrdata.ed.gov/ocr2006rv30/wdsdata.html.

Table 3.1   The Ten Worst States, by Percentage of Students Struck by Educators in the 2006–2007 School Year

Rank	State	Percentage
1	Mississippi	7.5
2	Arkansas	4.7
3	Alabama	4.5
4	Oklahoma	2.3
5	Louisiana	1.7
6	Tennessee	1.5
7	Texas	1.1
8	Georgia	1.1
9	Missouri	0.6
10	Florida	0.3

Source: U.S. Department of Education, Office for Civil Rights.

was used as a means of maintaining discipline. This form of punishment was permissible under Florida law and local school board regulations. Two students who had been corporally punished sued the school district both for individual damages and injunctive relief in federal district court. The students claimed that their beatings violated the Eighth Amendment's prohibition of cruel and unusual punishment. One student had been beaten so severely that he missed eleven days of school. The other lost the use of his arm for a week. The district court dismissed the complaint. The U.S. Court of Appeals, Fifth Circuit, reversed, but upon rehearing, affirmed the district court's decision. The U.S. Supreme Court granted review.

The Supreme Court held that the Eighth Amendment's cruel and unusual punishment clause did not apply to disciplinary corporal punishment in the public schools. The Court indicated that the Eighth Amendment was intended to protect accused criminals, not students. The High Court held that the openness of the public school and its supervision by the community afforded significant safeguards against the kind of abuses from which the Eighth Amendment protects convicted criminals. The High Court also held that the due process clause of the Fourteenth Amendment does not require notice and hearing prior to the imposition of corporal punishment. Imposing this burden would significantly intrude into the area of educational responsibility.[11]

In spite of this ruling, federal courts have subsequently ruled that excessive corporal punishment violates the substantive due process clause of the Fourteenth Amendment. The courts, however, have fallen short of determining exactly when corporal punishment becomes excessive. Although the *Ingraham* case upholds the legality of corporal punishment as an acceptable means of controlling student behavior, local school district policy in many cases has seriously limited its use. Nevertheless, according to a recent survey conducted by the National Center for the Study of Corporal Punishment and Alternatives in Schools, at least 2,000 U.S. schoolchildren are physically punished each day. States that have banned corporal punishment have sought alternative corrections to student misbehavior, such as developing character education programs, building social skills, instituting instructional peer mediation, and other types of behavior modification strategies designed to curb student misconduct. It should be noted that students with disabilities cannot be disciplined for behavior that is a manifestation of their disability as reflected in their Individual Education Plan (IEP). (See Chapter 5 regarding the discipline of students with disabilities.)

It is commonly accepted that the principal should possess the authority to discipline students and that the exercise of that authority should be safeguarded. No one disagrees with the point that a peaceful environment is essential to an effective learning climate and that it is the principal's primary responsibility to provide that environment for students.

The following case illustrates the court's support for corporal punishment in public schools. In February 2001, a third grader, Michael Setliff, was administered three blows to the buttocks with a wooden paddle for misbe-having at recess.[12] Prior to the punishment, Michael's parents had explicitly requested that he not be physically punished. Michael's family filed charges against the school board and principal claiming that he was injured when his principal administered the punishment. The court held that the school board and principal were not responsible for Michael's injuries. The court also found that their actions were far less severe than those of a teacher in an earlier case, *Harrell v. Daniels*, in which the court refused to award damages.[13] In *Harrell*, the child was paddled and taken to an emer-gency room shortly after the paddling. A medical report described two bluish-red bruises 2½ by 3 inches in width; one bruise was located on the buttocks, and the other over the left flank. In refusing to award damages, the court in *Harrell* took into account that the student's behavior at school was disruptive, aggressive, and bizarre and therefore merited such punish-ment. In relying on this holding, the *Setliff* court dismissed Michael's suit. The court stated that by permitting corporal punishment the legislature rec-ognized a need for it under certain conditions. Therefore, parents should yield to a higher duty and support what is best for all of the children, as must those who have the enormous responsibility of educating them.

Poor decisions regarding the use of corporal punishment by a princi-pal will not be supported by the courts and could result in civil damage suits or even criminal prosecution for assault and battery. An example of a poor decision is illustrated in an Alabama case. The U.S. Court of Appeals, Eleventh Circuit, upheld a federal district court order denying qualified immunity to an Alabama principal accused of beating a student. The court held that repeatedly striking a thirteen-year-old with a metal cane was an obvious constitutional violation. It rejected the principal's assertion that a prior incident involving weapons possession allowed him to beat the student.[14] (Assault usually involves a threat to use force. If bodily contact actually occurs, then a battery has been committed.)

In cases where corporal punishment is permitted, it should be used only as a last resort measure. Every reasonable method should be employed prior to administering corporal punishment, which may involve working very closely with teachers, parents, or guardians to resolve a child's deviant behavior. In all cases, students should be informed through student conduct codes beforehand of specific infractions that warrant corporal punishment.

When administered, the punishment should be reasonable and consis-tent with the gravity of the infraction. Corporal punishment should never be administered excessively or with malice. In the past, there have been numerous suits alleging that children were struck with double belts, lacrosse sticks, baseball bats, electrical cords, bamboo rods, hoses, and wooden drawer dividers. None of these practices could pass the test of reasonableness established by today's courts.

In districts that support corporal punishment, school officials and teachers should ensure that there is a direct relationship between the act committed by a student and the resulting physical punishment. In short, the punishment should fit the offense, and school personnel should not act arbitrarily or capriciously in either the formation or enforcement of regulations. Although school personnel have the power to enforce responsible regulations governing students, the administration of corporal punishment for behavior that is not clearly punishable violates the students' constitutional rights. School personnel should ensure that students are given adequate notice that paddling may result from certain types of conduct, and students should always know what to expect in these cases.

It is important that school personnel be aware of the physical condition of students who might be subject to corporal punishment. If, in the process of administering punishment, a student's physical condition is aggravated, the principal could face charges of assault and battery or more serious offenses. If a student appears to be frail or sickly, an alternative punishment should be considered. Where possible, punishment should be administered by those of the same gender, with men punishing male students and women punishing female students. In all cases, the age, size, maturity, and ability of the child to bear punishment should be carefully considered. Corporal punishment should not be administered in the presence of other students.

While the courts have not defined what constitutes a reasonable instrument, school personnel should not use one that can obviously injure the student. Many school boards prescribe the type of instrument that should be used. Obviously, the use of instruments that may cut or cause serious injury is wholly indefensible.

School personnel should always explain to the student prior to administering corporal punishment the reasons why the punishment is necessary. If the student professes ignorance of the rule allegedly broken or innocence of the offense, a brief but thorough informal hearing should be held to permit the student to present his or her side of the issue. This procedure ensures that minimal due process has been provided.

A witness should always be present when corporal punishment is administered. The witness should be a certified school employee who is informed of the infraction committed. It is important that this employee be able to verify exactly what occurred during the punishment process to counter possible allegations by the student that the teacher or administrator acted improperly.

Caution should be exercised to ensure that an intent to seriously harm the student is not present. There is greater probability that a teacher or administrator who is angry will exercise poor judgment that may result in injury to the student. School officials should avoid administering physical punishment when provoked by students, allowing a sufficient period of time to regain composure.

Corporal punishment should not be inflicted in a manner that might be considered cruel or excessive. Malicious use of corporal punishment is utterly indefensible, often occurring when frustrated school personnel administer punishment for an unreasonable period of time or use an improper instrument. School personnel should refrain from overusing corporal punishment. A good rule of thumb is not to administer more than three strikes for any single infraction.

Whenever possible, students should be provided punishment options for undesirable behavior. They are less likely to resist if they are given a choice. Corporal punishment should never be administered when the student is physically resisting it. To proceed in this situation may expose school personnel to charges of assault and battery. If a parent objects to the use of physical punishment, an effort should be made to accommodate the request through other alternatives involving collaboration with the parent.

School personnel should be knowledgeable about local or state policies and regulations governing the use of corporal punishment. For example, policies in some districts or states ban corporal punishment. Some states or districts permit such punishment only by administrators, whereas others allow teachers to administer punishment. In all cases, laws and prescribed procedures should be followed. Repeated failure to do so may be grounds for insubordination.

The controversy over the use of corporal punishment—banned in Poland, Holland, Austria, France, Italy, Japan, and other countries—continues to be a major issue in our schools today. In growing numbers, opponents are declaring that it is a fundamental breach of human rights and should be forbidden. Although the U.S. courts have not banned its use, corporal punishment should be a last resort measure administered in a rational and prudent manner.

The following cases exemplify court decisions on the use of corporal punishment in schools:

- A principal and assistant principal were held liable for inflicting excessive force when they corporally punished two students. The students experienced extensive bruising that lasted approximately one week. The Department of Health and Rehabilitative Services notified both that they were child abusers.[15]
- A principal was held liable for administering excessive corporal punishment to a sixth-grade student with disabilities. The corporal punishment resulted in the student being hospitalized and a lengthy stay in the psychiatric ward for mental trauma associated with the incident.[16]
- A principal was denied sovereign immunity when a student's arm was broken during the administration of corporal punishment. There was a question as to whether the child was punished in good faith and whether the punishment was too severe.[17]
- The Eighth U.S. Circuit Court of Appeals upheld a principal when he grabbed a student's neck and shirt collar, led him into the office, threw him on a bench for kicking a school machine and displaying disrespect to a teacher who asked him not to kick the machine. The

court ruled that school administrators are entitled to substantial deference in their efforts to maintain order and discipline. The principal responded quickly and decisively to an incident of serious student misbehavior.[18]

- A teacher was reinstated by the Oklahoma Supreme Court when it was determined that she did not mentally or physically abuse a special needs student by slapping him in his face to calm him down.[19]

- A district court in Georgia held that it is anticipated that corporal punishment will produce pain and the potential for bruising. The punishment is not considered excessive if the student experiences no more than short-term discomfort.[20]

- The Eighth U.S. Court of Appeals held that bruises that result from paddling a student's buttocks do not constitute a substantive due process violation.[21]

40. Do Teachers Have a Responsibility to Their Students in Situations Involving Bullying?

Yes. Bullying is a persistent problem in public schools and may involve physical injury to the victim, emotional harm, sexual harassment, or harassment in general. It is intentional and cruel behavior against victims. Commonly, students will inform the teacher that they have been threatened or bullied by another student. If the teacher does not take this information seriously and fails to act or to inform the principal, the teacher could face a liability suit if a student is then actually assaulted and injured.

41. Are Zero Tolerance Policies Supported by the Courts?

Yes, generally speaking, particularly when the focus is on school safety. However, there are Fourteenth Amendment standards to be considered by school officials who implement zero tolerance policies. Fundamental to any type of policy implementation process is fairness. School district policies meet the standard of fairness when the behaviors that fall under zero tolerance provisions are clearly specified. The consequences linked with these infractions and all policies must achieve consistent application. And, it would be prudent to inform students and parents in advance of the implementation process to ensure that everyone affected understands the policies and consequences for policy violations.

Zero tolerance policies carry predetermined punishment for specific offenses without regard for circumstances. These policies emerged in public schools as a means to reduce and prevent violence. From their inception, most zero tolerance policies were aimed at deterring serious student offenses involving possession of firearms, weapons other than firearms, drugs, assaults, violence, tobacco, alcohol use, and bullying. The implementation of zero tolerance policies is understandable in these instances based on the seriousness of the offenses and concerns for student safety.

42. How Did Zero Tolerance Emerge in Public Schools?

Zero tolerance emerged during the 1990s and was directed primarily at students who concealed weapons and drugs on school grounds. In fact, former President Clinton provided a major boost when he signed the Gun Free School Act of 1994 that mandates expulsion of students who bring a weapon to school. This federal statute affects each state that receives federal funds and requires local educational agencies to expel from school for a period of not less than one year any student found to have brought a weapon to school. However, the statute does provide the chief administrator of the district the latitude to modify the expulsion requirement for students on a case-by-case basis; therefore, even though this statute is a version of a "one strike, you're out" strategy, it does provide flexibility based on administrative discretion. Thus, in the strictest sense, it is not absolute zero tolerance.

Today's version of zero tolerance typically provides no flexibility, which is one of the criticisms of the concept. Historically when behavioral infractions were addressed by school officials, they tended to consider the student's age, history of behavior in the school, and the severity of the infraction when determining the type of punishment that should be imposed. Zero tolerance policies do not provide this type of latitude, which in some cases results in questionable punishment based on the nature of the infraction. It has become a "one-size-fits-all" response to every behavioral infraction in public schools. Zero tolerance generally results in suspension, expulsion, and even arrests. Additionally, zero tolerance policies tend to have a disproportionate impact on minority students. Nationally, African American students represent 17 percent of the population but account for 36 percent of school suspensions and 31 percent of expulsions according to the Office of Civil Rights in the Department of Education.

Some argue that school officials are confusing equal treatment with equality, even though students may receive equal treatment with respect to the application of zero tolerance. There is no equality when the seriousness of the offense is not considered. For example, there is a difference between marijuana and Tylenol, yet the possession of Tylenol carries the same level of punishment in some school districts under zero tolerance as does possession of marijuana. Students should be concerned with fairness; consequently, when they see minor offenses treated in the same manner as more serious offenses, a sense of unfairness is the logical result. There have been accounts of the misapplication of zero tolerance in a number of schools, a few of which are cited below:

- A high school student was expelled for shooting a paper clip at another student and inadvertently striking another person.[22]
- A fifth-grade student drew a bloody vampire for his art class assignment. He was told that he could not return to school unless he passed a psychological test.[23]

- A first grader was disciplined for smacking a classmate's bottom on the playground, and the police were summoned to the school.[24]
- One of the most unfortunate outcomes of zero tolerance occurred in Tennessee. Dustin Seal, then a high school senior, was expelled after authorities at his high school discovered a three-inch knife in his car. The knife did not belong to Dustin. A friend who left the knife in Dustin's car claimed responsibility for it. The administration, however, did not change its position. Under the school's zero tolerance policy, every student found with a weapon on campus had to be expelled. His father stated that Dustin became depressed and withdrawn after his expulsion. Dustin was distraught because he had done nothing wrong; however, he was not allowed to return to school. The Seals sued the school district and took the case all the way to the Supreme Court, winning at every step. But by the time the Court sent the case back to the local level for Dustin to claim damages, he was too exhausted to continue fighting. He settled for $30,000 in December 2001. Six months later, Dustin spent a June day with his father shooting pool. He went home that night, drew a bath, got in the bathtub, placed a pistol under his chin, and pulled the trigger. He was twenty-two years old. Almost two years after his son's suicide, Dennis Seal sued the Knox County School Board for wrongful death, claiming that Dustin's suicide was a direct result of his expulsion.[25]
- A six-year-old student removed a plastic butter knife from the school cafeteria and placed it in his book bag. A classmate saw the knife and reported it to the teacher, and he was suspended for ten days.[26]
- An honor student, cheerleader, and Student Council member violated the school's zero tolerance policy by bringing to school a twenty-ounce bottle of Cherry 7-Up mixed with a few drops of grain alcohol and faced five months in a military-style boot camp.[27]
- Students have been suspended from school for possession of Midol, Tylenol, Alka Seltzer, cough drops, and Scope mouthwash—contraband that violates zero tolerance and antidrug policies.[28]
- A second grader from Alexandria, Louisiana, was suspended for bringing her grandfather's gold-plated pocket watch to school because the timepiece had a tiny knife attached.[29]
- A ten-year-old student at a school in Colorado was expelled because her mother placed a small knife in her lunchbox to cut an apple. When the student realized the knife might violate the school's zero tolerance policy, she turned the knife in to the teacher, who told her she had done the right thing.[30]

These represent a few of the many questionable applications of zero tolerance policies.

43. Are Unorthodox Disciplinary Practices by Teachers Supported by the Courts?

It depends on the nature of the discipline and the probable impact it has on children. Courts generally do not support practices that demoralize or embarrass students. There is a view by some courts that emotional damages suffered by children are more serious than physical injury. Psychological effects stemming from these practices can be devastating to children. School personnel should be mindful of the need to respect students by not engaging in disciplinary practices that damage their self-esteem and overall emotional health. Disciplinary practices should never be employed that result in humiliation and negative consequences or maltreatment for children. Emotional pain might result in significant problems for children who crave love and acceptance from the teachers they look up to and depend on for support, safety, guidance, and direction.

A Hawaiian case illustrates the consequences of using an unorthodox practice. A Hawaiian elementary school teacher sent a student to the school office to be disciplined for fighting.[31] The student refused to stand still against a wall for a timeout punishment. The school's vice principal warned the student that he would take him outside and tape him to a tree if he did not stand still. He then taped the student to the tree with masking tape. A fifth-grade student told the vice principal that "she did not think he should be doing that." The vice principal allowed her to remove the tape from the student. The student's family sued the state education department and vice principal in a federal district court for constitutional rights violations. The court denied the vice principal's motion for summary judgment. He appealed to the Ninth Circuit Court of Appeals. The court held that taping an eight-year-old to a tree was objectively unreasonable conduct. Students have a clearly established right to be free from excessive force by their teachers. The district court had properly found a violation of the student's rights, and the court affirmed the judgment.

The following unorthodox practices raise serious questions regarding disciplinary actions by teachers that are not sanctioned by school or district policy. The individuals involved risked being charged with insubordination or unprofessional conduct, at least, and often dismissal.

- Haitian students were forced to eat on the floor with their hands and were called animals in New York.[32]
- A substitute teacher was dismissed when she tied a student to a chair and taped another student's mouth in Cobb County, Georgia.[33]
- A five-year-old male student in central Florida was required to put on a yellow dress because the teacher determined that he talked too much.[34]
- A student with disabilities was forced to eat oatmeal despite his allergic reaction to it. He was pinned down by one teacher while the other forced him to eat the oatmeal.[35]

- A fourteen-year-old ninth-grade choir member was allegedly told by her choir teacher that she looked bad, was a brat, and was ugly. The teacher allegedly kicked her on her buttocks. A lawsuit seeking damages is pending.[36]
- A teacher allowed kindergarten students to tell a fellow student what they disliked about him and to vote him out of the class. The student was voted out by a 14–2 margin.[37]

These represent just a few of the many incidents reported by students or their parents throughout the country. Degrading and abusive discipline can be very destructive to students and has a devastating impact on the development of their personality, self-esteem, and sense of belonging. Schools as educational institutions should strive to provide positive environments that respect the dignity and uniqueness of all children so that they can learn, grow, and reach their full potential.

Summary of Cases Involving Student Discipline

- The U.S. Court of Appeals for the Seventh Circuit held in an unpublished decision that a school official did not violate a student's Fourth Amendment rights regarding unreasonable search and seizure when he suspended the student for seven days for refusing to consent to have her purse searched.[38]

- The U.S. Court of Appeals for the Sixth Circuit held that school officials did not violate a student's due process rights by suspending her for one day without a notice and an opportunity to be heard.[39]

- The North Carolina appellate court concluded that a student's due process rights were violated when his attorney was excluded from a hearing involving long-term suspension. The student faced suspension for sexually harassing a female classmate when he pushed the lower part of his body in her face and grabbed his crotch while making sexual remarks.[40]

- The Virginia Supreme Court held that a student's due process rights were not violated when he was suspended and later expelled for bringing a pocketknife on a school field trip because the board provided him with notice and a hearing at each step in the disciplinary process.[41]

- Under zero tolerance, a student was suspended near the end of the fall semester for marijuana possession. The school's zero tolerance policy called for expulsion. The student was subsequently expelled until the following semester and was denied credit for courses taken during the fall semester. The student filed suit charging that the penalty was excessive under state law. The district court sided with the district in supporting the suspension and denial of credit.[42]

• The Eleventh Circuit Court of Appeals held that a teacher violated a student's substantive due process rights when he caused the student to lose vision in one eye by striking him with a metal weight in retaliation for the student having struck another student with the weight.[43]

Summary Guides

1. Control of disruptive student behavior is necessary to enhance teaching and learning.

2. Bullying can create a negative school climate and infringe upon the rights of students to learn in a safe school environment free of fear.

3. Bullying results in physical or psychological intimidation that may lead to a pattern of harassment and abuse.

4. Students are entitled to due process when school infractions result in disciplinary sanctions.

5. The burden of proof rests with school personnel to demonstrate that all aspects of due process are met during student disciplinary hearings.

6. *In loco parentis* does not relieve school personnel of the duty to exercise reasonable judgment in disciplining students.

7. Minimal due process is sufficient in student suspension cases, whereas full due process proceedings are required in student expulsion cases.

8. Serious student misconduct away from school can be addressed by school officials based on the nature of the misconduct and its impact on proper discipline and decorum in the school.

9. Excessive corporal punishment is a substantive due process violation and will not survive court scrutiny.

10. Zero tolerance policies are viewed as one-size-fits-all mandatory punishments, irrespective of legitimate explanations by students who have never been involved in disciplinary infractions.

11. Positive student-teacher relationships may minimize the execution of zero tolerance policies.

12. Unorthodox forms of punishment can result in psychological injury to students and will not be sanctioned by the courts.

NOTES

1. *Board of Regents v. Roth*, 408 U.S. 564, 572 (1972).
2. *Butler v. Rio Rancho Pub. Sch. Dist.*, 2002 WL 863141, at *1 (10th Cir. May 7, 2002).
3. *Goss v. Lopez*, 419 U.S. 565, 95 S.Ct. 729, 42 L.Ed. 2d 725 (1975).
4. *In re Gault*, 387 U.S. 1, 87 S.Ct. 1428 18 L. Ed. 2d 526 (1967).
5. *Woodman v. Litchfield Community School District No. 12*, 242 N.E. 2d 780 (Ill. App. 1968).
6. *Morris v. Ortiz*, 103 Ariz. 119, 437 P.2d 652 (1968).
7. Ibid.
8. *Burdick v. Babcock*, 31 Iowa 562 (1871).
9. *O'Rourke v. Walker*, 128 Atl. 25 (Conn. 1925).
10. *Douglas v. Campbell*, 116 S.W. 211 (Ark. 1909).
11. *Ingraham v. Wright*, 430 U.S. 651, 97 S.Ct. 1401, 51 L.Ed.2d 711 (1977).
12. *Setliff v. Rapides Parish Sch. Bd.*, 888 So. 2d 1156, 1158 (La. Ct. App. 2004).
13. *Harrell v. Daniels*, 499 So. 2d 482 (La. Ct. App. 1986).
14. *Kirkland v. Greene County Board of Educ.*, 347 F.3d 903 (11th Cir. 2003).
15. *B.L. v. Dept. of Health & Rehab. Serv.*, 545 So. 2d 289 (Fla. App. 1st Dist. 1989).
16. *Fee v. Herndon*, 900 F.2d 804, 59, Ed. Law Rptr. 7003 (5th Cir. 1990).
17. *Crews v. McQueen*, 385 S.E. 2d 712, 57 Ed. Law Rptr. 269 (Ga. App. 1989).
18. *Golden ex. rel. Balch v. Anders*, 324 R.3d 650 (8th Cir. 2003).
19. *Hagen v. Independent School Dist. No. I-004*, 738 3d 157 19 OK (2007).
20. *Maddox v. Boutwell*, 176 Ga. 492, 336 S.E. 2d 599 (1985).
21. *Wise v. Pea Ridge School District*, 855 F.2d 560 (8th Cir. 1988).
22. *Education Week*, June 2008.
23. *Savannah Morning News*, October 31, 2008.
24. *Education Week*, June 2008.
25. *Seal v. Morgan*, 229 F.3d 567 (6th Cir. 2000).
26. *The Vindicator*, Youngstown, Ohio, March 10, 2003.
27. *USA Today*, April 13, 1999.
28. Ibid.
29. Ibid.
30. Ibid.
31. *Doe v. State of Hawaii*, 334 F.3d 906 (9th Cir. 2003).
32. *New York News*, May 9, 2005.
33. *Atlanta Journal Constitution*, April 29, 1998.
34. WKMG Channel 6, Orlando, Florida.
35. *Eason v. Clark County School Dist.*, 303 F.3d 1137 (9th Cir. 2002).
36. *San Diego News*, July 23, 2008.
37. *Treasure Cost Palm News*, May 27, 2008.
38. *Maimonis v. Urbanski*, 143 Fed. Appx. 699, WL 1869208 (7th Cir. 2005).
39. *Laney v. Farley*, 2007 U.S. App. LEXIS 20553,*;501 F.3d 577;2007 FED App. 0344P (6th Cir.).
40. *In re Matter of Roberts*, WL 956370 (N.C. App. 2002).
41. *Wood v. Henry County Public Schools*, 495 S.E. 2d 255 (Va. 1998).
42. *South Gibson Sch. Bd. v. Sollman*, 768 N.E.2d 437, 441 (Ind. 2002).
43. *Neal v. Fulton County Board of Education*, 229 F.3d 1069 (11th Cir. 2000).

4

Liability and Student Records

Family Education Rights and Privacy Act (FERPA)

⁂ INTRODUCTION ⁂

Students enrolled in public schools are afforded a level of privacy with respect to their personally identifiable information. Prior to the passage of the Family Education and Privacy Act (FERPA) or the Buckley Amendment, there were significant conflicts and litigation involving lack of parental or student access to student records, as well as erroneous and irrelevant information contained in student files. Additionally, confidential information was frequently released to external groups without the knowledge or consent of the parent or student. These conflicts led to the passage of FERPA by Congress in 1974. Since FERPA is a federal statute with the expressed purpose of providing privacy protection for students, all school districts and educational institutions that receive federal funds are impacted by this law.

44. What Is the Buckley Amendment or Family Educational Rights and Privacy Act (FERPA), and How Does It Apply to Teachers?

The Buckley Amendment or Family Educational Rights and Privacy Act (FERPA) of 1974 was passed by Congress to protect the privacy rights of students regarding confidential information and to allow parents and eligible students, with a few exceptions, to determine whether confidential information will be released.

Teachers who wish to access a student's educational records are required to sign a prescribed form indicating the legitimate interest they have for making their request. Maintaining permanent records is the responsibility of school officials. Permanent records should indicate who has gained access to student records and specifically what information was reviewed by the party, as well as the basis for reviewing the specific information. Additionally, teachers must be informed by school policy that information reviewed may not be divulged to any other party without the expressed consent of the parent or eligible student. Parents, legal guardians, or eligible students must consent in written form to release confidential information to another party.

45. Are There Exceptions That Allow Other Parties to Access Records Without Consent?

Yes, the statute does include an exception that allows other parties to access student information contained in the file without consent. These include

- the eligible student or parent;
- school officials and teachers who have a legitimate interest in accessing students' personal information;
- the comptroller general of the United States;
- the secretary of education;
- the administrative head of an educational agency;
- officials who need access in conjunction with a student's financial aid;
- federal or state auditors; and
- court representatives in compliance with a judicial order or subpoena, upon the condition that parents are notified prior to the release of information.

Organizations that conduct studies on behalf of educational agencies for the purpose of developing and or validating predictive tests must not divulge the identity of students involved unless it is totally essential. Additionally, educational records may be forwarded to school officials in a district to which a student transfers without parental permission. Directory information can also be released without parental consent; however, if parents object to the release of directory information on their children, their request must be honored. Directory information includes, but is not limited to, the following:

- Student's name
- Address
- Telephone listing
- Date and place of birth
- Major field of study
- Participation in officially recognized school-sanctioned activities and sports
- Weight and height of members of athletic teams
- Dates of attendance
- Degrees and awards received
- Most recent educational institution attended by the student

46. What Is the Importance of the Public Notice Requirement Regarding FERPA?

Public notice is a requirement of the statute. The notice must be given annually in regard to the categories of information classified as directory. A reasonable period of time must be allowed for parents or legal guardians to have an opportunity to object to the release of the information designated as directory. Additionally, school districts must, on an annual basis, provide information regarding the content of the law, informing parents, legal guardians, and eligible students of their rights to due process when complaints are filed. They must also be informed of their right to file complaints with the Rights and Privacy Act Office of the Department of Education if a resolution to their challenges is not resolved. School districts are required to provide information in the native language of non-English-speaking parents.

47. Who Is Affected by FERPA Implementation?

FERPA applies to any educational institution that receives or distributes federal funds. Violation of any component of this act may result in the loss of federal funds. The following excerpt is taken from Public Law 93-380, commonly referred to as the Buckley Amendment:

> No funds shall be made available under any applicable program to any educational agency or institution unless the parents of students who are or have been in attendance at a school of such agency or at such institution are provided an opportunity for a hearing by such agency or institution, in accordance with regulations of the Secretary, to challenge the content of such student's education records, in order to insure that the records are not inaccurate, misleading, or

otherwise in violation of the privacy or other rights of students, and to provide an opportunity for the correction or deletion of any such inaccurate, misleading, or otherwise inappropriate data contained therein and to insert into such records a written explanation of the parents respecting the content of such records.

48. How Does No Child Left Behind Impact the Privacy Rights of Students?

The No Child Left Behind (NCLB) Act includes a provision that requires the secretary of education to inform each state education agency of its obligations under FERPA, including the rights of parents and eligible students. Notices must also be provided to local school districts. In light of these requirements, it will become increasingly difficult for school officials to justify not enforcing provisions of FERPA based on the defense that they were unaware of the requirement to provide annual notice.

49. What Rights Are Provided Parents and Legal Guardians Regarding Student Records?

Parents or legal guardians of students under age eighteen are entitled to the same rights as eligible students (eighteen years old) regarding their children's records. Parents can inspect educational records of their children and challenge the accuracy of any information contained in the files that they believe to be inaccurate. Upon request for a hearing, the school district must provide a hearing to allow parents the opportunity to challenge the accuracy of their child's record. Parents may engage an attorney if they wish to do so. Appropriate corrections and deletions must be made if it is determined that specific information contained in the files is inaccurate. If adjustments are not made because the school officials' view is that the information in question is accurate, parents may include a statement of disagreement regarding specific information in the student's file, which must be disclosed whenever records are released and kept as long as records are maintained by the school. Parents or legal guardians may also file a complaint with the Department of Education if they believe provisions of the act have been violated.

50. What Must Teachers Know Regarding Access Rights Afforded Students Under FERPA?

Eligible students have a right to

- inspect and review all educational records directly related to the student and maintained by an educational agency, institution, or party acting for the agency or institution;

- seek amendment of records that the student believes to be inaccurate, misleading, or otherwise in violation of the student's privacy rights;
- consent to disclosure of personally identifiable information contained in the student's educational records; and
- file a complaint with the Department of Education concerning alleged failures by the educational agency or institution to comply with the requirements of the act.

Eligible students must be provided with information regarding procedures for exercising their right to access, inspect, and challenge the accuracy of information contained in their file. The school must grant access within forty-five days. Although forty-five days constitute the maximum length of time under the statute, school officials should provide access as quickly as is feasible. If a request to amend records based on changes or inaccurate information is denied, a hearing must be scheduled to address the challenge. The person or persons designated by the school to hear the challenge should have no direct interest in the outcome of the hearing. Eligible students may, at their discretion, involve an attorney. A final decision regarding the challenge must be provided by the school in writing within a reasonable period of time. The final decision must be based solely on the evidence presented during the hearing. A summary of the evidence and the rationale for the final decision must be included in the summary. If the final decision results in denying the request to amend student records, eligible students must be advised that a statement of disagreement can be added to the record, which must be disclosed with any records as long as the record is maintained by the school. Copies of disclosed records must be provided upon request. Records protected under the Buckley Amendment include those directly related to a student and those maintained by the educational institution. It must be noted that personal records maintained by teachers are not subject to disclosure under FERPA. Table 4.1 indicates records considered to be educational versus those that are not.

51. Is There a FERPA Exception to Health Insurance Portability and Accountability Act (HIPAA) Regulations?

Yes. The U.S. Department of Health and Human Services issued the Privacy Rule to implement certain requirements of the Health Insurance Portability and Accountability Act (HIPAA) of 1996.[1] The Privacy Rule addresses the use and disclosure of individuals' health information by organizations subject to the rule as well as individuals' rights to understand and control how their health information is used. A major goal of the Privacy Rule is to assure that individuals' health information is properly protected. The act also permits the dissemination of health information that is needed to promote high-quality health care and to protect the public's health and well-being. The rule strikes a balance that permits important uses of information while protecting the privacy of people who seek health care.

Table 4.1   Educational Versus Noneducational Records

Educational Records	Noneducational Records
1. Records, files, documents, and other material that contain information directly related to a student	1. Institutional records
2. Records maintained by a public or private educational institution	2. Records maintained in the possession of teachers and administrators that are not accessible or revealed to other individuals except those serving as substitutes
3. Records maintained by an individual acting for a public or private institution	3. Records maintained by law enforcement agencies
	4. Records maintained by a law enforcement unit of an educational agency that were created by the law enforcement unit for the purpose of law enforcement
	5. Medical and psychological records of an eighteen-year-old student who attends a postsecondary institution that are maintained by a physician, psychiatrist, psychologist, or a recognized professional involved in the treatment of the student

Source: Family Educational Rights and Privacy Act, PL 93-380.

The law simply protects individuals from the risk that their personal health information will be inappropriately accessed, released, or misused. With respect to educational records, HIPAA's definition of protected health information excludes educational records protected by FERPA, meaning that the use and disclosure of educational records as defined by FERPA are not subject to HIPAA regulations. Simply stated, health information contained in a student's educational record that is subject to FERPA is exempt from HIPAA requirements.

52. What Must Teachers Know About Libel and Slander in Handling Student Records, and How Are They Affected?

Libel and slander are forms of defamation. Defamation typically occurs when certain statements are made by one person against another by which the defamed person incurs injury to his or her reputation or standing.

Libel is written defamation, whereas slander is oral defamation. Both forms constitute a tort in which recovery is possible. In both instances, communication of the harmful information must have been transmitted to a third party to incur liability.

Lawsuits are possible when

- a false or defamatory statement regarding a person is communicated to another party;
- the information communicated is unprivileged; and
- the person against whom the information was communicated was damaged.

Teachers run the risk of a lawsuit for defamation when they inadvertently leak personal, sensitive, or damaging information found in a student's educational record to another who is not privileged to receive the information. Student educational records generally contain family background information, health records, psychological reports, disciplinary records, and other confidential information. Additionally, the Portability and Accountability Act of 1996 requires the Department of Health and Human Services to establish national standards for effective healthcare transactions designed to protect the privacy rights of healthcare data. If the communication of sensitive information results in injury to a student's reputation or standing in school or results in mental distress, liability charges can be brought by the parents, legal guardian, or the student. The burden of proof rests with the individual who claims injury.

53. Should Teachers Record Information on Students' Records Based on Their Opinion?

No. Educators are legally vulnerable when they record damaging information with no documentation or basis for including it in the student's file. Sensitive information must be documented and specific if it is determined that the information must be placed in the student's file. Information that is subject to change, such as minor infractions, should not be placed in the student's permanent file but in a temporary file. Opinions regarding a student or stereotypical statements must be avoided. Only true, documentable, and defensible statements should be recorded in the file. It is important to recognize that truth within itself is not always a proper defense against liability claims. True statements that are communicated to a third party, because of the actual damage that may accrue from these statements, are libelous. Examples include the following:

- Statements that a student is infected with a sexually transmitted disease
- Statements accusing a student of unlawful activities in which there is no documented evidence

- Statements suggesting that a student has the propensity to steal or cheat in the absence of specific documentation
- Statements suggesting that a student has psychological problems in the absence of authority or expertise to justify such a statement

Teachers are entitled to a qualified privilege in communicating information regarding students as long as they act in good faith, convey truthful information that does not damage the student, and do not communicate information with malice or an intent to harm a student's reputation. Qualified privilege is based on truthful information conveyed in accordance with the teacher's prescribed duties. This privilege is lost if the teacher had knowledge that the defamatory statement was false or the teacher had no reasonable grounds to believe that the statement was truthful.[2] It is important to remember that truth is only valid in the absence of intent to harm a student. Educators must maintain strict confidentiality regarding personal information involving students and refrain from communicating personal or sensitive information to others who have no need to receive this information.

54. What Are the Consequences for Teacher Errors on Confidential Student Records?

Teachers are responsible for errors made on student records when the error is detected either by school officials, the teacher, or eligible students or parents. The teacher must correct the error, date the correction(s), and affix his or her signature to the corrected document. If the error resulted in damages to the student, it can be pursued legally; however, the burden of proof resides with the student, who must demonstrate that the error was deliberate and designed to injure.

55. What Legal Options Are Available to Parents or Students for FERPA Violations?

Violations of FERPA provisions typically result in injunctive relief by the courts as well as denial of federal funds by the U.S. Department of Education to the educational agency found to be in violation. Individual monetary damages are not available under FERPA since the U.S. Department of Education's Family Compliance Office represents the vehicle for enforcing compliance. In a landmark case, *Gonzaga University v. Doe,*[3] the U.S. Supreme Court ruled that FERPA does not provide a private right of action to sue for damages. Chief Justice Rehnquist expressed the view that the law fell short of conferring enforceable rights. The language of the law only denies federal funds to the institution or district that improperly discloses a student's personal information. The case arose when Doe, a student, claimed that his reputation was damaged when

Gonzaga University failed to recommend him for a teacher's license due to a lack of moral character. This assessment stemmed from a conversation among students regarding sexual misconduct by Doe that was overheard by a university official. Since no private course of action was available to Doe, his only recourse was to file a complaint with the U.S. Department of Education.

56. Does a FERPA Violation Occur When Teachers Allow Students to Score Each Other's Papers?

Probably not. *Owasso Independent School District No. I-011 v. Falvo* was a leading FERPA case regarding confidentiality of students' grades that reached the U.S. Supreme Court. In *Owasso*, teachers occasionally requested students to score each other's tests, papers, and assignments as teachers explained the correct answers to the entire class. Plaintiffs who were parents of minor children enrolled in the class filed suit against the school district claiming that peer grading violated FERPA.[4] Plaintiffs argued that FERPA authorizes federal funds to be withheld from school districts that permit students' educational records or personally identifiable information to be released without parents' written consent. Educational records are defined as records, files, documents, and other materials containing information directly related to students that are maintained by an educational agency or a person acting for the agency. The district court held that grades recorded on paper by another student are not educational records. The Tenth Circuit Court of Appeals reversed, concluding that FERPA provided the respondent with a cause of action enforceable under § 1983 and finding that grades marked by other students are educational records and that the very act of grading in this way is an impermissible release of information.

The U.S. Supreme Court rejected the Tenth Circuit's reasoning that the teacher's gradebooks and grades within them are covered by the act. The High Court indicated that "maintain" suggests that FERPA records will be kept in a file in a school's record room. Student graders only handle an assignment for a few minutes until the teacher records it. The Tenth Circuit Court of Appeals erred in concluding that a student grader is "a person acting for an institution." The High Court ruled that the practice used by teachers of involving students in recording grades does not violate the tenets of FERPA. The Tenth Circuit ruling was reversed and remanded.

In a slightly different case, *C. N. v. Ridgewood Bd. of Education*, the court reached a similar conclusion. During the fall of the 1999 school year, school officials in the Ridgewood Public School District of New Jersey administered a survey titled "Profiles of Student Life: Attitudes and Behaviors" to students in the seventh through twelfth grades. The survey solicited information regarding students' drug and alcohol use, sexual activity, experience of physical violence, attempts at suicide, personal associations and relationships (including their parental relationship), and views on matters of public interest. The survey was designed to be voluntary and anonymous. Survey results were released only in the aggregate with no identifying information.

Three students and their mothers brought suit against the Ridgewood Board of Education and school administrators. Plaintiffs claimed that the survey had been administered in a way that was involuntary and not anonymous and had thus violated their rights under FERPA, the Protection of Pupil Rights Amendment, and the U.S. Constitution. Prior to any discovery, the U.S. District Court of New Jersey denied the plaintiffs' motion to enjoin release of the survey results and granted summary judgment to the school defendants on the merits of the statutory and constitutional claims. On appeal, this court reversed in part and remanded for further proceedings. Following discovery and voluntary dismissal of the statutory claims, the district court granted the school defendants' motion for summary judgment on the remaining constitutional claims. The court concluded that the survey did not violate the provisions of FERPA or the privacy rights of students.[5]

An interesting challenge arose in Florida regarding access to student discipline forms. A Florida appellate court held that student transportation discipline forms and bus surveillance videotapes are confidential and exempt from the Florida Public Records Act (FPRA) and that such records could not be released to a television station, even if personally identifying information had been redacted. WFTV, a local television station, had requested access to Seminole County School District's student transportation discipline forms and bus surveillance videotapes. When the school board denied the request, WFTV sued the school board, requesting a state trial court to order the board to disclose the records. The trial court dismissed the case. The station appealed. The appellate court rejected the station's argument that the "confidential and exempt" provision of the FPRA applies only to personally identifiable information contained in the records. Even if the personally identifiable information were redacted, the court held, the forms and videotapes would still be confidential and exempt, and the school board would be prohibited from disclosing the information without written parental consent. The court stated that, if the records merely were exempt from the FPRA, the board would not be prohibited from disclosing them; however, because the records also were confidential, disclosure was prohibited. The appellate court also rejected WFTV's argument that the FPRA must be compatible with the federal FERPA. While FERPA protects only personally identifiable information contained in student records, the FPRA goes further than FERPA by "preventing the release of 'any personal information' contained in records or reports which permit the personal identification of a student."[6]

Finally, in a special education case involving FERPA, a California federal district court held that a provision in the state's education code requiring local school districts to provide the parents of special education students with copies of standardized achievement test protocols is not preempted by federal copyright law. Even though the test materials enjoy copyright protection, the court held that providing parents access based on state law constitutes a "fair use" under federal copyright law. The parent of a special education student in the Newport-Mesa Unified School District requested copies of his son's test protocols before a scheduled individualized education program (IEP) meeting. When school district officials denied his request, he filed a complaint with the California Department of Education. The California Department of Education ruled that the school district had failed to comply with the education code provision. The district sued the California Department of Education, seeking to overturn the decision. The school district argued that federal law prohibited it from providing copies of copyrighted test records. The court framed the central issue in the case by asking whether "the doctrine of 'fair use' avoids preemption" of the state education code provision by federal copyright law. Under the fair use doctrine, the court explained, the reproduction of copyrighted material for purposes such as reporting or teaching is a fair use and not a copyright infringement. The purpose of the use was noncommercial, the nature of the work when the students' answers were added was informational rather than creative, and only those portions of the test identifiable with the student were to be copied. In addition, the court found no substantial risk of widespread public access or adverse marketing. The court observed in a footnote that the federal FERPA also provides parents the right to examine original test protocols.[7]

57. Under What Circumstances May Teachers Be Held Liable When They Write Letters of Recommendation for Students?

Teachers may be liable when they include information intended to harm a student's reputation, expose the student to public scorn, or deter third parties from establishing an association. Harmful statements based on opinion only may also create legal challenges for teachers, particularly if such statements imply undisclosed defamatory facts as a basis for the opinion. The primary issue is the important distinction between statements of fact and derogatory or defamatory expressions of opinion about others. This distinction is important for several reasons: truth is a justifiable defense for someone who publishes defamatory statements; there is a vast difference between statements of documented fact and statements of opinion with respect to what is the truth; and truth is best validated through documented statements of fact. False or unsubstantiated statements with harmful intent may create liability challenges for teachers.

58. Should Teachers Share Sensitive Information With Coworkers Involving Student Information That Is Found in Student Records?

No. Sensitive information is deemed to be confidential. Information should not be shared with a coworker who has no need to be informed. Information contained in the student's file should be used exclusively by the teacher who accessed the information. Additionally, the information accessed should be used to assist the student in achieving success in school. Sharing confidential information without consent will result in a violation of the statute and trigger sanctions by the Department of Education as well as possible legal actions against the teacher who shared the information.

Court Cases Involving Liability and Student Records

• A school district did not violate the privacy rights of a student according to the New York Supreme Court when it released the name of a student and a picture of her class to a trucker who participated in the school building program that was a part of the school's geography project.[8]

• The Montana State Supreme Court ruled that a local newspaper was entitled to a school board's disciplinary records on two *unidentified* students found guilty of shooting classmates with a BB gun. The court concluded that FERPA does, however, apply to records of disciplinary hearings.[9] In other words, disciplinary records are considered to be educational records.

• The Arizona Court of Appeals ruled that disclosure of a special education student's records was appropriate in a medical malpractice case because the records were not totally protected by the Arizona Medical Records Privilege Act.[10]

• An Ohio court ruled that the case of identifying student information involving alleged misconduct by a school superintendent did not fall within the disclosure exemption for student records because the file was not prepared in the normal course of business or maintained in a central location with educational records.[11]

• A Virginia circuit court concluded that a defendant was entitled to discover the original version of an injury report that had been altered by school officials at a student's request. Accordingly, FERPA permitted the release of student records that had been subpoenaed by the court when the student sought to use the edited record to his advantage.[12]

Summary Guides

1. FERPA is designed to provide privacy protection for parents, legal guardians, and eligible students.

2. Parents, legal guardians, and students eighteen years old or attending postsecondary institutions are entitled to inspect the student's record and challenge the accuracy of information contained in the student's file. If the challenge is unsuccessful, a note of disagreement with specific content may be included in the student's record file as long as the records are maintained.

3. Parents or legal-age students who make a request must be provided a hearing to contest inaccurate student information.

4. Parents of students under eighteen years old must be granted access to their child's records and must consent to the release of confidential information regarding their child.

5. Teachers, school officials, and federal and state officials may access student records without consent if access is required to execute their duties and responsibilities.

6. Consent exceptions involve federal and state agencies who are enforcing federal and state laws.

7. Students must not be personally identified by federal or state agencies unless it becomes necessary to enforce federal and state laws.

8. Student information can be released through a court-ordered subpoena as long as parents are informed prior to its release.

9. Directory information may be released as long as parents are informed through public media that the information will be released. Parental objections to withhold directory information must be honored.

10. Statements placed in a student's record must be properly documented and legally defensible.

11. Educators are subject to defamation charges when they release or discuss confidential information regarding a student when the disclosure results in injury to the student's good name and reputation or creates mental distress for the student.

NOTES

1. P.L. 104-191.
2. *Gardner v. Hollifield*, 549 P.2d 266 (Idaho, 1976).
3. *Gonzaga University v. Doe*, 536 U.S. 273 (2002).

4. *Owasso Independent School District No. I-011 v. Falvo*, 534 U.S. 426; 122 S.Ct. 934; 151 L.Ed. 2d 896 (2002).

5. *C.N. v. Ridgewood Bd. of Educ.*, 146 F. Supp. 2d 528 (D.N.J. 2001), 319 F. Supp. 2d 483 (D.N.J. 2004).

6. *WFTV v. School Board of Seminole County*, 2004 WL 1072839 (Fla. App. May 14, 2004).

7. *Newport-Mesa Unified School District*, 2005 WL 1274384 (C.D. Cal. May 24, 2005).

8. *Goins v. Rome City Sch. Dist.*, 27 A.D.3d 1149 (N.Y. App. Div. 4th Dept. 2006).

9. *Board of Trustees, Cut Bank Pub. School. v. Cut Bank Pioneer Press*, No. 06-0074 (Mont. May 8, 2007).

10. *Catrone v. Miles*, 160 P.3d 1204; 2007 Ariz. App. LEXIS 113; 507 Ariz. Adv. Rep. 27.

11. *BRV, Inc. v. Superior Court of California*, 143 Cal. App. 4th 742; 49 Cal. Rptr. 3d 519; 2006.

12. *Bunch v. Artz*, 71 Va. Cir. 358; 2006 Va. Cir. LEXIS 252.

5

Rights of Students With Special Needs

▦ INTRODUCTION ▦

The Individuals with Disabilities Education Act (IDEA), formerly referred to as Public Law 94-142 or the Education for All Handicapped Children Act of 1975, was enacted to address the growing needs of children with disabilities in the nation. Prior to its passage, many students with disabilities were either receiving inappropriate educational services or no services at all. All students, including special needs students, have a property right to receive an education. This act places a leading obligation on each state to ensure that children with disabilities are provided equal access to a public school education. Individuals with disabilities may not be discriminated against or denied equal educational opportunities based on their disability.

59. What Federal Laws Protect the Rights of Students With Disabilities?

There are three major federal laws that provide protection for individuals with disabilities:

> *Public Law 94-142* served as the forerunner to the reauthorized Individuals with Disabilities Education Act of 1990, 1997, and 2004. This law ensures that students with disabilities receive a free, appropriate education.

The Rehabilitation of Act of 1973, Section 504, protects individuals from discrimination based on their disability in any program or activity receiving federal funds.

Americans with Disabilities Act of 1990 prohibits discrimination against any qualified individual who has a disability with respect to employment, training compensation benefits, promotions, and terms and conditions of employment.

These statutes were enacted to provide protection from discrimination for individuals with disabilities and to provide them equal access to educational opportunities, facility utilization, and employment opportunities.

60. How Do States Qualify for Funding Under IDEA?

States must develop and implement a plan to ensure a free appropriate education for all children with disabilities. States must also formulate a policy that guarantees certain due process rights for all such children. This plan must include goals, timelines for meeting goals, personnel, facilities, and related services necessary to meet the needs of children with disabilities. Last, the state's plan must include a defensible system for allocating funds to local school districts, which, in turn, are required to submit an application to their state indicating how they will comply with the requirements of IDEA.

61. What Is Meant by Zero Rejection Regarding Students With Disabilities?

Under IDEA's zero rejection policy, no child with disabilities can be denied a free, appropriate public education. In fact, students who have not received an education must become the first priority for funding, followed by children with the most severe disabilities.

62. Must Students With Disabilities Demonstrate That They Can Benefit From Special Education Instruction?

No, children with disabilities are not required to demonstrate that they will benefit from special education as a condition to receive it. This point was stressed in *Timothy v. Rochester*. In 1980, school officials held meetings to determine whether Timothy was educationally disabled for purposes of the act and entitled to special education. Timothy had been born two months' prematurely and subsequently suffered severe respiratory problems. He later experienced hemorrhaging and seizures, which resulted in a classification of profoundly mentally retarded.

Upon the evidence presented at the meetings, Rochester concluded that Timothy did not fall within the act because he could not benefit from special education. Timothy filed suit alleging that the denial of special education violated his rights under the act. The district court disagreed, holding that Rochester's denial was proper. Timothy appealed. The First Circuit Court of Appeals reversed the district court's ruling and held that the act does not require a disabled child to demonstrate that he can benefit from special education to be entitled to receive it. The language of the act clearly guarantees all children with disabilities the right to a free appropriate education (FAPE). There is no exception for children with severe disabilities. In fact, IDEA requires that the most severe cases be given priority. There was no question that Timothy, having multiple disabilities and being profoundly mentally retarded, qualified under the act's definition of a child with disabilities.[1]

IDEA is not an affirmative action law but one that requires an absence of discrimination. School districts are required, under the law, to provide a FAPE that includes additional special educational services as well as procedural safeguards to protect the rights of special needs students and their parents. School districts are not, however, required to maximize a student's education to a level comparable to students without disabilities, as illustrated by the *Rowley* case.

Rowley, who was almost completely deaf, was admitted to kindergarten. She was provided a hearing aid, with which she achieved a measure of academic success. The school board, however, rejected her request that a sign language interpreter be provided. A suit was filed in a U.S. district court contending that Rowley's educational opportunities could not be maximized without the interpreter. The district court agreed. The court of appeals affirmed, and the U.S. Supreme Court granted a review. The Supreme Court reversed the district court's ruling by stating that the Education of the Handicapped Act does not require special services that maximize a disabled child's education to a level commensurate with children without disabilities. The act provides that special services are to be offered as necessary to permit the child to benefit from instruction; there is no language stating that benefits are to be maximized. The Court stated that, although Rowley may be correct in her argument that the act was passed with a desire to promote equal educational opportunity, achieving equality of result is an impossible goal not likely to have been contemplated by the act.[2]

IDEA is very specific in identifying categories of disabilities that qualify for services (discussed later in this chapter). If students have one or more disabilities that adversely affect their ability to perform adequately in school, they qualify for special education services. In terms of priority, special education services are provided first to those children who are without services and second to students who have the most severe disabilities.

63. What Is the Basic Purpose of the Individuals with Disabilities Education Act of 2004 (IDEA)?

The initial landmark Education for All Handicapped Children Act of 1975 was enacted to address the educational needs of millions of children with disabilities who were not receiving an appropriate education. The act was reauthorized in 1990, 1997, and 2004. Although modifications have been made to the act, the basic intent remains intact. Prior to this act, children with disabilities were excluded entirely from public schools and were not being educated with their peers. Undiagnosed disabilities by school personnel also prevented children who were attending public schools from receiving the benefits of an appropriate education.

64. How Is the Term "Children With Disabilities" Defined by the Act?

The act covers infants and toddlers with disabilities (birth to age two) and their families. This group receives early intervention services under IDEA, Part C. Children and youth (ages three to twenty-one) receive special education and related services under IDEA, Part B.

The act identifies the following disability categories: autism, deafness or hearing impaired, mental retardation, multiple disabilities, orthopedic impairment, serious emotional disturbance, specific learning disabilities, speech or language impairment, traumatic brain injury, visual impairment including blindness, and other health impairments. To be eligible, a student must have a disability that adversely affects his or her educational performance and need special education and/or a related service to receive an appropriate education. See Figure 5.1 for the percentages of students with disabilities receiving services.

65. What Mandatory Requirements Apply to School Districts?

To qualify for funds, each state must develop an approved plan outlining the goals, timetables, personnel, facilities, and other services for children with special needs. They must also assure through policy that the substantive rights of these children are protected. Funds are allocated to state and local educational agencies for special education and related services based on average pupil expenditure and the educational needs of the child.

66. What Is Meant by Response to Intervention Regarding Students With Disabilities?

Response to Intervention (RTI) is a method of academic intervention used to provide early, effective assistance to children who are experiencing difficulty with learning. RTI is also referred to as a data-based process of diagnosing learning disabilities. The RTI method is often used as an alternative means of identifying learning disabilities besides requiring children to demonstrate

Figure 5.1   Students With Disabilities: Percentage of Youth Ages Three to Twenty-One in Early Education Centers or Public Schools Receiving Services Under the Individuals with Disabilities Education Act (IDEA), by Primary Disability Type (Selected Years, 1976–1977 Through 2005–2006)

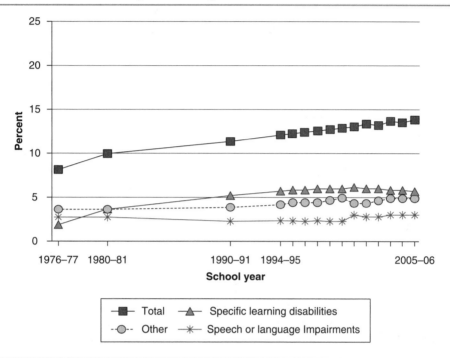

Source: U.S. Department of Education, Office of Special Education and Rehabilitative Services (OSERS), Office of Special Education Programs (OSEP) (2006). *26th Annual (2004) Report to Congress on the Implementation of the Individuals With Disabilities Education Act*, vols. 1 and 2; data from OSERS, OSEP, Data Analysis System (DANS), 1976–2005. Retrieved September 22, 2006, from http://www.ed.gov/about/reports/annual/osep/2004/introduction.html and https://www.ideadata.org/index.html.

a notable inconsistency between their IQ and academic achievement as determined by standardized tests. An RTI assessment more clearly defines the Specific Learning Disability (SLD) category from the Individuals with Disabilities Education Act (IDEA, 2004).

RTI essentially minimizes academic failure due to early intervention, regular progress reports, and intensive, research-based instructional interventions for children who continue to experience difficulty. Students who do not respond to effective interventions are more likely to experience learning disabilities that require special education. For children with learning disabilities, RTI can be used to assist teachers in minimizing student failures by providing appropriate intervention as soon as children exhibit signs of difficulty.

67. What Role Does a Regular Teacher Play in Identifying Students Who May Need Special Services?

Teachers have the responsibility of identifying students who may need special services in order to receive the full benefits of an appropriate education.

This appraisal should be conducted prior to any formal assessment or special programming. The teacher, carefully working with the student over a reasonable period of time using alternative assessment measures, should determine whether he or she needs special assistance beyond what is provided in the regular classroom. When the regular classroom teacher has worked with a student and feels that the student needs special assistance, a request is normally made in the form of a referral.

The referral form should be as thorough as possible, providing the information needed to conduct a formal assessment of the student. Data requested on the referral form may include the student's name, present grade level, age, gender, standardized test scores, local test data, strengths and weaknesses in key subject areas, reading ability, behavior and relationships with fellow students, pertinent family data, and teaching methods or strategies that have been successful, as well as those that have been unsuccessful. If a formal assessment procedure is contemplated, the student's parent must grant consent and be informed of personal rights under due process procedures. It is commonplace for districts to hold pre-referral conferences to discuss concerns regarding the student's academic and social performance. These meetings usually involve the referring teacher, a special education professional, the principal, the counselor, and, in many instances, the parent. They may also be used as an intermediate measure to discuss the implementation of new and different strategies regarding the student's progress before a formal assessment is contemplated and decisions made regarding the need for special services. These measures, if implemented appropriately, can reduce the occurrence of overreferrals and misclassifications and can result in the best education program for the student, particularly when new strategies and interventions are implemented and evaluated over a reasonable period of time. Some school districts have also implemented positive behavior support plans aimed at preventing inappropriate behavior through teaching and reinforcing appropriate behaviors.

68. How Is the Individualized Education Plan (IEP) Developed for Children With Disabilities?

An Individual Education Plan (IEP) must be developed for each child with disabilities, utilizing a team approach that involves the child's teacher, parents, special education representatives for the district, and other professionals as needed. The team should consider the

- strengths and weaknesses of the child,
- parent concerns for enhancing the child's education,
- results of the initial evaluation or most recent evaluation of the child,
- academic development of the child, and
- functional needs of the child.

The IEP is developed based on extensive data using a battery of appropriate tests, the teacher's notes and observations, samples of the student's work, and interventions used by the teacher to support the child's progress in the classroom. A sixty-day timeline is established for receipt of parental consent for the evaluation, which will determine the child's eligibility for special services and educational needs. If parental consent is not provided, the school district must initiate an impartial hearing through a hearing officer to receive approval.

When the evaluation process has been completed, the child's IEP is developed. Each IEP should minimally contain the following components:

1. Child's present level of academic and functional performance

2. Measurable annual goals and short-term instructional objectives

3. How the child's progress toward meeting annual goals is to be measured and reported to parents

4. Specific educational services to be provided and some indication regarding the child's ability to participate in the regular educational program

5. Explanation of the periods during which the child will not participate with children without disabilities

6. Schedule of services to be provided, including when services are to begin and the frequency, duration, and location of the provision of services

7. Identification of transitional services, including interagencies that may be involved when the student leaves the school

8. Accommodations to be provided during state and district assessments that are necessary to measure the child's academic and functional performance

9. When transition services will be initiated and concluded (required when the child reaches age sixteen)

10. Appropriate criteria and procedures to be used to determine, on an annual basis, whether instructional objectives are being met

69. How Often Must the IEP Be Reviewed?

Each IEP must be reviewed annually, and a determination must be made as to whether revisions are necessary. Consistent with procedural safeguards, parents must be informed of any proposed changes in placement. If they disagree, an impartial hearing must be held to address the objection. The secretary of education, however, with the 2004 reauthorization of IDEA, approved proposals from fifteen states to allow school districts to develop a multi-year IEP for a maximum of three years with parental consent. The IEP thus might not be reviewed annually. Under this provision, short-term objectives are no longer required except for children who are meeting alternative assessment requirements and/or for students with the most significant cognitive disabilities. Additionally, a member of the IEP team may not be required to attend the annual meeting if the parent consents in writing (and the district agrees) that the teacher's curricular area is not being modified.

An interesting IEP attendance challenge arose in Washington. A Washington student with autism and low cognitive ability attended kindergarten with an IEP that allowed placement in an integrated class. His teacher was certified in both regular and special education. The student's mother attended class with him for most of the five days he was in school. She observed that he was teased on several occasions and reported the teasing to the teacher, though she admitted that her son might not have noticed one incident and was happy during another. She also reported the teasing to the vice principal and removed the child from school after his fifth day of attendance. The district offered to place the student in a self-contained classroom in another school, but the parents rejected the proposal. They also refused to attend the IEP meeting, at which time a self-contained classroom with mainstream opportunities was proposed. The parents requested a due process hearing, claiming that the absence of a regular education teacher at the meeting violated IDEA.

The case reached the Ninth Circuit Court of Appeals, which held that the school district had violated IDEA by failing to have the regular education teacher present at the IEP team meeting. It was not sufficient that the teacher was a member of the IEP team; she had to attend the meeting. However, her absence did not cause a loss of educational opportunity for the student because a self-contained classroom was the best placement for him, and the placement would not have changed had the regular education teacher been present at the meeting. Further, the district was deprived of the opportunity to end the teasing when the parents removed the student from school after only five days of attendance. The district's procedural violation of IDEA did not result in the denial of a FAPE.[3]

---

70. What Must Teachers Know About the Least Restrictive Environment (LRE) and Free Appropriate Public Education (FAPE)?

There are two basic requirements regarding IDEA: a child with disabilities must receive a free appropriate public education (FAPE), and it must be in the least restrictive environment (LRE). A FAPE calls for an educational program tailored to the special needs of children that imposes no expense to parents. A FAPE is a right of students with disabilities, and IDEA ensures that this education is made available for all students with disabilities, provided at public expense under the supervision of public schools. The

IEP is the vehicle used to meet the requirements of a FAPE, as established by IDEA. The procedures used must allow parents of students with disabilities to examine school records, participate in IEP meetings, and register complaints regarding any aspect of the act that is not viewed as having been met by the school or district.

A least restrictive environment or LRE essentially means that students who have a disability should have the opportunity to be educated in a regular classroom to the greatest extent possible. They should have access to the general education curriculum, to extracurricular activities, or to any other program that those without disabilities are able to access. The special needs student should be provided with the supplementary aids and services necessary to achieve educational goals while in this setting. If the nature or severity of a child's disability prevents the student from achieving these goals in a regular education setting, then the student would be placed in a more restrictive environment such as a special classroom or a more restrictive placement. Generally, the less opportunity a student has to interact and learn with students without disabilities, the more restrictive the setting is considered to be. LRE requires that children with disabilities be placed in educational environments with the least number of restrictions consistent with the child's IEP. LRE thus suggests that children with disabilities, when appropriate, be placed in a regular classroom, which is tantamount to inclusion.

A least restrictive challenge arose in Kansas when a student with Down syndrome scored in the 0.1 percentile on the knowledge and skills portion of the Woodcock-Johnson achievement test. His district proposed placing him in a self-contained classroom. His parents objected, and a trial placement was made in a regular classroom. The student could not keep pace with his classmates, however, and became frustrated and disruptive. A hearing officer determined that a self-contained classroom was his LRE. A federal court and the Tenth Circuit Court of Appeals agreed. The student would continue to have interaction with regular education students in nonacademic classes.[4]

The amended version of IDEA, however, does not require inclusion. The law simply requires that children with disabilities receive an education in the LRE designed to meet their specific needs. IDEA requires school districts to develop a continuum of available placements with a range of options to include regular classrooms, special classrooms, residential settings, extended school year placement, private school placement, and other options based on the unique needs of the child. However, parents may, in some instances, receive tuition reimbursement if they unilaterally place their child in a nonapproved private school, as demonstrated in *Florence County School District Four v. Carter*.[5]

In that legal case, a South Carolina ninth grader with a learning disability attended special education classes. Her parents disagreed with the IEP established by their public school district. The IEP called for inclusion in regular education classes for most subjects, with individual instruction three periods per week and specific goals of increasing the student's reading and mathematics levels by four months for the entire school year. The student's parents requested a due process hearing under IDEA. Meanwhile, they unilaterally placed the child in a private school that specialized in teaching students with disabilities. The hearing officer held that the IEP was adequate. After the student raised her reading comprehension three full grades in one year at the private school, the parents sued the school district for tuition reimbursement. The U.S. District Court in South Carolina held that the educational program and achievement goals of the proposed IEP were grossly inadequate and that, even though the private school did not comply with all IDEA requirements, it provided the student with an excellent education that complied with IDEA's substantive requirements. It held that the parents were entitled to tuition reimbursement. The district court's decision was upheld by the U.S. Court of Appeals, Fourth Circuit. The school district appealed to the U.S. Supreme Court. The Supreme Court held that the parents were entitled to tuition reimbursement because the public school placement violated IDEA and because the child received an otherwise proper education from the private school.

All options must be funded by the state in which the child resides. The starting point regarding placement, however, begins with the regular classroom teacher through the IEP process.

71. What Should Teachers Know About Inclusion?

Inclusion is an integral component associated with LRE. It requires school officials to educate children with disabilities in regular classrooms to the fullest extent possible. An exception is granted if the nature and severity of the student's disability is such that placement in a regular classroom with the use of supplementary aids and services cannot be achieved satisfactorily. Consequently, all teachers must be prepared to teach students with disabilities who are placed in their classrooms. Teachers must balance their teaching strategies in a manner that allows them to meet the educational needs of students with disabilities as well as those without disabilities. These teaching strategies require considerable instructional and time management skills by teachers. There is no consensus regarding the concept of inclusion. Some educators believe that all students benefit from learning together and becoming a part of the school community. Other educators feel that students with disabilities are being placed in unsupportive environments with minimal opportunities to learn.

72. What Is the Importance of Special Education–Related Services?

Related services must be provided for children with special needs. A related service is one that is necessary for the child to benefit from an education. Examples of related services include but are not limited to the following: audiology, counseling services, medical services, occupational therapy, orientation and mobility services for children who are visually impaired or blind, parent counseling, rehabilitative counseling, school health services, speech/language pathology, transportation, recreation, and other services based on the child's needs. The IEP will identify the related services necessary to facilitate the child's educational experience. Comparable related services must be provided for a child with disabilities who transfers to a new school district in his or her state within the same school year.

Medical services are not considered related services unless they are linked with diagnostic evaluation. A landmark U.S. Supreme Court ruling provided clarity regarding a related service versus a medical service. In Texas, school officials refused to provide catheterization for Tatro, an eight-year-old child born with spina bifida.[6] The parents filed suit against the school district requesting that this service be provided. A U.S. district court supported the school. Parents appealed to a U.S. court of appeals, who reversed the district court's ruling. The school district appealed to the U.S. Supreme Court. The Supreme Court held that a clean intermittent catheter is a supportive service, not a medical service. The school district had argued that catheterization was a medical service because it was pre-scribed and supervised by a physician, even though it could be adminis-tered by a nurse or a trained lay person. The Supreme Court was not convinced by the school district's argument. The Supreme Court noted that the parents were not requesting equipment but merely a service that any trained lay person could perform.

73. Why Are Transition Services Important to Students With Disabilities?

Transition services for students with disabilities must be provided through the IEP to create a smooth transfer from school to work. Transition services must be provided when students reach age sixteen or at a younger age if determined to be appropriate. Transition services include but are not limited to instruction regarding community experiences, development of employment and other postschool opportunities, determination of adult living objectives, and, if appropriate, acquisition of daily living skills and a functional vocational evaluation. Services must include a statement of the needed transition services, including, if appropriate, a statement of each public and each participating agency's responsibilities in helping to develop the work skills needed for the student's chosen occupation prior to the student leaving the school setting.

Under the 1997 reauthorization, transition services were required to be included in the student's IEP beginning as early as age fourteen, with annual updates to ensure that needed services are provided. Besides a description of transition services, a timetable and an explanation of rele-vant criteria and procedures to be employed each year to determine if objectives are or have been achieved must be included in the student's IEP. Transition services should be tailored to the needs and interests of individual student needs. The requirements of IDEA stipulate that transition services should be provided across a variety of locations within the community, as befitting the needs of the student and the particular skills or knowledge he or she needs to acquire.

74. What Role Does Assistive Technology Play for Students With Disabilities?

IDEA includes an assistive technology component. Assistive technology is defined by the act as any item, piece of equipment, product, or system, whether acquired commercially off the shelf, modified, or customized, that is used to increase, maintain, or improve the functional capabilities of a child with a disability.[7] The term does not include a medical device that is surgically implanted or the replacement of the device. The term *assistive technology service* means any service that directly assists a child with a disability in the selection, acquisition, or use of an assistive technology device. Assistive teaching includes:

- evaluating the needs of the child, including a functional evaluation in the child's customary environment;
- purchasing, leasing, or otherwise providing for the acquisition of assistive technology devices for the child;
- selecting, designing, fitting, customizing, adapting, applying, maintaining, repairing, or replacing assistive technology services;
- coordinating and using other therapies, interventions, or services with assistive technology devices, such as those associated with existing education and rehabilitation plans and programs;
- training or technical assistance for the child or, where appropriate, the family of the child; and
- training or technical assistance for professionals (including individuals providing education and rehabilitation services, employers, or other individuals substantially involved in the major life functions of the student).[8]

75. What Is Meant by Highly Qualified Special Education Teachers Under No Child Left Behind?

All special education teachers must meet No Child Left Behind provisions that state that teachers in core academic areas must be highly qualified in the academic subjects they teach. This requirement became effective at the end of the 2005–2006 school year; therefore, all new teachers must immediately be highly qualified. The law outlines a list of minimum requirements related to content knowledge and teaching skills that a highly qualified teacher must meet. Special education teachers must instruct students to the appropriate level of proficiency. If a special education teacher teaches a core subject, he or she must meet the standard of a highly qualified teacher in that subject. The minimum requirements of highly qualified teachers are listed below:

- Must be certified (may also hold alternative certification)
- Must hold a bachelor's degree
- Must possess demonstrated subject area competency

76. What Due Process Rights Are Parents and Students Afforded Under IDEA?

Schools are required under IDEA to provide a notice of procedural safeguards to parents of children with disabilities. This document includes a description of their legal rights. The document must be provided only one time each school year, unless a complaint is filed or a request made for an evaluation.

Prior written notice must be provided to parents at least five school days prior to initiating decisions or actions in regard to their child. The purpose is to provide parents with information so that they will be able to participate in the decision-making process. The notice must be written in language that is understandable; that is, it must be translated into the parents' native language or put into another mode of communication, unless it clearly is not feasible to do so.

A prior written notice should describe and explain what action the school is proposing to initiate or refusing to initiate. It should describe other options that were considered by the review committee and why those options were rejected. The notice should also describe each evaluation procedure, assessment, record, or report the school used as a basis for what it proposes or refuses to provide and should include other factors relevant to the services being proposed or refused. The school must inform parents that they are protected under procedural safeguards. If the parents request it, before the school obtains their consent for a psychological examination or test, it must provide them with the name and type of test and with an explanation of how it will be used to develop an appropriate IEP for their child. A reasonable effort should be made to obtain the parents' informed consent before determining whether the student has a disability.

School districts must exercise caution during the IEP development process, as illustrated by an Alabama case. An Alabama school board violated IDEA by writing improper IEPs for a student with autism. A federal district court held that the unquantifiable goals in the student's IEPs violated IDEA objectives. The student's mother signed his IEP but objected to the school's failure to include behavioral interventions or a behavior intention plan. The school board asserted that autism cannot be treated and that any inappropriate behaviors were being managed via instruction in a predictable, structured environment. The mother claimed that the student's inappropriate, self-injurious, and aggressive behavior was increasing and requested a due process hearing. The hearing officer found that the student's most recent IEP was improperly written and violated his right to a FAPE. None of the IEPs prepared for the student had a behavior management component. In fact, the board had never conducted a Functional Behavior Assessment for him. The hearing officer sharply criticized the IEPs for lacking notations on the mastery of benchmarks and for vague statements about the student's present levels of performance, which made it impossible for the student's parents and IEP team members to track his progress.

The board appealed to a federal district court, which agreed with the hearing officer that the student's behaviors were directly related to autism, which did not excuse the board from providing behavior management techniques in his IEP or in a separate behavior intervention plan. The court found that the hearing officer had correctly rejected the board's argument that no behavior plan was warranted. There was an array of technical defects in the student's IEPs, most notably the lack of mastery dates for benchmarks and inadequacy of annual goals. The annual goals section of the IEP did not identify measurable goals and, instead, referred to an 80 percent accuracy objective, never identifying to what this objective applied. The court held that, without a clear statement of present levels of performance, the student's annual goals were "unmoored, untethered and meaningless." While the court found that technical perfection was not the objective of the statute, procedural defects can violate IDEA if they cause a loss in educational opportunities or benefits or if the parents are deprived of participation. The defects in the student's IEP invalidated the suitability of his entire program. Vague and immeasurable goals could not confer educational benefit and made it impossible to measure achievement. The court upheld the hearing officer's decision.[9]

Schools also need parental consent to provide children with special education services. If parents refuse to consent to the initial provision of services, the school is then not considered to be in violation of the requirement to provide a FAPE. Additionally, the school will not be required to convene a meeting or develop an IEP for the child. If parents consent and then revoke it, the revocation will not be retroactive. The school must also obtain parental consent to reevaluate children after special education services have been received. However, if the school is able to demonstrate that it used reasonable measures to obtain parental consent and the parents failed to respond, then the school may proceed without consent.

The school must use a variety of evaluation tools and strategies when it conducts a full and individual evaluation of a student. The evaluation must assess the child in all areas related to the suspected disability. It must be sufficiently comprehensive to identify all of the child's needs for special education and related services, even if the needs are not commonly related to the child's particular category of disability. At least every three years after the first evaluation, the school must reevaluate the child unless the parents and the school agree that a reevaluation is unnecessary. The results of the review and any new evaluations will be used to determine whether the child will continue to be eligible for special education services and to update the content of the child's IEP.

Parents are important members of their child's IEP committee. They have a right to be actively involved in the committee meeting and to discuss any aspect of their child's educational program. Although they are not required to attend, the parents must be invited to each meeting of their child's IEP committee.

77. Can Students With Disabilities Be Disciplined?

It depends on whether the student's conduct is related to his or her disability. If it is related, the student may not be disciplined. If the student's conduct is unrelated to his or her condition, then the school may use regular disciplinary measures that it would use with students without disabilities. If a child's behavior interferes with learning, the IEP committee must consider the use of positive behavioral interventions and supports and other strategies to address those behaviors. If the committee decides that behavioral strategies are needed, the interventions to be used must be documented in the IEP. If the child violates school rules, the child has certain rights throughout the school's disciplinary process. If a child with disabilities violates the student code of conduct, the school may remove the child from the current placement for ten school days or less during a school year, just as it does when disciplining children without disabilities. However, the "stay put" provision applies, which means that a student with disabilities remains in his or her educational placement pending a full review of the student's IEP. The school is not required to provide educational services during these short-term removal periods, which must not total more than ten days in a school year, unless such services are provided to students without disabilities.

The child with disabilities has certain additional rights when there is a change of placement for disciplinary reasons. A change in placement occurs if the removal of a student is extended beyond ten consecutive school days or if a series of shorter removals totaling more than ten school days forms a pattern. When the decision is made to remove a child and thus a change of placement occurs based on a violation of the student code of conduct, the school must notify parents of that decision and provide them notice of procedural safeguards. Additionally, within ten school days of any such decision, the Local Education Agency (LEA), parent, and relevant members of the IEP committee must conduct a manifestation determination review. While conducting the review, the members must evaluate all relevant information in the child's file, including the child's IEP, any teacher observations, and any relevant information provided by the parent. The members determine if the child's conduct was (1) the direct result of the school's failure to implement the child's IEP or (2) caused by or had a direct and substantial relationship to the child's disability. If IEP members determine that either condition is applicable, then the child's conduct must be considered a manifestation of the child's disability.

Prior to the 1997 reauthorization of IDEA, the U.S. Supreme Court in a landmark decision addressed the suspension of disabled students in the *Honig v. Doe* case.[10] Smith and Doe, both emotionally disturbed students, were suspended indefinitely for violent conduct related to their disabilities pending the outcome of expulsion proceedings. Doe had a history of reacting aggressively to peer ridicule; he had responded to the taunts of a fellow student by choking him with sufficient force to leave neck abrasions and had kicked out a school window while being escorted to the principal's office. Doe filed suit seeking to dismiss his suspension and the expulsion proceedings. Smith experienced academic and social difficulties as a result of hyperactivity and low self-esteem. Smith had a propensity for verbal hostility, and his disruptive behavior included stealing or extorting money from fellow students and making sexual comments to female students. Smith alleged that the suspension and proposed expulsion violated the "stay put" provision of IDEA. The district court agreed and enjoined the action. The court of appeals affirmed. The U.S. Supreme Court granted review. The Supreme Court ruled that states may not remove children with disabilities from classrooms for violent or disruptive conduct related to their disability under the act, which prohibits removing the child while any proceedings are pending. However, schools may still use their normal procedures for dealing with children who endanger themselves or others. Students who pose an immediate threat to the safety of others may be temporarily suspended for up to ten school days. These measures provide schools with an adequate means of ensuring the safety of others. Thus, the lower courts properly balanced the schools' interest in maintaining a safe learning environment and the mandates of the act.

78. How Does Manifestation Impact Discipline of Students With Disabilities?

A student may not be disciplined for behavior that is a manifestation of his or her disability. If the child's conduct is a result of a disability, the IEP committee must conduct a Functional Behavioral Assessment (FBA), unless it has already done so. An FBA is used to determine the cause of student behavior prior to developing a behavioral intervention plan (BIP). If a BIP has already been developed, the IEP committee must review it and modify it as necessary to address the behavior. If the child's conduct was the direct result of the school's failure to implement his or her IEP, the school must initiate immediate steps to remedy those deficiencies. Finally, except in special circumstances, the IEP committee must return the child to the placement from which he or she was removed, unless there is agreement between parents and the school to a change of placement as part of the modification of the BIP.

By way of illustration, a school district was not supported in a manifestation case in New York. This case arose when classmates called a New York student with learning disabilities "faggot" and "PLC," which stood for prescriptive learning class. A fight broke out between the student and a classmate, and the disabled student was suspended for five days. The district notified him of a hearing to consider a longer suspension. The superintendent accepted the hearing officer's recommendation for another five-day suspension pending a manifestation hearing. The school's committee on special education found that the student's behavior was not a manifestation of his disability, and the superintendent then planned to suspend the student for the rest of the year. The student sued the district in a federal district court, which ruled in his favor. The court found that the term "PLC" was a reference to his learning disability, thus making the incident related to his disability. In addition, the district had treated the manifestation determination dismissively and did not afford the student due process under IDEA.[11]

79. Why Would Students With Disabilities Be Placed in an Interim Alternative Educational Setting (IAES)?

In special circumstances, a school may remove a child to an interim alternative educational setting (IAES) for not more than forty-five school days without regard to whether the behavior is a manifestation of the student's disability. These conditions arise when the student (1) carries a weapon to or possesses a weapon on school premises or at a school function; (2) knowingly possesses or uses illegal drugs, or sells or solicits the sale of a controlled substance, while on school premises or at a school function; or (3) has inflicted serious bodily injury upon another person while on school premises or at a school function. The "stay put" rule does not apply in these specific circumstances.

If the student's behavior is not a manifestation of his or her disability, then the child may be disciplined in the same manner and for the same duration as for students without disabilities, except that the student must continue to receive a FAPE.

If the student is removed from his or her current educational placement either because of special circumstances or because the behavior is not a manifestation of the student's disability, the IAES will be determined by the student's IEP committee. If parents disagree with any decision regarding disciplinary placement or manifestation determination, they have the right to request an expedited due process hearing through the state hearing officer. If the school believes that maintaining the student in his or her current placement is substantially likely to result in injury to the student or to others, the school may request an expedited due process hearing. The hearing should occur within twenty school days of the date the hearing is requested. The hearing officer must make a determination within ten school days after the hearing. Unless the parents and the school agree otherwise, the student must remain in an IAES until a determination is made by the hearing officer or until the school's IAES placement expires, whichever occurs first. Remaining in a current setting is commonly referred to as "stay put." In this situation, the "stay put" is the IAES.

When the school requests an expedited due process hearing due to a substantial likelihood of injury to the student or to others, the hearing officer may order continued placement in an appropriate IAES for not more than forty-five school days. The hearing officer can order the IAES placement even if the student's behavior is a manifestation of his or her disability. Alternatively, the hearing officer may decide to return the child to the IEP placement from which he or she was removed. These measures are designed to assist school authorities in dealing with substantial disruption to the educational process and to provide due process for the affected student.

80. What Should Teachers Know About the Rehabilitation Act of 1973, Section 504?

The Rehabilitation Act of 1973, Section 504, also provides equal access and opportunity regarding an appropriate education in public school. This act affects any agency receiving federal funds. Section 504 does not require affirmative action regarding children with disabilities; it essentially requires the absence of discrimination against them.

There are public school students who possess certain disabilities that do not receive coverage under IDEA but may be covered under Section 504 of the Rehabilitation Act of 1973. For example, students with attention deficit hyperactivity disorder (ADHD) may receive special education services if there is evidence that they have a learning disability or any other type of impairment adversely affecting their ability to capitalize on an equal education opportunity. Students who are covered by Section 504 may receive regular or special education and related services that allow them to receive an appropriate education. Students are evaluated and placed based on documented needs. The assessment process is not as extensive as the process related to IDEA, but the objectives are very similar. Section 504 requires that

- assessment or evaluation of students with special needs be conducted,
- parents be provided a right to contest evaluation results,
- the school district develop an IEP for either regular or special education–related services,

- the child receive an education in a regular class setting unless it is determined that regular instruction along with supplemental aids are insufficient to achieve satisfactory results, and
- teachers make necessary adjustments in regular classroom instruction to meet the educational needs of students covered under the Rehabilitation Act.

The essence of IDEA and Section 504 is to ensure that children with disabilities are not treated unfairly in regard to their educational opportunities.

Summary of Cases Involving Students With Special Needs

- The U.S. Court of Appeals for the Fourth Circuit has ruled that the terms written into a student's IEP supersede any oral representations that may have been made to the parents before the IEP was finalized.[12]

- The U.S. Court of Appeals for the Ninth Circuit upheld a federal district court's ruling that a Washington parent could not seek monetary damages under Section 1983 for lost income and emotional distress suffered while pursuing relief under the Individual With Disabilities Education Act (IDEA).[13]

- The U.S. Court of Appeals for the Fourth Circuit held that a Virginia school district failed to provide a special education student with a FAPE as required by IDEA because the district's IEP did not identify a particular school at which it anticipated the student would be educated.[14]

- A federal district court in New York denied a motion by a student who was hearing impaired for a preliminary injunction ordering school officials to allow him to bring his service dog to school.[15]

- The U.S. Court of Appeals for the Second Circuit ruled that IDEA does not preclude public reimbursement of private school tuition for a student who never received any special education or related services from the school district.[16]

- A court in Connecticut ruled that suspension of a student with disabilities is tantamount to a change in placement, thus triggering the "stay put" provision of IDEA.[17]

- The Fifth Circuit Court of Appeals ruled that a student with mental retardation may not be expelled without a hearing to determine whether the conduct exhibited was related to her disability.[18]

Summary Guides

1. The Individuals with Disabilities Education Act (IDEA) is a leading source of disability-related legislation that provides a free appropriate public education (FAPE) for children with disabilities.

2. IDEA requires that each child with disabilities is guaranteed equal access to a public school education.

3. Educational services should be provided first to students who have received no services and second to students with disabilities who possess the most severe disabilities.

4. No child with disabilities may be excluded from receiving a FAPE.

5. Each state has the responsibility to identify and develop appropriate educational strategies to address the needs of children with disabilities. States may delegate these responsibilities to local school districts within each state.

6. Each local school district must develop well-tailored plans designed to ensure that children with disabilities receive the benefit of educational programs.

7. The child with disabilities does not need to demonstrate that he or she will benefit from special education and related services to be entitled to receive them.

8. IDEA does not guarantee equality of results but equality of opportunity for children with disabilities.

9. Parents must be provided due process guarantees with respect to assessment, IEP development, placement, and annual review of their special needs child.

10. Students may not be punished for behavior that is a manifestation of their disability.

11. Students with disabilities must be provided procedural and substantive due process guarantees.

12. Schools can remove a student with disabilities for conduct that creates a danger or substantial disruption for the student or others for up to ten days without having to determine manifestation. Schools may also place students with disabilities in an interim alternative education setting for up to forty-five days.

NOTES

1. *Timothy v. Rochester, New Hampshire School District,* 875 F.2d 954 (1st Cir. 1989).

2. *Hendrick Hudson District Board of Education v. Rowley,* 458 U.S. 179 (1982).

3. *M.L. v. Federal Way School Dist.*, 341 F.3d 1052 (9th Cir. 2003).

4. *T.W. v. Unified School Dist. No. 259*, Wichita, Kansas, No. 04-3093, 136 Fed. Appx. 122 (10th Cir. 2005).

5. *Florence County School District Four v. Carter*, 510 U.S. 7, 114 S.Ct. 361 126 L.Ed 2d 284 (1993).

6. *Irving Independent School District v. Tatro*, 468 U.S. 883, 104 S.Ct. 3371 (1984).

7. 20 U.S.C. § 1400 (C) (1988).

8. Ibid.

9. *Escambia County Board of Educ. v. Benton*, 406 F. Supp. 2d 1248 (S.D. Ala. 2005).

10. *Honig, California Superintendent of Public Instruction v. Doe*, 484 U.S. 305, 108 S.Ct. 592 (1988).

11. *Coleman v. Newburgh Enlarged City School Dist.*, 319 F. Supp. 2d 446 (S.D.N.Y. 2004).

12. *Avjian v. Weast*, No. 05-2236, 2007 U.S. App. LEXIS 16689,*;242 Fed. Appx. 77.

13. *Blanchard v. Morton Sch. Dist.*, No. 06-35388, 2007 U.S. App. LEXIS 27940,*.

14. *A.K. v. Alexandria City Sch. Bd.*, No. 06-1130, 2007 U.S. App. LEXIS 17925,*;497 F.3d 409.

15. *Cave v. East Meadows Union Free Sch. Dist.*, 2007 WL 878497 (E. D. N.Y. Mar. 19, 2007).

16. *Frank G. v. Board of Educ. of Hyde Park*, No. 04-4981-CV, 2006 U.S. App. LEXIS 19029,*;459 F.3d 356.

17. *Stuart v Nappi*, 443 F. Supp. 1235 (D. Conn., 1978).

18. *S-1 v. Turlington*, 635 F.2d 342 (5th Cir.), cert. denied, 454 U.S. 1030 (1981).

6

Teacher Constitutional Rights and Freedoms

▦ INTRODUCTION ▦

Public school teachers occupy a significant role in the lives of the students they instruct. They are often viewed as role models, surrogate parents, counselors, and mentors for students in their care. Although teachers exercise significant influence over students and occupy a special role as public school employees, they enjoy the same constitutional rights as do other citizens. They may exercise those rights as long as they demonstrate a high regard for the sensitive nature of their profession and the impact their actions may have on students. In this sense, the exercise of teacher rights is not totally unlimited but must be balanced against the public interest of the school district. If teachers' constitutional rights are restricted by school officials, they must be able to demonstrate a compelling need to do so.

81. How Does the First Amendment Guarantee to Free Speech Apply to Public School Teachers' Speech Outside the Classroom?

Public school teachers are citizens under the U.S. Constitution; consequently, they do not relinquish their freedom of expression rights as a condition of accepting a teaching position. Teachers may exercise their freedom of expression rights in a variety of ways. For example, they may speak on issues of common concern to the community. They may express their views through editorial comments regarding important local, state, or national issues. As teachers express their views, they should always preface their statements by indicating that they are speaking as private citizens rather than as employees of the school district so that their speech is clearly viewed as individual speech and not endorsed by the school district.

82. Can Teachers Be Dismissed for Speaking Out on Controversial Issues Involving the School District Outside of the Classroom?

It depends. Teachers must avoid comments that may be considered defamatory; therefore, their statements should be directed toward issues as opposed to personal attacks on individuals. Teacher expression should also meet standards of professionalism based on the important role teachers play in relation to students and the community.

Pickering v. Board of Education is one of the leading cases regarding teacher freedom of expression rights.[1] Marvin L. Pickering, a teacher in Township High School District 205 in Illinois, was dismissed from his position by the school board for sending a letter to a local newspaper in connection with a recently proposed tax increase. His letter was critical of the manner in which the board and superintendent had handled past proposals to raise new revenue for the schools. Pickering was dismissed following a full hearing based on the board's determination that the letter was detrimental to the efficient operation and administration of the schools in the district. Under Illinois statute, the interests of the school thus required his dismissal.

Pickering claimed that writing his letter was protected by both the First and Fourteenth amendments. The board rejected his claim and was supported by the Circuit Court of Will County. On appeal, the Illinois State Supreme Court upheld his dismissal, ruling that the teacher was unprotected by the First Amendment because he had accepted a position that required him to refrain from making statements regarding school operations. The U.S. Supreme Court reversed and remanded the case, finding no support for the state supreme court's ruling that public employment subjected the teacher to deprivation of his constitutional rights. The following points were pivotal to the Supreme Court's ruling:

- The state's interest in regulating employee speech has to be balanced against individual rights.
- School personnel are entitled to constitutional protection when they comment on matters of community concern.
- The public interest in free speech and debate on matters of community interest outweigh school officials' concern regarding allegations of defamation.
- Pickering's statements were not made with reckless disregard for the truth.

- No evidence was presented that demonstrated that a board member's professional reputation was damaged.
- Pickering's comments only constituted a difference of opinion on matters of public concern.

In *Pickering*, the U.S. Supreme Court generated the following guidelines regarding restrictions on freedom of expression by teachers. Speech may be restricted if it

1. creates disruption of the superior-subordinate relationship,

2. results in a disruption of public service, or

3. renders the teacher unfit based on the content of his or her speech.[2]

Essentially, if a teacher's speech adversely affects a substantial public interest, it can be restricted, and the teacher can be disciplined.

The U.S. Supreme Court addressed another landmark speech case in *Mt. Healthy City School District Board of Education v. Doyle*.[3] Doyle was an untenured teacher who was not renewed following a number of incidents involving what the school board viewed as a lack of tact in handling professional matters. Doyle engaged in a shouting match with a cafeteria employee over the amount of spaghetti he was served. He was involved in an argument with a fellow teacher, which resulted in face slapping and obscene gestures made by Doyle to two female students when they failed to obey his directives. Doyle also called a local radio station to render his opinion regarding a new school dress code.

When the board failed to renew his contract, Doyle requested and received a list of reasons for his nonrenewal. The board included concerns regarding his general behavior but also cited his phone call to the radio station. Doyle sued, claiming that his discussion with the radio station was protected speech and that his nonrenewal was a result of his exercising his First Amendment rights. The U.S. district court concurred, as did the court of appeals, that his First Amendment rights were violated. The board appealed to the U.S. Supreme Court, which overturned the decisions by the district court and the court of appeals. The U.S. Supreme Court held that the board could have made its decision based on several other incidents involving Doyle, despite his claim of First Amendment protection. The radio incident, while clearly implicating First Amendment rights protection, was not the sole reason for his nonrenewal.

The following points were pivotal to the High Court's ruling:

- No reasons are required for nonrenewal of a nontenured teacher's contract.
- The school board would have reached the same decision had Doyle not engaged in constitutionally protected conduct.
- An otherwise marginal employee should not be renewed simply because he engages in constitutionally protected speech.

- Marginal employees should not be able to prevent dismissal by hiding behind a constitutional shield as protection from other actions that do not receive constitutional protection.

Since the board had sufficient reasons not to renew Doyle's contract, it was improper to have mentioned the radio incident since it did not substantially contribute to the board's decision.

Connick v. Myers is a leading nonpublic speech case that has been cited by the courts in speech cases involving public school employees.[4] The Supreme Court upheld Myers's dismissal based on charges of insubordination. Myers, an assistant district attorney, was informed that she would be transferred to a different area of criminal law. She opposed the transfer and distributed questionnaires to coworkers soliciting information regarding morale and pressure to be involved in political campaigns. The High Court based its decision on the fact that Myers's communication was personal in nature rather than a matter of public concern. While the question raised may have fallen under the claim of public concern, her First Amendment interest was overridden by the disruptive nature of her questions.

The following points were pivotal in the High Court's decision:

- Communication that creates disruption, undermines authority, and adversely affects relationships will not receive First Amendment protection.
- Communication that affects employees' discipline and creates controversy will not receive First Amendment protection.
- The extent of Myers's interest in exercising free speech did not meet the standard of public concern.
- Speech involving private concerns requires a lower standard of proof by the state to justify dismissal.

A significant ruling by the Eleventh Circuit Court of Appeals defined the limits of speech that can be exercised by public school teachers. An Alabama teacher wrote numerous insulting letters to members of his school board, including one that accused a board member of being grand wizard of the Ku Klux Klan. He also released information on special education students in his classes, and one of his students burned his hand while he was working without safety gloves. The board voted to terminate the teacher's contract, which resulted in the teacher filing a federal district court action for discrimination, speech rights violations, and retaliation. The court found that his speech was protected by the First Amendment but held that the board would have discharged him regardless of his speech.

Upon appeal, the U.S. Court of Appeals, Eleventh District, held that the board did not offer any legitimate nondiscriminatory reason for its action. The case was remanded to the district court, which held a trial. The jury returned a $186,000 verdict for the teacher, but the court ordered a new trial when it learned that a jury member lied about her criminal history. The case was reassigned to a different judge, who awarded judgment to the board. The teacher appealed again to the Eleventh Circuit Court of Appeals, which considered his speech claim under *Pickering* and *Mt. Healthy City School Dist. v. Doyle*.[5] *Mt. Healthy* permits a school district to discharge a teacher who brings speech rights claims if the district shows it would have done so regardless of speech. The Eleventh Circuit Court of Appeals held that the evidence before it now was far different than what was presented earlier. In contrast to the limited record at the first appeal, there were now two trial transcripts of evidence about the teacher's demeaning letter-writing campaign and its effect on the school. Since the new evidence indicated that the teacher could cause discipline problems, undermine morale, and impair workplace harmony, the court had permissibly held in the board's favor on remand. The teacher's inflammatory letter-writing campaign was itself a legitimate basis for termination. The board had abundant nonracial reasons for its action, and the appeals court affirmed the judgment.[6]

83. How Do Free Speech Rights of Teachers Apply to Speech Inside the Classroom (Academic Freedom)?

Teachers are viewed as representatives of the school district when they speak in the classroom; consequently, school officials have an interest in the content spoken by teachers as they instruct students. On the other hand, public school teachers do enjoy a degree of freedom to instruct their students. This freedom is not as prominent as that in higher educational institutions, however.

The legal concept of academic freedom originated in Germany. The basic premise supporting academic freedom is that teachers have a right to teach and students have a right to learn. However, this concept is limited in public schools. Classrooms should be a marketplace of ideas where teachers are empowered to pursue freedom of inquiry, research, and discussion on a variety of issues in their academic disciplines. Professional educators must, however, be mindful of the age, maturity, and readiness of children to absorb the information introduced. Teachers must also confine their teaching to the prescribed areas in which they are certified and assigned to teach. Controversial material unrelated to the teacher's discipline or certification will not likely receive support by the courts, as was illustrated in a ruling by the Seventh Circuit Court of Appeals, which failed to support a teacher who distributed brochures regarding the pleasures associated with drugs and sex to eighth graders. The court ruled that the information was unrelated to class activities and did not serve a legitimate educational purpose. The teacher was subsequently dismissed.[7] Since public school curriculum is prescribed by the state, public school teachers do not enjoy broad latitude to deviate from the course of study or basic curriculum they are obligated to teach. Teachers should refrain from expressing their personal views unrelated to course content since the classroom is not considered to be a public forum. Where curriculum is prescribed, teachers, for the most part, enjoy latitude in determining teaching methods and strategies to meet the diverse needs of students, unless specific teaching methodologies are also prescribed by the school district.

A teaching methodology case arose when a Jewish student in a choir class alleged that her music teacher's choice of explicitly Christian religious music and Christian religious sites for performance of the high school a cappella choir violated her rights under the U.S. and Utah constitutions. The court, in *Bauchman v. West High School*, held that these actions did not violate the student's establishment clause rights since the teacher's selection had the primary purpose of teaching music appreciation and the effect of the curriculum was not to advance or promote religion or constitute excessive entanglement.[8] In a similar case, *Bradley v. Pittsburgh Board of Education*, a court held that a teacher did not have a First Amendment right to academic freedom to employ a technique called "Learnball," which involved using a sports format, peer approval, teams, and team leaders that had been banned by the board.[9]

84. Can School Officials Interfere With the Privacy Rights of Public School Teachers?

No, generally speaking, teachers as citizens enjoy a measure of privacy in their personal lives. If a challenge emerges regarding a teacher's private life, school officials must be able to demonstrate that the teacher's behavior has a detrimental impact on the teacher's effectiveness in performing professional duties and responsibilities. Although personal privacy is not addressed by the U.S. Constitution, the courts have recognized that citizens are entitled to a degree of constitutional protection in their personal lives. Personal privacy rights may include issues involving single teachers of the opposite sex living together, private homosexual acts, lifestyle choices, and childbirth out of wedlock. When school officials challenge private matters involving teachers, the burden of proof rests with them to demonstrate that private matters have an adverse affect on teaching performance. It should be clearly understood, however, that private sexual activities involving teachers and students are totally unacceptable and in most cases illegal. Teachers who are found guilty of improper sexual conduct involving students may face dismissal, decertification, and criminal prosecution.

For example, a tenured middle school teacher was dismissed for repeated offensive sexual comments toward female students and for placing his hand on a female student's back and snapping her bra.[10] A more extensive case arose in Michigan when a high school senior and a teacher began communicating outside class via emails and instant messages. As the student neared graduation, the teacher told her she was gay. The student's mother discovered an email from the teacher to the student with sexual innuendoes. The teacher informed the principal that the email was sent to all her email address book recipients and was mistakenly sent to the student. She denied any inappropriate relationship with the student. However, the two continued to correspond after the student enrolled in college. The principal recommended the teacher for tenure. Days later, the mother informed the principal that the explicit email was sent to her daughter alone, not to each address in the teacher's book. She revealed an instant messaging session between the teacher and student with explicit sexual and romantic content. The principal suspended the teacher and recommended denying her tenure for her lack of candor. The school board upheld his recommendation. The teacher sued the district, its board, and district officials in a federal district court for due process violations relating to rights, to privacy and intimate associations, and to freedom from arbitrary state action. The court held that the Constitution did not protect the teacher's relationship with the student, after which the teacher appealed.

The U.S. Court of Appeals, Sixth Circuit, held that schools may act to prevent teachers from having intimate relationships with students. While the due process clause protects personal decisions relating to marriage, family, and intimate relationships, only rules prohibiting all personal relationships violate due process rights. The court had previously upheld an anti-nepotism rule barring school employees from marrying. Just as that rule did not directly burden an employee's right to marry, the board's action in this case did not directly and substantially affect the teacher's intimate association rights. The principal's assessment of the teacher's candor was alone a legitimate explanation for denying her tenure. A policy against relationships between teachers and recent graduates would prevent high school seniors from being perceived as prospective dates after graduating. Because the board did not violate the teacher's due process or privacy rights, the judgment was affirmed.[11]

85. What Political Rights, if Any, Can Public School Teachers Exercise?

Teachers possess political rights just as ordinary citizens do. They may openly support candidates for public office, vote for candidates of their choice, and, in certain instances, run for public office. State laws that prohibit public employees from participating in all types of political activities have been determined to be unconstitutional. Teachers may engage in peaceful political debate. Teachers may be required to request a leave of absence if they elect to run for public office. While exercising their political rights, teachers should be certain that school resources are not utilized to support political activities. Additionally, the classroom should never be used as a forum to espouse political views or ideologies. Teachers should also be certain that political activities do not adversely affect their ability to perform assigned duties and responsibilities.

86. Can a Teacher Hold Public Office?

Yes. However, if a teacher is elected to public office, he or she may be required to resign the teaching position. State statutes usually address issues involving the occupation of elected office by school personnel. Courts tend to be divided on the issue. Some courts support a requirement that the teacher resign before actually campaigning for public office. Other courts do not support a general ban against running for public office and view such actions as unconstitutional.

As teachers pursue political offices or exercise their political rights, they should be mindful of the sensitive positions they hold as professionals and the impact their behavior may have on impressionable students. They should always adhere to the highest standards of professionalism and integrity.

87. Can Legitimate Restrictions Be Placed on School Personnel Rights to Freedom of Association?

No, as a general rule, school personnel are afforded freedom of association rights. Although freedom of association is not implicitly addressed by the First Amendment, courts tend to recognize that rights to association are related to freedom of speech and assembly. Freedom of association permits individuals to associate with others of their choice without fear of reprisal. If teachers' associations do not involve subversive or illegal acts or create a negative impact on the school district, they should be able to associate with individuals or organizations without jeopardizing their teaching positions. Public school educators cannot be treated arbitrarily or capriciously by school officials for participating in collective negotiations or affiliating with legally sanctioned teacher unions. Teachers may not be dismissed, denied tenure, demoted, or reassigned based on organizational affiliations. At the same time, teachers should always be mindful of their professional positions and the responsibilities associated with professionalism. They must also ensure that membership and affiliation with professional organizations do not impair their ability to satisfactorily perform their duties. They must be certain that they do not promote illegal or unethical goals that might be embraced by the organization with which they decide to affiliate.

Increasingly, courts have been willing to intervene in matters involving freedom of association rights of teachers. The Court of Appeals in Tennessee addressed a conflict regarding the Education Professional Negotiations Act (EPNA) and the Open Shop Law of 1947. The Open Shop Law made it unlawful to deny employment based on union membership or to exclude any person from a labor organization because of failure to pay dues, fees, or other charges. The teacher, who objected to his dues being used in support of certain causes, argued that the teachers' association was a "state actor," since the EPNA authorized it as the exclusive bargaining agent for all district teachers. The court agreed, finding sufficient state action to allow four of his constitutional claims to proceed. The court rejected the association's claim that the teacher had no constitutional right to join a labor union. The EPNA required a professional employees' organization to open its membership to professional employees to qualify as a collective bargaining agent. The court remanded the teacher's claims relating to the use of his dues in violation of his rights. It rejected his claim that the EPNA violated the portion of the Tennessee constitution that bars monopolies, however. No monopoly was created by the recognition of collective bargaining under the EPNA.[12]

88. Do Teachers Have an Option Not to Recite the Pledge of Allegiance?

Probably so. If the Pledge of Allegiance conflicts with the teacher's religious beliefs or conscience, he or she cannot be required to recite it. If the teacher elects to abstain, someone else should be assigned to lead the pledge while the teacher stands silently and respectfully. The teacher should never attempt to influence students not to participate, nor should the teacher engage in a discussion with students regarding his or her failure to participate. The First Amendment provides freedom of speech protection as well as freedom of religion protections. This point was stressed by the court in *Hanover v. Northrup* by its ruling, based on the *Tinker* test, that a teacher's refusal to lead or recite the pledge was an expression that could not be forbidden at the risk of loss of employment.[13]

89. What Latitude Are Teachers Provided Regarding Their Lifestyle Choices?

Teachers are provided considerable latitude to exercise personal lifestyle choices that are implicitly associated with Fourteenth Amendment personal rights. When conflicts arise regarding lifestyle choices, the courts attempt to balance the personal rights of teachers against the compelling interests of school boards. Compelling interests generally involve a peaceful school district free of substantial or material disruption. Consequently, if a teacher's lifestyle choice creates significant disruption or raises questions regarding the teacher's ability to perform assigned duties effectively, thus resulting in a negative impact on the teaching and learning process, the school board may pursue the matter legally. School officials, however, may not legally challenge lifestyle choice issues based solely on personal disapproval. A case in Maryland addressed the consequences that arose when private homosexuality became public. A Maryland teacher not only acknowledged his homosexuality but also appeared on various local and national television programs in his role as a homosexual. A U.S. district court held that a school district could not discriminate in any way against a teacher because of his homosexuality. However, in this case, the teacher went far beyond merely letting his preferences be known. He failed to exercise discretion, and his public activities such as appearing on national television went beyond the bounds of propriety that, of necessity, must govern any teacher regardless of sexual preferences.[14]

In a related case, a middle school teacher worked for a Wisconsin school district for many years before disclosing his homosexuality. After the disclosure, he reported being subjected to derogatory comments, insults, name calling, lavatory graffiti, and obscene and harassing phone calls. The school disciplined students who engaged in offensive behavior such as using inappropriate or offensive racial- and/or gender-related language. It also granted the teacher's request to transfer to an elementary school where the level of student harassment dropped, although parental taunts and threats increased. The teacher experienced a mental breakdown and resigned. He then sued the district in a federal district court for failing to take effective steps to prevent harassment. The court held for the district, and the teacher appealed.

The Seventh Circuit Court of Appeals stated that homosexuals do not enjoy a heightened level of constitutional protection. Title VII does not provide a private right of action based on sexual orientation discrimination, and there is no remedy under 42 U.S.C. § 1983 for sexual orientation discrimination.[15]

Issues involving homosexuality, pregnant unwed teachers, and other controversial private acts are decided on an individual case-by-case basis. The key question involves how the act committed by the teacher impairs his or her effectiveness as a teacher. In the absence of overall fitness to teach, the courts have been quite liberal but not consistent in supporting private acts of teachers. For example, an appeals court in Florida held that a single teacher could not be dismissed because she lived with a man. The school board claimed that the teacher violated the moral standards of the community and that her conduct rendered her ineffective as a teacher. The board, however, produced no evidence to support its claim. Additionally, there was testimony that she was an excellent teacher. Therefore, the private sexual relationship was an insufficient cause for dismissal.[16]

A very different decision was reached in an earlier case in South Dakota when the federal appeals court upheld the dismissal of an elementary teacher who began living with a male friend in a small rural town. She was requested to change her living arrangement but refused to do so, citing privacy rights and lifestyle choices. The teacher was dismissed based on the view that she was a bad example for students and violated the moral standards of the community. Even though the court acknowledged that this case posed very difficult constitutional issues, it nonetheless held for the school board.[17]

90. Can Public School Teachers Exercise Their Religious Beliefs in Public Schools?

No, teachers are not free to exercise their religious beliefs based on an establishment clause violation. The establishment clause states that school personnel cannot establish religion in public schools or aid one religion, aid all religions, or prefer one over the others. The requirements of the First Amendment mandate that school personnel maintain a neutral position in all matters regarding religion. Teachers, however, are free to exercise their religious beliefs outside the school environment. Teachers cannot be discriminated against by school boards based on their religious beliefs or affiliations; therefore, school officials cannot refuse to employ teachers based on religious considerations. They also cannot be demoted, nonrenewed, or dismissed based on religious beliefs. However, teachers are permitted to request religious holiday leave provided that his or her absence is not excessive and does not disrupt students' education. Continuity of instruction is important to students' academic success. Consequently, school officials may deny leave based on the special interests of students to learn if excessive absences occur.

91. Can School Officials Require Teachers to Instruct the Prescribed Curriculum Irrespective of Their Religious Views?

Yes, teachers cannot refuse to follow the prescribed school curriculum based on religious beliefs. The First Amendment does not grant a teacher the liberty of uncontrolled exercise that conflicts with approved curriculum. This point was emphasized in *Palmer v. Board of Education for the City of Chicago*.[18] Palmer refused to teach certain components of the curriculum based on religious beliefs. The court recognized his religious belief but indicated that the state's interest in properly educating children outweighed his religious freedoms. The court stated that teachers have no constitutional right to subject others to their views by foregoing a portion of their education that they would otherwise be entitled to.

92. Do Teachers Have Explicit Rights to Express Themselves Through Religious Dress and Appearance?

No, as a general rule, teachers may not wear religious clothing in public schools. The First Amendment prohibits schools from creating a religious atmosphere in public schools. Religious clothing does, in fact, create a potential establishment clause issue. Many state statutes prohibit religious dress by teachers so that they will understand the religious dress prohibitions as a condition of employment within the state. Wearing religious dress in the classroom may have a proselytizing effect on young, impressionable children and convey the belief that the school supports a particular religion. In *Cooper v. Eugene School District No. 41*, the court upheld the constitutionality of a state law prohibiting public school teachers from wearing religious dress while engaged in their teaching duties and the revocation of the teaching certificate of teachers who violated the rule. This case involved overt and repeated displays of religious garb by the teacher.[19]

Summary of Court Decisions Regarding Educators' Speech

• The U.S. Supreme Court upheld the First Amendment right of a Mississippi teacher to voice her opposition to racial policies within her school district because her communication with her employer was private.[20]

• When public employees make statements in accordance with their official duties, they are not speaking as citizens. Their communication is thus not insulated from employer discipline.[21]

• A school district was upheld when it removed materials posted on the bulletin board by a teacher in the classroom after it was determined that the posting was a curricular dispute in nature and thus did not constitute speech as a matter of public concern.[22]

• A U.S. district court held that a teacher had a right to participate in a political demonstration by honking her horn in response to a "honk for peace" sign protesting the war in Iraq because military intervention is an issue of public importance. The teacher shared her response in class when asked by students. Since parents complained and the school principal requested that the teacher not take sides in any political controversy, her right was qualified by the requirement that the expression not disrupt an employer's business unduly.[23]

Summary of Cases Involving Teachers' Rights

• A South Carolina federal district court ruled that the actions of a substitute teacher who had worn a button with the slogan "War is Not the Answer" and was alleged to have made other negative statements during her classes regarding American military policy in Panama and Iraq were not protected by the First Amendment.[24]

- A high school teacher in Virginia was ordered to remove pamphlets he had placed outside of the classroom describing a number of banned books. Although they were designed to create discussion on an important public policy, the judge found that posting the material was an extension of the curriculum, which is the responsibility of the school.[25]

- The Fifth Circuit Court of Appeals held that a superintendent who supported one candidate for the school board over another and then lost the election must suffer the consequences. The nature of the working relationship between the superintendent and board is of necessity a close one. The efficiency and effectiveness of the school district depends on harmony between the superintendent and school board. When the superintendent publicly speaks out, these bonds are broken, and there is no First Amendment shelter provided him.[26]

- The Eighth Circuit Court of Appeals held that a teacher's letter to the Arkansas Department of Education regarding the school's delay in implementing federally mandated programs for students with disabilities was a matter of public concern and therefore protected.[27]

- A federal district court upheld the dismissal of a teacher who made homosexual advances to a salesman in the teacher's lounge. While there was no direct evidence that his behavior negatively affected his teaching effectiveness, it nevertheless depicted a flaw in moral behavior and professionalism that indicated general unfitness to teach.[28]

- The Eighth Circuit Court of Appeals held that the school district's refusal to renew a probationary teacher's contract based on statements regarding consensual sexual relationships between teachers and students during compelling testimony did not violate her free speech rights. Her statements did not constitute a matter of public concern.[29]

Summary Guides

1. Teachers, just as other U.S. citizens, possess constitutional rights that must be respected by school officials.

2. Teachers may legally express their views on issues of community concerns without fear of reprisal by school officials.

3. Teachers must avoid defamatory statements and avoid personal attacks on their supervisors or school boards.

4. Teachers can be penalized for speech content that is unprofessional or that renders the teacher ineffective in his or her relationship with students.

(Continued)

5. Teacher statements may not materially or substantially create disruption in the school system.

6. Teachers cannot invoke freedom of expression violations when their professional behavior otherwise warrants dismissal by the school board.

7. Disruptive interoffice communication that serves a personal interest does not receive First Amendment coverage.

8. Academic freedom of public school teachers is limited to appropriate content based on their licensure or teaching assignment and must consider the age, maturity, and readiness of students to be exposed to certain content.

9. Teachers' privacy rights should be respected, unless there is evidence that suggests general unfitness to teach.

10. Teachers possess the same political rights as do other citizens but should exercise them in a manner consistent with their professional positions. They may not use school resources to support their political objectives, nor may they use the classroom as a forum to promote them.

11. Teachers might be required to use a leave of absence when they pursue a public or political office.

12. Teachers' religious rights must be respected but should not infringe on the rights of students.

13. Teachers cannot be required to pledge allegiance to the flag if contrary to their religious beliefs or conscience.

14. Teachers are required to teach the approved curriculum irrespective of their religion or beliefs.

NOTES

1. *Pickering v. Board of Education*, 225 N.E. 2d 16 (Ill. 1967).
2. Ibid.
3. *Mt. Healthy City School District Board of Education v. Doyle*, 429 U.S. 274, 97 S.Ct. 568 (1977).
4. *Connick v. Myers*, 461 U.S. 138, 147, 103 S.Ct. 1684, 1690, 75 L.Ed. 2d 708 (1983).
5. *Mt. Healthy City School District Board of Education v. Doyle*, 429 U.S. 274, 97 S.CT. 568 (1977).
6. *Jackson v. State of Alabama State Tenure Comm'n*, 405 F.3d 1276 (11th Cir. 2005).
7. *Webster v. New Lennox School Dist. No. 122*, 917 F.2d 1004 (7th Cir. 1990).
8. *Bauchman v. West High School*, 900 F. Supp. 254 (Utah 1995).
9. *Bradley v. Pittsburgh Board of Education*, 910 F.2d, 1172 (3rd Cir. 1990).

10. *Knowles v. Board of Education*, 857 P.2d 553 (Cal. Ct. App. 1993).

11. *Flaskamp v. Dearborn Public Schools*, 385 F.3d 935 (6th Cir. 2004).

12. *Esquinance v. Polk County Educ. Ass'n*, No. E2004-02408-COA-R3-CV, 2005 WL 1798625 (Tenn. Ct. App. 2005).

13. *Hanover v. Northrup*, 325 F. Supp 170 (D Conn 1970).

14. *Jantz v. Muci*, 976 F.2d 623, 10th Cir. Ct. App. (1992).

15. *Schroeder v. Hamilton School Dist.*, 282 F.3d 946 (7th Cir. 2002).

16. *Sherburne v. Sch. Bd. of Suwannee Co.*, 455 So. 2d 1057 (Fla. Dist. Ct. App. 1984).

17. *Sullivan v. Meade Indep. Sch. Dist. No. 101*, 530 F.2d 799 (8th Cir. 1976).

18. *Palmer v. Board of Education for the City of Chicago*, 603 F.2d 1271, 1274 (7th Cir. 1979), Cert. denied, 444 U.S. 1026, 100 S.Ct. 689 (1980).

19. *Cooper v. Eugene Sch. Dist. No. 41*, 301 Ore. 358 (1986), app. dismissed, 480 U.S. 942 (1987).

20. *Givhan v. Western Line Consolidated School District*, 439 U.S. 410, 99 S.Ct 693, 58 L.Ed. 2d 619 (1978).

21. *Mills v. Evansville*, 452 F.3d 646 (7th Cir. 2006).

22. *Lee v. York County Sch. Dist.*, 418 F. Supp. 2d 816 (E.D. Va. 2006).

23. *Mayer v. Monroe County Community School Corp.*, U.S. Dist. Lexis 26137 (S.D. Ind.) (2006).

24. *Calef v. Budden*, 361 F. Supp. 493 (S.C. 2005).

25. *Newton v. Slye*, 116 F. Supp. 2d 677 (2000).

26. *Kinsey v. Salado Independent School Dist.*, 950 F.2d 988 (5th Cir. 1992).

27. *Southside Public Schools v. Hill*, 827 F.2d 270 (8th Cir. 1987).

28. *Stephens v. Board of Education*, 429 N. W. 2d 722 (Neb. 1988).

29. *Padilla v. South Harrison R-II School District*, 181 F.3d 992 (8th Cir. 1999).

7

Terms and Conditions of Employment

⚎ INTRODUCTION ⚎

Teachers are contract employees. The local school board is the only legal entity authorized to issue contracts to teachers. School boards are provided considerable discretion in deciding to whom a contract is offered. Courts are reluctant to interfere with school board authority and generally will not intrude on school board employment decisions unless there is substantial evidence of capriciousness or political or discriminatory intent.

The employment contract essentially defines expectations and responsibilities between school personnel and school boards. Teachers must fulfill licensure requirements to be considered for an employment position. The teacher's license does not, necessarily, assure employment in local school districts. As long as contracts are issued in a fair and defensible manner consistent with the employment needs of the district, there is no legal basis to challenge school board decisions. The burden of proof initially resides with the prospective employee to establish a bona fide case of employment discrimination, after which the board must provide a defensible basis for not awarding a contract. The affected teacher thus must demonstrate that the board's action is a pretext for discrimination. Most contractual agreements are subject to applicable state laws, rules, and regulations of the state board of education and the local school district in which the contract is issued.

93. What Are the Essential Components of a Teacher's Contract, and When Does It Become Binding?

The first essential element of a contract is the offer and acceptance. When an offer is made, the person to whom the offer is made must accept the offer to consummate an agreement. Typically, there is a prescribed time-frame in which the offer must be accepted. The offer is null and void if the designated timeframe is not met unless otherwise agreed upon by the party extending the offer.

COMPETENT PARTIES

The second element involves competent parties, meaning that those involved in the offer and acceptance must have the legal authority to enter into a contract. For example, the school board is the legal entity that offers contracts. School principals lack the legal authority to enter into a contract with a teacher. They can be delegated the responsibility to recommend employment to the superintendent, who in turn must recommend and receive school board approval to establish a valid contractual agreement. A teacher who is not duly licensed lacks the legal authority to enter into a contract because he or she is not legally considered to be a competent party.

CONSIDERATION

A valid contract must include an element of value provided for an act or promised by the person to whom the offer is extended. For example, a teacher makes a commitment to teach, and the school board agrees to offer remuneration for his or her services. These components bind the contract.

LEGAL SUBJECT MATTER

All valid contracts contain legal subject matter. Illegal subject matter invalidates a contract. The offer and acceptance must involve legally sanctioned activities. Teaching and supervising children are legally sanctioned activities.

PROPER FORM

Legal enforcement of a contract requires that the document be framed in a manner consistent with statutory law. Proper form requires that contracts between the school and the teacher be provided in written form. Again, the contract becomes legal when all of the conditions stated above are met. More specifically, it becomes binding when the written agreement is signed by those legally authorized to make an offer and to accept the offer.

94. Is the Contract Void if It Is Not Written?

No, not necessarily, if the particular state does not require that it be in written form. Although verbal contracts may be allowable in some states, they are generally more difficult to enforce than those produced in writing; there is no written documentation validating that an agreement has been reached and that all the elements of a contract have been incorporated into the agreement.

95. Can Supplemental Contracts Create Special Problems for Teachers?

Maybe, it depends on the facts and circumstances surrounding the contract agreement. Supplemental contracts usually involve the performance of extra services by a regular teacher that consumes considerable time and for which the teacher receives compensation. Supplemental contracts are typically issued to teachers such as band directors and athletic coaches. Conflicts often arise regarding whether two separate contracts are required and whether breach of one constitutes breach of the other. For example, if a teacher is employed by written contract to teach science and direct the school's band, the teacher would be required to do both. In this case, two services are written into one contract; therefore, a breach in the performance of one service constitutes a breach of the entire contract. Conversely, if a teacher is actually employed to teach social studies and the school board requests that she coach girls' softball, the teacher is not required to continue coaching in future years because coaching softball was not a condition of her initial employment contract. Typically, teachers earn tenure as a teacher rather than as a coach or band director. Supplemental contracts do not carry tenure rights. Thus, a tenured teacher can be relieved of coaching duties but maintain tenure as a classroom teacher.

96. Are Oral Contracts Legally Enforceable?

Yes. Oral contracts are legally enforceable, but it is often difficult to prove what was agreed upon by either party. Also, the details of the contract could prove to be even more difficult to enforce because of the challenges of recalling them. In such legal challenges, the courts face a very difficult task in determining if a breach of contract has occurred. Courts typically rely on the concept of fairness, which may be viewed as subjective and unfair by parties who do not agree with the court's ruling. Written contracts are thus preferred because the terms and conditions are documented and legally binding when all the requirements of a valid contract are met.

An example of an oral contract dispute occurred in *Sonnichsen v. Baylor University*. Sonnichsen was hired by Baylor University as its women's volleyball coach. Under an oral contract, the university informed Sonnichsen and the coaching staff that it planned to provide written contracts after six years of employment. When the university failed to do so, Sonnichsen sued for breach of contract and fraud. Baylor University was awarded summary judgment by the trial court; however, the court of appeals remanded the case to the trial court. The trial court granted Baylor an exception and dismissed the contract claim without giving Sonnichsen an opportunity to amend his pleading, because it contained incurable defects. The trial court's decision was affirmed by the supreme court of Texas.[1]

97. When Does a Teacher Breach a Contract?

A teacher breaches a contract when he or she fails to meet the requirements set forth in the contract. When the contract is signed, the teacher has a legal obligation to fulfill the expectations expressed in the contract. Should the teacher leave the contract position before the contract expires, a breach of contract has occurred.

An example of a breach of contract arose when two mathematics teachers challenged the Talbot County Board of Education for withholding accrued salary of $4,312 and $3,467, respectively, based on their breach of contract. Both teachers submitted resignation letters well past the May 1 deadline specified in their contracts. The Maryland Court of Appeals, in its ruling against the teachers, stated that the state board of education has very significant and broad powers in determining how best to educate children in the state. The court of appeals thus reversed a lower court ruling holding that forfeiture provisions included in Maryland public school teachers' employment contracts were unenforceable. The appellate court stated that the forfeiture provision was indeed a valid and enforceable liquidated damages clause.[2]

98. What Consequences Can Teachers Face for Breach of Contract?

Consequences vary from state to state. Legal remedies available to the party against whom the contract was breached normally involve compensatory remedies. Courts tend to support compensatory damages in the amount that restores the injured party for losses. Other states have the authority to revoke the teacher's certificate upon breach of contract.

99. How Does No Child Left Behind Legislation Affect Teacher Employment?

No Child Left Behind (NCLB) outlines minimum requirements that teachers must meet to be employed in public schools and be deemed highly qualified. They must achieve the following minimum requirements:

- Earned a bachelor's degree
- Achieved full state certification
- Demonstrated subject-matter competency for each subject they are assigned to teach

These requirements were implemented at the end of the 2005–2006 school year. Consequently, all new teachers must now immediately meet the highly qualified standard mandated by NCLB. Newly hired teachers in Title I programs or schools must also be highly qualified immediately. A more flexible timeline, however, has been allowed for teachers in eligible small, rural schools who often teach multiple subjects. The statute requires states to ensure that Title I schools provide instruction by a highly qualified instructional staff. States must develop plans with annual measurable objectives to ensure that all teachers of core academic subjects are highly qualified. Core academic subjects include English, reading or language arts, mathematics, science, foreign language, civics and government, economics, arts, history, and geography.[3]

100. How Should Teacher Evaluations Impact Professional Development of Teachers?

Teacher evaluation is essential to lifelong learning and teacher development. The primary purpose of teacher evaluations should be centered on the improvement of teaching effectiveness. Consequently, teacher evaluations should be linked to the school district's mission and viewed as a continuous process of growth and development. The evaluation itself should serve as a direct connection between the manner in which the teacher is performing and the desired level of performance. The evaluation process should be a positive and constructive one involving the teacher and the principal, including joint agreement on evaluation objectives, methodology, and how results will be processed and utilized. The teacher's performance plan should be a product of his or her evaluation process. Evaluation systems that are developed to promote teacher growth and development using formalized evaluation strategies are considered to be a more effective means of enhancing reflective practice and increased accountability for performance.

The evaluation process should be viewed as a collaborative decision-making process involving the principal and the teacher receiving the evaluation. The principal, as instructional leader, must understand teaching and learning, the complexities of teaching, collaborative decision making, and focused student outcomes. Evaluation systems that center on regimented sets of behaviors do not tend to facilitate teacher involvement, collaboration, or development. Evaluation is considered to be more positive and effective when it is included as an integral component of the teacher's daily practice. Typical components of an evaluation include a demonstration of content knowledge, teaching techniques, methodology, and resources. Communications with students, student participation, classroom management and recognition of student diversity, demonstrated knowledge of student groups, student development, and other relevant measures should also be components of the teacher evaluation process. Teaching skills should reflect best practices based on research regarding student learning.

Several national organizations such as the National Board for Professional Teaching Standards (NBPTS) and the National Commission on Teaching and America's Future (NCTAF) have created blueprints for preparing teachers and supporting excellence in the classroom. Additionally, the Interstate New Teacher Assessment and Support Consortium (INTASC) has developed, in conjunction with the National Council for the Accreditation of Teacher Education (NCATE), a set of core standards that identify knowledge, dispositions, and performance standards for new teachers. School districts can therefore draw on research-based standards developed by national organizations in designing and implementing meaningful outcomes-based evaluation systems that will contribute to more effective teacher development plans.

101. When Do Teachers Achieve Tenure?

Tenure is granted based on state statute in states that support it. While there may be variations among states, tenure is normally awarded after the teacher has successfully completed the probationary period. The probationary period typically is a two- to four-year process depending on the particular state in which a probationary teacher is seeking tenure. A teacher must therefore successfully complete two to four consecutive years in the same district and receive an offer for reemployment for the succeeding year. This point was emphasized in a California case when a school district hired a teacher in the middle of the 1998–1999 school year. The teacher held a valid state teaching certificate but needed to complete coursework and obtain a Bilingual, Cross-Cultural, Language and Academic Development (BCLAD) certificate. He replaced a certificated employee on leave of absence and was classified as a temporary employee. The district employed him fulltime during the next two school years under the same terms. At the same time, it employed many more temporary teachers than the number of permanent teachers on leave. The teacher obtained his BCLAD certificate in 2001, and the district rehired him for 2001–2002. In February 2002, midway through his third full year of employment by the district under a temporary designation, the district notified him that he would not be reemployed. The teacher petitioned a state court to grant him permanent status.

The state court ruled that he became a permanent employee before receiving the nonrenewal notice. The appeals court held that a certified probationary employee who works for two full consecutive years is deemed to have permanent status by operation of law if he or she is reemployed by the district for the succeeding year. The first year of employment as a temporary employee is deemed probationary. "Temporary teachers" include those employed due to a leave of absence by another certified employee. If a temporary teacher's duties continue, the teacher is considered a "probationary employee." State law deemed that all certified teachers who were not classified as permanent or substitute employees were "probationary employees." In this case, the teacher had worked for over a full school year as a temporary employee by the end of the 1999–2000 school year and was then reemployed in 2000–2001, when he became a probationary employee. He completed the year in a certified position and received proper credentials. For this reason, when the district rehired him for 2001–2002, he became a permanent employee by operation of law. The court affirmed the judgment in his favor.[4]

Teachers are not guaranteed tenure. School boards, at their discretion, may decide to grant or deny tenure. As long as their decisions are not arbitrary, capricious, or based on political grounds, they are free to render tenure decisions. Tenure is considered to be a security measure that protects teachers from arbitrary and capricious actions by school officials. It essentially means that, if teachers continue to meet prescribed performance standards, they should be secure in their employment positions. Tenure is not a guarantee of employment if teachers fail to effectively meet performance standards. It simply means that teachers may not be removed from their employment positions in the absence of a specific or valid cause and full due process proceedings.

In many states, there is a statutory timeframe by which nontenured teachers must be notified through certified or registered mail if they will not be reemployed for the succeeding year. This concept is referred to as "spring notification" in some states. For example, if the school district fails to notify a teacher who is eligible for tenure as prescribed by law, the teacher will have earned tenure by default for lack of a timely notice, even if the board had not intended to award it. There have been instances in which teachers have alleged that notification was not received within the statutory timeframe. In such cases, the district must only demonstrate that the notice was forwarded by certified mail during the prescribed timeframe to the latest known address of the teacher to be supported by the courts if litigation arises.

Tenure should protect effective teachers and not those who have demonstrated ineffectiveness. There is agreement in theory with this view, but operationally it may not always be the practice. When principals fail to effectively evaluate teachers who are allowed to perform at unacceptable levels, there is a strong probability that these teachers may receive tenure. If incompetent or ineffective teachers are awarded tenure, children do not receive the equal educational opportunity to which they are entitled.

There is a perception that it is difficult to dismiss a tenured teacher. While generally true that dismissal is difficult, it is not impossible. Once teachers have been awarded tenure, they have gained a property right or a legitimate claim to a teaching position. Even though a property right exists, with systematic evaluations, feedback, and administrative support over a sufficient period of time to substantiate and document ineffectiveness, a tenured teacher may successfully be dismissed for cause. If the principal assumes leadership in removing ineffective teachers while observing school district procedures, state statutes, and all constitutional provisions, ineffective tenured teachers can be successfully dismissed.

102. Can a Teacher Earn Tenure by Default?

It depends on the state involved. Some states award tenure to a probationary teacher who has met the statutory requirements to earn tenure in cases where the school board fails to meet the statutory time notification requirement, which is referred to as spring notification.

103. Is It Legal for a State to Abolish Tenure?

Yes, if the state elects to do so. Teachers do not have a constitutional right to be awarded tenure. If a state grants tenure based on statute, it may abolish it as well. State legislatures are provided broad powers by the courts to change tenure laws.

104. Do Nontenured Teachers Have Legal Protection Regarding Nonrenewal of Their Teaching Contract?

Generally not, unless they can demonstrate that nonrenewal was motivated by personal or political reasons. They may claim a liberty interest violation by showing that the particulars of their nonrenewal were discussed by board members outside of the board meeting, hence resulting in limited opportunities to be awarded another position. The burden of proof, however, rests with the nontenured teacher.

105. What Does Nontenured Status Really Mean?

Nontenured status essentially means that a teacher is a probationary teacher who is awarded a contract by the school board to provide designated services during a particular contract year. When the service requirement has been met at the end of the contract year, the teacher may or may not, at the board's discretion, be renewed for the succeeding year because both the teacher and the district have met their legal obligations to each other. Nontenured status, therefore, carries no expectation of employment beyond the contract year. When the school board elects to do so, it may issue annual contracts to probationary teachers if they are performing effectively. As indicated earlier, if a nontenured teacher meets the statutory requirements for consecutive year contracts, which vary by state from two to four years, and is reemployed during the succeeding year, he or she has attained tenure. When a nontenured teacher is not renewed, no reasons need be given since the teacher's property right does not extend beyond the contract year, unless prescribed by a particular state statute. However, if a nontenured teacher is dismissed during the contract year, his or her property right has been violated. For legal purposes, the nontenured teacher must receive the same level of due process as a dismissed tenured teacher would receive since both involve a legitimate property interest in employment.

In summation, nontenured status is characterized as follows:

- No legitimate expectation of employment beyond the contracted year
- No right to receive reasons for nonrenewal
- No right to due process
- No hearing

An interesting probationary case arose in Oklahoma when a probationary teacher nearing completion of her third year of employment in a district was offered a temporary contract for the next school year.[5] The district did not offer her a permanent contract due to performance concerns. The temporary contract had a resignation clause effective at the end of the school year and waived the teacher's right to further notice for contract termination. At the end of her fourth year, the board decided not to renew the temporary contract. The teacher sued the district in an Oklahoma trial court for an order compelling tenured status. The court granted the district's summary judgment motion, and the case reached the supreme court of Oklahoma.

The supreme court held that the teacher was not tenured either before or after she completed the temporary contract. As she was not tenured, the district could offer her a temporary contract instead of not rehiring her. Teachers employed under temporary contracts are exempt from the state tenure law. The court rejected the teacher's assertion that she was entitled to tenure rights prior to the completion of three years of employment under a written contract. Under Oklahoma law, teachers gain tenure after the completion of three consecutive complete school years under a written teaching contract. The court affirmed the district court judgment.

A teacher who has been nonrenewed may claim a liberty interest violation if there is evidence that his or her range of potential job opportunities has been adversely affected based on negative comments communicated by board members regarding the teacher. In this case, the nontenured teacher is claiming injury to his or her professional reputation or standing. Courts will generally address liberty interest claims to ensure that fundamental fairness prevails. It is important to recognize that the burden of proof rests with the nontenured teacher who alleges a liberty interest violation.

106. Can Teachers Be Legally Assigned Duties Outside the Normal School Day?

Yes, as long as the duties are not overly burdensome, are professional in nature, and are beneficial to children. The courts generally place three legal duties on the shoulders of teachers. All teachers are expected to:

- Instruct
- Supervise
- Provide a safe environment for students

Repeated failure to perform these important duties may result in teacher dismissal. In addition to these three legal duties, the courts also have defined other nonteaching duties that teachers may be expected to perform. For example, lead cases in Illinois, California, and New York indicate that teachers may be required to perform any duties, including nonteaching assignments, that are reasonable adjuncts to normal school activities provided such duties are not demeaning to professional status, unreasonably time consuming, or discriminatory in the manner in which they are assigned among teachers.

These criteria were used by the court in the *Thomas v. Board of Education* case, in which the court upheld the school district's assignment of extra duties involving teachers. This case emerged when a teacher filed suit contesting the assignment of nonclassroom duties beyond the normal school day. The teacher further challenged the legality of such duties because they were not clarified in school district policy. The district court, in ruling for the school district, stated:

Teaching duties are not solely confined to the classroom and additional responsibilities may be properly imposed so long as they are within the scope of the license held by the teacher. Extra duty assignments do not need to be specified in school board rules in order to be valid. If duties are not onerous, demeaning, unusually time-consuming, or assigned in a discriminatory manner, they may be assigned even though the teacher considers them an inconvenience.[6]

Therefore, teachers may be required to perform extra duty assignments if they are professional in nature, not unduly time consuming, and related to the teacher's area of specialization, even though they may not be spelled out in district policy. The absence of policy statements regarding extra duty does not relieve teachers of the obligation to perform the assignment.

The *McGrath* case offers a further illustration of the types of cocurricular duties generally accepted by the courts as professional in nature and reasonably related to the teaching function. In *McGrath v. Burkhard*, the plaintiff requested that the court clarify the rights and duties under the contract of employment. He had suggested to the school board that non-classroom work was not within the scope of employment, that he must not be assigned duties on a teaching day that required more than eight hours per day to perform competently, and that no duties must be assigned on days for which he was not paid, that is, Saturdays, holidays, and non-teaching days. The board had responded by stating that

- it had the right to assign the teacher any teaching duties within the scope of his credentials;
- it had the right to assign the teacher to assist in the supervision of athletic and social activities conducted under the auspices of the Sacramento Senior High School, provided the assignments were made impartially and without discrimination; and
- since the teacher was a professional, the services could not be arbitrarily measured but were dependent on the reasonable needs of the school's program.

The court, in ruling for the school district, stated:

In view of the foregoing, the court is convinced that the respondent school board had the right to assign plaintiff to assist in the supervision of any and all athletic or social activities, wherever held, when conducted under the name or auspices of the school or any class or organization thereof, provided such assignment is made impartially and without discrimination against plaintiff with relation to the other teachers employed at said school. . . . We find nothing unreasonable in the assignment objected to by the appellant. We must presume that school authorities were acting for what they considered the best interest of the students and the people of the district.[7]

This particular court did suggest that the hours involved in nonteaching duties must be reasonable; however, the court did not find an occasional

Saturday assignment to be unreasonable. A teacher may therefore be required to provide supervision for any extended school activities sanctioned by the school in which students benefit, as long as the duties are reasonable and nondiscriminatory in nature. In addition, teachers may be asked to perform extra-duty assignments sponsored by the school even when those activities take place off school grounds and consume more than the eight-hour school day.

The language used by the court in the *McGrath* case is very similar to the language used in an earlier case, *Parrish v. Moss.* In that case, a teacher contested the right of the school board to assign incidental duties outside the instructional program. The court held that teachers could be assigned those duties when they are related to their respective fields. English teachers could be required to coach drama plays and assist debate teams, band leaders could be expected to travel with the band on field excursions, and physical education instructors could be required to coach intramural and interschool athletic teams. The court in ruling for the school district said:

> The hours established in any case must be reasonable. The board's grant of authority to fix "duties" of teachers is not restricted to classroom instruction. Any teaching duty within the scope of the license held by a teacher may properly be imposed. The day in which the concept was held that teaching duty was limited to the classroom instruction has long since passed. Children are being trained for citizenship and the inspiration and leadership in such training is the teacher. Of course, it is recognized that any bylaw of a board outlining teachers' duties must stand the test of reasonableness.[8]

The *Blair v. Robstown* case illustrates the serious consequences that can occur from failing to execute cocurricular duties generally accepted by the courts as reasonable and professional in nature.[9] The plaintiff in this case refused to take tickets and supervise conduct at high school football games, although male teachers were required to perform these functions as a condition of employment. Refusal on two occasions was held by the Fifth Circuit Court of Appeals to constitute insubordination. The teacher admitted that his refusals were retaliatory in nature for what he considered to be mistreatment by school officials. Coupled with an incident of violating another rule, these acts were sufficient to warrant nonrenewal of the teacher's contract.

Among other cocurricular duties implied by the court as professional in nature and reasonably related to the teaching function are supervision of study halls and cafeteria, monitoring school-sponsored events (social and athletic), attendance at open house, participation in teacher workshops, and service on various school or district committees. Repeated failure to perform these important duties may form grounds for dismissal on charges of insubordination.

In summarizing the courts' position in these cases, it seems quite clear that teachers may not be assigned menial tasks that can be performed by nonprofessionals. Such tasks may include but not be limited to police or traffic duties, ticket-selling duties, custodial duties, and so on. If such duties are requested, teachers must be provided reasonable compensation. By no means must nonteaching assignments be used as punitive measures against teachers by school officials. Furthermore, these duties may not be assigned for personal or political reasons. Assignments must be reasonably related to the teacher's area of specialty and assigned on a fair and defensible basis. Teacher assignments that extend beyond the school day and are outside the scope of reasonableness will not likely receive support by the courts when challenged by teachers.

107. Can School Boards Legally Transfer Teachers From One School or Position to Another?

Yes, if there is a justifiable basis for doing so. Most teacher transfers are governed by individual state statutes that prescribe procedures that must be followed to ensure that transfer decisions are not based on personal or political grounds but rather on the needs of the district. Teachers are not entitled to be assigned to a specific school within a district. The school board may, based on the superintendent's recommendation, transfer or refuse to transfer a teacher to a different school. Personnel transfers should not be initiated as a punitive measure but must be based on good faith and district needs. Most state statutes outline due process procedures that must be followed if teachers wish to contest a transfer based on their view that the transfer is motivated by personal or political considerations. Good faith and uncontested transfers do not require a formal due process hearing.

As a West Virginia court stated decades ago,

> it is conceivable that many teachers are transferred by boards of education not because of inefficiency, misconduct or unfitness but rather because of the mere fact that they are competent, effective teachers and that, therefore, a proper administration of the public school system dictates the basis of transfers to places and positions where the teacher's special qualifications will better promote the entire public school program of the district.[10]

However, some personnel transfers occur based on personality conflicts and incompatible relationships. Courts tend to support these types of transfers when there is evidence that supports conflicts or incompatibility. Transfers should result in positions of equal status and compensation consistent with the licensure area(s) in which the teacher was employed to teach.

Tenure should not be affected by teacher transfer as long as the teacher meets the requirements to be awarded continuing service status. In some states, when a continuing service teacher is transferred to an administrative position, he or she retains tenure status as a teacher even though there may be a new set of requirements for being awarded tenure as an administrator (in states where administrative tenure is granted).

A case involving teacher transfer arose in New Jersey when a teacher was certificated to teach English, social studies, and sciences and taught seventh-grade social studies until his position was eliminated. He was reassigned to a computer applications class and other duties during the next two school years with no reduction in benefits or salary. Within two years, the board reinstated a seventh-grade social studies teaching position for which the teacher applied but was not selected. The teacher petitioned the state commissioner of education, who held that the district had properly transferred the teacher to a position for which he was certified and that no reduction in force had taken place. The state education board reversed the commissioner's decision, finding that a reduction in force had occurred, and ordered the local board to reassign the teacher to the social studies position.

The local board appealed to the Superior Court of New Jersey, Appellate Division, where it argued that no reduction in force occurred when the position was abolished since there had been no layoff of teaching staff, a prerequisite to the creation of a preferred eligibility list under state law. The court agreed with the local board's finding that the teacher's seniority rights were not affected. Although the board had abolished the position, it had reassigned the teacher to teach different subjects within his certification without any reduction in salary or benefits. The transfer was not a demotion because the teacher's new duties were within the scope of his certification. The reasons stated by the board for the reassignment were permissible, and abolishment of the position did not affect the teacher's seniority rights. The court reversed the state board's decision.[11]

School boards may reassign teachers in areas where their services are needed. They are not required to reinstate a teacher to a previous assignment unless there is evidence of arbitrary and capricious decisions by the board. Teachers may also request voluntary transfers based on state or district policy. There are required procedures to be followed along with established timeframes in which voluntary transfers must be requested. In many cases, teachers are not required to submit reasons for requesting the transfer but may voluntarily provide reasons if they wish. If the transfer is denied, specific reasons must be provided consistent with fundamental fairness.

108. Are School Boards Required to Legally Grant Leaves of Absence for Teachers?

Yes and no. It depends on the type of leave involved and the subsequent impact it has on the school or district. There are mandatory leaves of absence such as military, maternity, Family Medical and Leave Act, paternity, and peace corps to name a few. Other leaves are considered discretionary, such as sabbatical and personal leave. Leaves of absences are reflected in district policy. The courts view continuity of instruction as important for an effective teaching and learning environment; consequently, they are reluctant to intrude on the decisions of school officials regarding leave unless there is evidence of arbitrary or capricious decisions that create equal protection challenges. Criteria governing leaves of absence must be stated clearly and concisely in school board policy so that teachers are well versed and knowledgeable of the conditions that surround personal leaves.

Some leaves are granted with pay, whereas others are granted without pay. Teachers must be familiar with all regulations governing leaves prior to requesting a leave. For example, a conflict arose in Arkansas regarding paid leave. After working for an Arkansas school district for almost twenty years, a teacher resigned to work as a school counselor in Missouri. She sought payment for ninety days of unused sick leave, but the district refused because she did not meet either of the criteria for such a payment—retirement or employment in another Arkansas school district. The teacher sued the district in a state court asserting that the law and her collective bargaining agreement required payment for accumulated, unused sick leave. The court dismissed the complaint, and the teacher appealed. The Arkansas Court of Appeals held that state law allowed teachers to take unused sick leave as pay only when they retired or as a credit upon their employment by another Arkansas district. The teacher appealed to the state supreme court.

The state supreme court held that the teacher's interpretation of state law could devastate school district budgets with "a sudden onslaught of requests for cash payments." The terms of the teacher's employment provided for payment for unused sick leave only in the two circumstances identified by the lower courts. Although the Arkansas legislature had amended state law in 1979 to allow such payments for unused sick leave, a payment was not required in this case as the teacher was ineligible for retirement and had not been reemployed by another Arkansas district. The court rejected her alternative argument that she had a vested contractual right to be paid for the sick leave. It affirmed the judgment.[12]

Many district policies include provisions for extended leave beyond the prescribed leave period. Applicable criteria are typically included in policies that govern extended leaves of absence.

109. What Happens to Teachers Who Are Injured at School in the Course of Executing Their Assigned Duties?

Teachers are eligible for workers' compensation if they are injured or disabled while executing their job-related professional responsibilities. The requirement that the injury be work related is a major aspect of workers' compensation; that is, an injured employee must be compensated for injury incurred in the line of duty. The agency in which the individual is employed assumes responsibility for the injury based on the view that such an injury would not have occurred had the individual not been involved in a particular work-related situation. Workers' compensation does not typically address issues involving negligence on the part of the injured teacher, administrator, or the school board as the employing agency.

A teacher, depending on the circumstances, may recover for a job-related injury that occurs over a period of time because of moving equipment or other types of physical exertion when there is documented evidence to support the extended injury. A number of workers' compensation plans provides benefits for dependents of workers who are killed during work-related incidents. State statutes include guidelines for workers' compensation. While there are variations among the states, most establish a timeframe in which an injury must be reported. Each state has an agency that administers the workers' compensation program. If an injured party is unsuccessful in receiving compensation for a job-related injury, the next option is to pursue the matter in court after all available remedies have been exhausted.

It is important to remember that the injury sustained must be work related, as emphasized by a case in South Dakota. The supreme court of South Dakota upheld an administrative decision denying workers' compensation benefits to a school bus driver injured while snow skiing on a school field trip. She was receiving downtime pay during the student activity and was free to do whatever she wished when she accepted a free lift pass. The court held that the driver's injury was not work related as it did not arise out of her employment. She was not expected to supervise students after they left the bus. The driver had stepped aside from her employment purpose when she went skiing and was not entitled to workers' compensation benefits.[13]

110. What Legal Duties Do Teachers Have in Reporting Suspected Cases of Child Abuse and Neglect?

Teachers have a legal duty to report suspected cases of child abuse and neglect to the appropriate state agency. Child abuse and neglect are based on the Child Abuse Prevention and Treatment Act that was originally enacted in P.L. 93-247. It was completely rewritten in the Child Abuse Prevention Adoption and Family Services Act of 1988 (P.L. 100-294) and further amended by the Child Abuse Prevention Challenge Grants Reauthorization Act of 1989 (P.L. 101-126). The act defines child abuse and neglect in the following manner:

> The physical or mental injury, sexual abuse or exploitation, negligent treatment or maltreatment of a child under the age of eighteen

or the age specified by the child protection law of the state in question by a person who is responsible for the child's welfare under the circumstances which indicate that the child's health or welfare is harmed thereby.[14]

This act was amended in 1992, 1994, and 1996 and resulted in larger appropriations to implement various program components. The law applies to professionals such as physicians, nurses, counselors, educators, and others who have frequent contact with children. Each state has specific procedures for reporting suspected cases, most of which call for reporting immediately upon suspecting that a child has been abused or neglected.

111. What Are the Consequences if No Child Abuse and Neglect Is Found After Teachers Report It?

All states have passed child abuse laws requiring school personnel to report suspected cases. Those convicted of failing to report child abuse and neglect may be fined as well as receive jail time. Additionally, school districts may impose districtwide penalties on teachers who fail to report suspected cases. The reporting professional does not need absolute proof that a child has been abused. Suspicion is all that is necessary to trigger reporting requirements. If the report fails to establish that abuse or neglect is present, the teacher or principal is not liable for reporting it. In fact, liability may stem from not reporting suspected cases. School personnel are granted immunity and protection against disclosure when they report suspected child abuse, as illustrated in a New York case.

New York parents sought the names of school employees who reported them for suspected child abuse and maltreatment to the statewide central register. In response to the report, the parents sued the school district in a state court asserting claims for defamation and intentional infliction of emotional distress. They sought to compel the disclosure of the names of the persons who reported the incidents. The court granted the motion, and the district appealed. The New York Supreme Court, Appellate Division, stated that Social Services Law Section 422 provides that reports to the central register are confidential and available only to persons and agencies listed by statute.

The court stated that the parents, as the subjects of the report, were entitled to see the report but not the names of the reporters. It rejected the trial court's reasoning that, because a court could obtain these names, it had an implied right to release them to the subject. Although the parents might encounter difficulty bringing a civil action against the reporters, social services laws did not permit the release of their names based on allegations that they acted with willful misconduct or gross negligence. This holding was consistent with the intent of the statute to protect the confidentiality of reporters of suspected child abuse. Disclosure of the names might have a chilling effect on reporting and hamper agency efforts to help families. The court reversed the trial court order.[15]

Summary of Cases Involving Terms and Conditions of Employment

- The supreme court of South Dakota held that a school district was not required to provide a hearing or other due process protection to a retired teacher who claimed she retained her continuing service status upon returning to the district under a probationary contract.[16]

- The U.S. Supreme Court held that the nonrenewal of a tenured teacher's contract based on her failure to earn certain continuing education credits was not a disruption of her due process and equal protection rights.[17]

- A court of appeals in Iowa held that the board only needed proof of a founded child abuse report to suspend or revoke a teaching certificate. It was not necessary for the board to determine if a teacher actually committed the acts substantiating a founded report.[18]

- A Florida district court held that it could not substitute its judgment for the state commission that was vested with discretion to make certificate decisions.[19]

Summary Guides

1. State licensure does not entitle a teacher to employment in public schools. It only qualifies them for consideration for an employment position.

2. Courts are reluctant to interfere with the school board's authority regarding employment decisions absent proof of arbitrary, capricious, or discriminatory intent.

3. A legal contract must involve competent parties. An uncertified teacher who enters into a contract under the assumption that the certificate will be granted does not constitute a competent party. The contract is only binding if the teacher is properly certified.

4. Tenure is a security measure that is granted when a teacher meets all requirements during the probationary period and is awarded tenure. Once earned, the teacher may not be dismissed except for cause involving due process.

5. Nontenured teachers have no legitimate expectation of employment beyond the contract year. Due process must be provided if the contract is cancelled during the particular contract year.

6. Teachers may be required to perform extra duties even though they are not stated in their contracts. Extra duties must not be excessive, must be assigned fairly, must be professional in nature, and must serve to benefit students.

7. Teachers may be transferred from one school to another consistent with the needs of the district. Transfers may not be based on personal or political grounds.

8. Leaves of absence may be granted to teachers based on district policy. School boards exercise discretion in granting nonmandatory leaves according to the instructional needs of the district.

9. Teachers are eligible for worker's compensation if they are injured or disabled while performing their job-related duties.

10. Teachers are required to report suspected cases of child abuse and may be fined for failure to do so as defined by state statute. No liability is imposed if reporting the abuse does not result in a bona fide case of child abuse.

NOTES

1. *Sonnichsen v. Baylor Univ.*, 47 S.W.3d 122, 127 (Tex. App.—Waco 2001, no pet.).

2. *Board of Education of Talbot County Maryland v. James D. Heister, et al.*, CA No. 56, 306 A.2d 216 (Maryland, 2005).

3. P.L. 107-110, No Child Left Behind Act of 2001.

4. *Rossi v. Salinas City Elementary School Dist.*, No. H024943, 2003 WL 22373464 (Cal. Ct. App. 2003).

5. *Scheer v. Independent School Dist. No. I-26*, Ottawa County, Oklahoma, 1997 OK 115, 948 P. 2d 275 (Okla. 1997).

6. *Thomas v. Board of Education*, 453, N.E. 2d 151 Ill. 1983.

7. *McGrath v. Burkhard*, 280 p. 2d 865 Cal. 1955.

8. *Parrish v. Moss*, 106 NYS 2d 577, 1951.

9. *Blair v. Robstown Indiana School District*, 556 F.2d. 1333 5th Cir. 1977.

10. *State ex. rel. Withers v. Board of Education of Mason County*, 172 S.E. 2d 796, 803 (W.Va. 1970).

11. *Carpenito v. Board of Educ. of Borough of Rumson*, 322 N.J. Super. 522, 731 A. 2d 538 (N.J. Super. Ct. App. Div. 1999).

12. *Turnbough v. Mammoth Spring School Dist. No. 2*, 78 S. W. 2d 89 (Ark. 2002).

13. *Norton v. Deuel School Dist. #19-4*, 674 N. W. 2d 518 (S D. 2004).

14. 42 U.S.C.A. § 5101 (1996), No. 100-294§§ 101-401 72 U. (§ 5101).

15. *Selapack v. Iroquois Cent. School Dist.*, 794 N.Y.S. 2d 547 (N.Y. App. Div. 2005).

16. *Wirt v. Parker School District*, 689 N.W. 2d 901 (S.D. 2004).

17. *Harrah Independent School District v. Martin*, 440 U.S. 194, 198, 99 S.Ct. 1062, 1064, 59 L.Ed.2d 248 (1979).

18. *Halter v. Iowa Board of Education Examiners No. 04-0427*, WL 97413, 698 N.W. 2d 337 (Iowa Ct. App. 2005).

19. *Wax v. Horne*, 844 So. 2d 797 (Fla. Dist. Ct. App. 2003).

8

School and District Liability

⚏ INTRODUCTION ⚏

A tort is a civil wrong independent of contract that occurs when one individual fails to meet a duty owed to another, resulting in injury. Parents and their children expect public schools to be safe places. In fact, courts have determined that schools are safe places since they are supervised by certified professionals properly trained to provide a safe and orderly environment where teaching and learning occur. *In loco parentis* (in place of parents) establishes a responsibility for teachers to exercise prudence in ensuring that all reasonable efforts are made to protect students under their care. Consequently, they must foresee that certain activities or conditions at school might create danger for students. Once determined, they must initiate reasonable steps to prevent harm to students. The courts, in designating schools as safe places, have assumed that parents need not be overly concerned that their children are unsafe while under the supervision of licensed school personnel whose legal duties include instruction, supervision, and student safety.

When liability charges are filed against school personnel, it is necessary to determine the nature and extent of legal duties required of teachers by the law. Liability is not automatic but is based on specific facts surrounding each situation. Teachers are not guarantors of student safety, but they are charged with reasonable care such as a parent of ordinary prudence would exercise under comparable conditions.[1] An analysis of specific facts and a determination of the magnitude of injuries will ultimately determine if liability charges are actionable. In all cases, reasonable decisions and prudence by teachers will minimize charges of liability and create a wholesome and safe school environment.

112. What Is an Intentional Tort, and How Does It Impact Teachers?

Teachers are responsible for their own tortious acts. They also have a legal responsibility to supervise and provide a safe environment for students under their care to the greatest degree possible. Teachers may face liability charges if their failure to act or improper actions result in injury to students. Intentional torts stem from committing an avoidable act that results in injury. The teacher's actions do not need to be malicious for an injured student to recover damages. In fact, the injury itself may not result from any intent to harm yet may, nevertheless, result in harm. All teachers are expected to meet a standard of care and to exercise the same level of care that other prudent school personnel would exercise under the same or similar circumstances. The standard of care will vary depending on the age, maturity, experience, and mental capacity of the students involved and the type of activity in which students are engaged. For example, teachers of kindergarten students must meet a higher standard of care than would an eleventh-grade teacher based on the obvious difference in the age and maturity of these two student groups. Additionally, teachers who supervise students in laboratory classes involving dangerous chemicals and equipment, in gym classes, and in vocational shops must meet a higher standard than would English teachers based on the nature of classroom activities in which the students are engaged. Teachers are expected to foresee or anticipate that certain activities may be harmful to students. Once foreseeability is established, they must act responsibly to prevent harm to students. Intentional torts include *assault, battery, defamation, mental distress,* and *false imprisonment.*

113. What Constitutes an Assault?

An *assault* is an offer to use force that creates apprehension within the victim of immediate offensive bodily contact. The person who commits an assault must be viewed as one who is capable of carrying it out. Assault constitutes a tort against the victim's mind, resulting in fear for one's safety, and is often associated with a threat to commit bodily harm.

It is important to note that no physical harm is necessary to commit an assault, and one has not occurred if no immediate fear results from the threat to use force. Again, the person who threatens force must be viewed as being capable of doing so. Therefore, if the offer is not accompanied by an immediate sense of fear or if the person is not capable of executing it, no tort has occurred. All conditions must be present to constitute an assault. Teachers or students can be charged with an assault if they meet all of the criteria listed previously. For example, if a larger male student who has a reputation for misbehavior threatens a female teacher by conveying that he will "get her" after school, an assault has occurred if the conditions stated above are present.

114. What Constitutes a Battery?

A *battery*, a companion tort, is a successful assault wherein an offer to use force actually occurs. A battery is unlawful bodily contact inflicted in a hostile manner, resulting in injury to another person. A battery therefore involves actual physical contact. Oftentimes, assault and battery are linked because the assault precedes the battery.

Teachers are most often charged with assault and battery during the administration of corporal punishment when there is evidence that the punishment was administered with malice and considered excessive. School personnel can also be charged with a battery if they fail to provide adequate student supervision and an aggressive student injures another. Liability occurs when teachers are expected to foresee or should have foreseen that a student might be injured by an aggressive student and do not take reasonable steps to prevent it. To sustain charges involving a battery, there must be illegal or unprivileged contact.

115. When Does Defamation Occur?

Defamation occurs when false statements are directed against another person that result in hatred, contempt, or injury to the person's standing and reputation. Defamation can be written (libel) or oral (slander). In either case, the communication must be transmitted to a third party. Defamation involves intent to harm another's reputation, and the concept is derived from the belief that people have a right to protect their reputation from false or malicious statements by others.

Teachers are entitled to qualified privilege if statements are communicated in conjunction with their professional duties, as long as statements meet good faith requirements. Good faith requires that statements be made without malice or intent to harm. Truth is a defense for defamation when statements are based on reasonable grounds. Teachers must refrain from intentionally spreading rumors concerning students or colleagues that may be injurious to their reputations. It should be emphasized that truth is not necessarily a defense when malice is present. Additionally, certain statements, even when true, can be libelous. For example, it is defamatory to convey that a colleague attempted suicide or that he or she is immoral, gay, or has a contagious disease. The very nature of these statements can cause others to be shunned, ridiculed, or ostracized and result in injury to their reputation. Obviously, the burden of proof rests with the party who alleges injury to demonstrate that injury did, in fact, occur. For example, a principal conveys to other teachers that a teacher misused school funds by purchasing materials without proper authorization and that he falsified invoices. If evidence shows, based on the teacher's allegation, that the principal harbored ill will against him based on his involvement with the teacher's union, then qualified privilege may be lost by the principal.

116. What Type of Behavior by Teachers May Result in Mental Distress Involving Students?

Mental distress is a tort regarding conduct that exceeds the boundaries of decency as defined by society. The conduct exhibited by the perpetrator is calculated to cause and actually does create mental distress. Teachers can be implicated in situations involving mental distress when they utilize unorthodox forms of punishment that result in emotional duress for students.

In loco parentis allows teachers to discipline students, but their actions must not be calculated to embarrass them in the presence of their peers, resulting in fear or anxiety. For example, locking a young child in a dark closet, taping him or her to a chair or a tree, or placing tape over a student's mouth are indefensible acts that might have an adverse affect on students' self-esteem. Students should not be degraded in a manner that creates mental distress, which may, in some instances, be more devastating than physical punishment. Teachers should seek guidance from school or district policies in discipline matters to avoid claims that they created mental distress for students.

117. What Must Teachers Know About False Imprisonment?

A teacher guilty of false imprisonment is one who illegally detains a student in a manner that confines the student within the boundaries prescribed by the teacher. False imprisonment typically occurs when students are detained after school for infractions that do not warrant detention or are held for an unreasonable amount of time. Teachers must be guided by school or district policy to ensure that detention is legally sanctioned. Even when detention is sanctioned, parents should be informed of the detention so that arrangements can be made to transport the student if he or she uses school-sponsored transportation. Additionally, teachers should refrain from being isolated with a student to minimize allegations of improper conduct.

Detention must not occur in a dangerous area such as a laboratory or vocational shop without adequate supervision since it is foreseeable that a student could be injured if dangerous equipment or chemicals are accessible.

Adherence to school district policy should minimize liability regarding false imprisonment. The charge does not usually result in significant compensatory damages unless there is evidence of wanton or reckless behavior by school personnel.

118. Do Teachers Incur a Lower Degree of Liability if the Tort Is Unintentional?

Not necessarily. Liability depends on the nature of the injury and the specific facts surrounding each incident. Liability judgments tend to compensate the injured party; consequently, most plaintiffs who succeed in a lawsuit are awarded compensatory damages designed to restore them to their status prior to the injury. Only in cases of willful or wanton negligence that results in very serious harm does the court award punitive damages. Punitive damages are awarded to convey to the defendant that his or her action was indefensible and beyond the boundaries of prudent behavior.

An unintentional tort involves negligence and occurs when one fails one's duty to exercise the standard of care needed to prevent harm to the person to whom the duty is owed. Most negligence cases fall into the category of civil wrongs; however, there may be instances where criminal charges are brought. An example might involve a teacher who is transporting a student, drives at a high rate of speed, and runs a stop sign, resulting in the death of the student. Criminal charges may then be brought against the teacher for reckless endangerment and vehicular homicide. Negligence is the most prevalent charge brought against school personnel.

Negligence charges are not valid unless certain conditions are met. Those who file charges of negligence must demonstrate that the following elements were present:

Standard of care: A legal duty or standard of care is owed to one by the other. For example, a teacher or principal owes a legal duty to students to provide adequate supervision and to provide for their safety.

Breach of duty: A legal breach occurred wherein the teacher or the principal failed to meet that duty.

Injury: The injured party has proven that an actual injury has been sustained.

Proximate cause: There is a direct link between the injury sustained and the breach of duty. If the injury is unrelated to the breach, there is no valid liability claim.

If any of the elements stated above are not present, there can be no valid liability claim. As an example, a negligence challenge arose in Arizona when a school district policy allowed some students to check out during lunch periods if certain conditions, including obtaining parental permission, were met.[2] A student informed a security guard that he was going off campus to retrieve books from his car. Although the student did not have permission to leave, the guard did not attempt to stop him, and he drove to a shopping mall. On the return trip to school, he drove his vehicle into oncoming traffic and collided with another vehicle. The driver and passengers of the other vehicle sued the school district in a state trial court. They asserted that the district had a duty to protect the public from the risk of negligent driving by students who left campus and that the policy of allowing students to leave created an unreasonable risk of harm. The court awarded judgment to the district.

In a related duty-of-care case, a Louisiana student alleged he was sexually assaulted by three other male kindergartners in a school lavatory.[3] According to the student's grandmother, school officials did not contact her about the incident and did not mention it until the following week when the student observed police at the school. The grandmother stated that the principal attempted to hold the student just as guilty as the other students because he did not pull his pants up and run out. She claimed the student suffered severe emotional distress that was exacerbated when the principal denied a request to transfer him from the classroom. The student's family sued the school board in state court for negligent supervision. The court awarded summary judgment to the board finding that the incident was sudden and unforeseeable. The family appealed to the state court of appeals.

The appeals court noted the teacher's admissions that the student had been assaulted by a student and that student assaults occurred at the school on a monthly basis. The teacher did not follow the school's procedure of providing hall passes to students for access to the lavatory. The court held that school boards through their agents and employees owe students a reasonable duty of supervision. It noted that boards cannot ensure student safety, and constant supervision is impossible. To find a board liable for failing to adequately supervise students, there must be a showing that the board knew of a foreseeable risk of unreasonable injury that could have been prevented by appropriate supervision. The court found, however, that the teacher's admissions and the principal's conduct made summary judgment improper. The principal failed to promptly advise the family of the incident, and the trial court was ordered to further review whether the assault was foreseeable.

119. May School Personnel Legitimately Claim Legal Defenses for Liability Charges?

Yes, if facts reveal that the defense is valid. There are legal defenses against liability; however, none of the defenses relieves school personnel of negligent acts. The most common defense against liability charges are *contributory negligence, comparative negligence, assumption of risk*, and *immunity*.

120. What Must Teachers Know About Contributory Negligence?

If a student who claims injury failed to meet a reasonable standard regarding his or her conduct and, hence, injury resulted, liability charges against teachers will not usually be supported. In other words, contributory negligence occurs when a student who is harmed contributed to the injury based on his or her decisions and actions. Contributory negligence tends to be the most frequently used defense against liability by school personnel. However, there is a common law presumption that contributory claims are invalid if the injured party is between the ages of seven and fourteen based on the view that the child's maturity level renders him or her incapable of knowingly contributing to the injury; a child beyond the age of fourteen may reasonably contribute to an injury. Although this age range is not absolute, it is relied upon as a guideline in contributory liability cases. The following case illustrates the court's view regarding contributory negligence.

A seventeen-year-old Indiana student agreed to assist a school music teacher with an elementary school production of *Peter Pan*. The student enjoyed rock climbing, and the teacher assisted him in building a zip-line for the Peter Pan character to use while flying onto the stage. At a dress rehearsal, the student was injured in a fall while testing the zip-line. He suffered facial fractures, a severed facial nerve, a lacerated spleen, and nerve damage to his hands and wrists. The student's mother sued the school district for negligence in a state court. The jury found for the student and awarded him $200,000. The district appealed to the Indiana Court of Appeals.

The court of appeals court explained that jury instructions must correctly state the law. The trial court had instructed the jury that the student had to exercise the reasonable care that a person of like age, intelligence, and experience would normally exercise under the same or similar conditions. The state supreme court had held that children over the age of fourteen must exercise the reasonable and ordinary care of an adult, unless special circumstances are present. The court explained that the "last clear chance" doctrine involves situations where a known danger can be avoided by due care. The doctrine applies if, among other things, the district knew the student was in a perilous position but was oblivious to it and had the "last opportunity" to avoid injury by using reasonable care. The court found no evidence that the school had the last chance to avoid the student's fall. He clearly had the choice of whether or not to attempt the stunt and the last opportunity to avoid it. The court rejected the student's arguments.[4]

121. What Is Comparative Negligence?

Comparative negligence is relatively new in relation to contributory negligence. It applies when there is a slight injury to a student, and the teacher is not totally relieved of the responsibility for contributing to the injury. In this case, the acts of the teacher are considered based on the degree of negligence attributed to the incident. The degree of harm may range from slight to ordinary to gross, depending on the specific facts. A jury will determine the degree to which the teacher or the student contributed to an injury. If one contributed more heavily than the other, damages are assessed proportionally based on the degree of fault. Comparative negligence does not prevent recovery for damages by an injured student but reduces the damages based on the degree of fault attributed to the student. For example, if the facts reveal that the student's action attributed 30 percent to an injury, then the teacher would be assessed 70 percent of the total damages. Liability cases are heard by juries, who examine and analyze all relevant facts surrounding a liability claim and render a decision based on factual circumstances.

122. How Does Assumption of Risk Affect Coaches and Teachers Who Supervise Contact-Related Activities Involving Students?

Assumption of risk is most frequently relied upon by coaches of athletic teams, cheerleader sponsors, and other professional personnel who supervise contact-related activities. The basic premise supporting assumption of risk is that the student assumes a degree of inherent risk while participating in the desired school activity. There is an additional presumption that students who chose to participate have prior knowledge of the potential danger associated with the activity. The courts recognize that an element of risk is involved when students participate in certain contact sports and other related activities; however, their participation does not relieve teachers and coaches of valid liability charges when they fail to meet a reasonable standard of care or fail to protect students from unreasonable risk. Coaches and teachers who supervise activity-oriented student groups must be aware of the health conditions, age, maturity, skill, coordination, and ability of students participating in various contact-related activities and be certain that they exercise the proper standard of care in providing proper instruction and supervision based on these factors. The critical standard that must be met by teachers who supervise student contact-related activities is to properly instruct students regarding the fundamental techniques associated with the activity and to provide proper supervision to ensure that appropriate techniques are employed by the student.

An assumption of risk case arose in New York when a student on his high school wrestling team was instructed before a match to wrestle an opponent in the next higher weight class. The student agreed to do so and was injured when the opponent hit his jaw during a takedown maneuver. The student voluntarily continued participating in the match after a medical timeout. He later filed a personal injury lawsuit against the school district in a New York trial court, which denied the district's dismissal motion.

On appeal, the New York Supreme Court stated that the student had assumed the risk of incurring a blow to the jaw and that the injury was reasonably foreseeable in a wrestling match. There was evidence that the size of the opponent had not caused the injury and that the student was aware of the risks involved in wrestling. The district's duty of care was limited to protecting the student from unassumed, concealed, or unreasonable risks. The trial court judgment was reversed.[5] As seen from this case, assumption of risk is a valid defense in the absence of negligence. Although the district was supported by the court, encouraging a student to wrestle a large opponent was not advisable based on the risk of injury and liability.

123. Does Immunity Protect Teachers in Liability Cases?

Probably not. Immunity as a legal concept has significantly diminished. Historically, school districts and their agents have enjoyed immunity from liability claims. Sovereign immunity evolved from England based on the belief that "the King could do no wrong." In modern times, the concept that state or federal government should receive protection from suits and be exempt from liability has not received unanimous court support, although some courts are supportive of this view. Public schools as state agencies have historically relied on this doctrine to avoid lawsuits.

Some states have recently offered immunity to teachers in corporal punishment cases. A number of states have abrogated school district immunity, whereas others have recognized it based on whether the act in question was ministerial or proprietary. Ministerial acts are those in which no discretion is allowed; consequently, they are required by law or policy. Proprietary acts are those in which school districts are not statutorily required to perform. Ministerial acts are inclined to receive immunity under this philosophy, whereas proprietary acts typically will not receive immunity coverage. Some states support immunity laws, but others do not. In either case, immunity does not generally apply to acts committed by teachers unless prescribed by state statute. Teachers may be sued as individuals even if a state claims immunity. Thus, they are responsible for their own acts. In general, immunity does not enjoy the level of court support it has experienced in past years. The following case in Illinois illustrates this point.

An Illinois craft fair patron who slipped on a sidewalk adjoining a junior high school gymnasium sued the school district for negligence. A state circuit court granted summary judgment to the school district finding that the district was entitled to immunity under the Illinois Tort Immunity Act's recreational purposes exclusion. The court denied the patron's motion to amend her claim to incorporate willful and wanton conduct as the cause of her injuries. On appeal, the appellate court of Illinois discussed whether the sidewalk was public property intended or permitted to be used for recreational purposes within the meaning of the exclusion. The court rejected the school's claim that use of the sidewalk for gymnasium access and occasional student recreation precluded a factual inquiry by a jury. It reversed and remanded the circuit court decision.[6] The ruling in this case supports the view that schools are responsible for ensuring that property used by the school is also safe for use by school patrons.

124. Can Teachers Transport Students in Their Personal Vehicles?

Yes, they may do so, but it is not advisable. To the greatest extent possible, school district–sponsored transportation or commercial transportation should be used to transport students. Teachers typically do not carry automobile liability insurance coverage for student transportation; consequently, if they use personal vehicles and are involved in an accident, they may be without coverage. They run the added risk of facing liability charges based on negligence if the facts reveal that the teacher failed to meet the standard of care necessary to avoid the injury. They can also be faced with the appearance to others of inappropriate relations between themselves and students, as well as accusations by a student of improper conduct. If teachers have no option other than to operate personal vehicles, they should secure an insurance premium that includes transportation provisions regarding students. In many cases, these policies can be issued on a trip-by-trip basis at a nominal fee. It is also advisable to secure personal liability coverage through membership in state and national education associations in the event that such coverage may be needed.

125. Do Permission Slips or Release Forms Relieve a School and Its Teachers From Liability?

Probably not. Release forms have no legal standing and do not relieve teachers and school personnel of negligent liability charges. Additionally, many states view waivers or release forms as invalid based on public policy grounds. A ruling by the court in *Doe v. Archbishop Stepinac High School* held that a release form was unenforceable based on its failure to clearly convey the intention of the plaintiffs to relieve school defendants from liability for negligence.[7]

126. Does the Same Standard of Care Apply to Supervision of Students on Field Trips as It Does on School Grounds?

Yes, the standard of care applies and may be even higher on field trips due to the fact that students are visiting unfamiliar environments that may require greater supervision. Additionally, it is foreseeable that students may be injured more readily because they are in a different environment from which they are accustomed. Because foreseeability is established, teachers must act to minimize the potential for injury to students under their supervision.

The courts view field trips as important extensions to the regular school program where learning is reinforced, but they also expect teachers to foresee the circumstances under which students might be injured and to take reasonable steps to prevent harm. Teachers should ensure that all students are briefed on the nature of the field trip they will experience and the specific expectations they must meet regarding acceptable behavior. Parent volunteers, if used, should also be familiar with the nature of the field trip and informed specifically of their duties and assignments regarding supervision. Students in need of close supervision should be assigned to teachers rather than to parents. The standard of care will vary depending on the nature of the activities related to the trip, the age, maturity, and mental capacity of the students involved, and the propensity of students to misbehave. Teachers must be certain there is sufficient supervision in terms of quality and quantity. Reasonable ratios of teachers to students and parents to students must consequently be determined, as well as supervisors who are prudent in monitoring students.

When classes are invited to a facility, they become *invitees*, which suggests that those who invited them are responsible for their safety. Students and teachers should be protected from any known hazards. However, if teachers request to visit an establishment, the standard of care is lower for the agency. The visitors are *licensees*. The agency in this case is only responsible for ensuring that the facility itself is safe and that there are no known hazards on the property that might contribute to injury.

127. What Should Teachers Understand About Playground Supervision to Avoid Liability?

Teachers should understand that a higher standard of care exists regarding playground supervision based on the fact that playgrounds are activity-oriented areas where students are engaged in a number of potentially dangerous activities involving the use of equipment. Teachers should inspect all playground equipment to ensure that it is in good repair prior to allowing student use. Additionally, they must provide appropriate instruction to students regarding the proper operation of the equipment. Last, teachers must provide adequate supervision to ensure that students are handling equipment properly. The standard of care will again vary depending on the age, maturity, and mental capacity of students and the types of activities in which they are engaged. Teachers must caution students to refrain from activities when they observe them engaged in a potentially dangerous manner. Playground supervision requires active supervision by teachers. It is difficult to build a defense if teachers are not actively moving about the playground observing and directing student activities in the use of playground equipment, as illustrated by a case that arose in the Louisiana Supreme Court.

In this case, *Rollins v. Concordia*, one teacher assumed the playground supervision load of another teacher, thus supervising both her class and her fellow teacher's class. While the teacher was attempting to supervise the two classes, a nine-year-old girl broke her leg while jumping off a merry-go-round. The state supreme court compared the negligence of the students as well as the school board. The court determined that the school board was negligent in failing to ensure that there was proper supervision based on quality and quantity measures. The court further found the student to be negligent in jumping off the merry-go-round. Since the student was equally responsible for the injury she sustained, the compensation she received was reduced by 50 percent under a comparative negligence ruling.[8]

Teachers should inform their principal if they believe that the number of students they are supervising exceeds reasonable limits, particularly when experiencing problems managing large numbers of students during any given time. Teachers should never leave unsupervised students on the playground since it is foreseeable that injury might occur in the teacher's absence. Liability charges against the teacher and the administration may result if they are aware of unattended students on the playground and fail to take reasonable measures to ensure proper supervision.

128. What Responsibility Do Teachers Have Regarding the Use of School Equipment by Students?

Teachers who instruct students where equipment is used, such as in science laboratories, vocational laboratories, or physical education, must inspect the equipment daily to ensure that it is in good repair and ready for student use. If faulty equipment is found, obviously students should not be allowed to use it. Some type of signage should be posted to designate that the damaged equipment is unsafe for students. Additionally, written requests should be submitted through the appropriate channels in an attempt to have faulty equipment repaired or replaced as quickly as possible. Students must be taught to operate the equipment based on the manufacturer's directions and should not be allowed to experiment with it inappropriately. Proper instruction and supervision are vital to ensuring that students who use school equipment do not increase their risk for injury. Accidents are commonly associated with equipment used by students; consequently, teachers should post rules and instructions governing the operation of equipment and supervise adequately to ensure that proper directions are followed.

A case in Georgia illustrates the dangers associated with a vocational laboratory. A shop teacher demonstrated a voltmeter by stretching insulated wire across student desks. Parts of the wire were then exposed so that students could attach probes to measure the voltage. The teacher explained that touching the wire with both hands could cause death. After turning on a transfer that sent seven hundred volts of electricity through the wire, the teacher noticed a student slumping over with both hands on the wire. The staff performed CPR on the student and called emergency personnel, but he died from electrical shock. A federal district court dismissed an action by his parents against the school district, teacher, school principal, and superintendent for constitutional rights violations.

The parents appealed to the U.S. Court of Appeals, Eleventh Circuit, which explained that a governmental agency or employee can be liable for substantive due process violations only if official conduct is so extreme that it "shocks the conscience." The U.S. Supreme Court has admonished lower courts to refrain from making the due process clause a "surrogate for conventional tort principles." Deliberate indifference by officials and unsafe working conditions do not implicate due process rights. The student's death did not result from intentional conduct by the teacher and did not shock the conscience. The district court had correctly awarded summary judgment to the teacher and district.[9] This case was not a due process case but one that addressed whether a required standard of care was met by the teacher, who had alerted students of the dangers of touching the exposed wiring.

If special clothing or protection is required to be worn by students, they should not be permitted to operate the equipment if they fail to wear it. Excessively long hair and certain types of jewelry worn by students should be monitored or disallowed to prevent potential harm to students. It may be advisable for teachers to provide parents with copies of the rules governing laboratory classes and equipment use so that they are aware of the efforts to create and maintain a safe environment for students. Prudence, foreseeability, proper instruction, and supervision are key ingredients to establishing and maintaining a safe learning environment for students.

129. What Precautions Should Teachers Follow Regarding Students' Science Fair Projects?

Science fair projects, if not supervised, can pose a threat to student safety. Teachers should develop specific guidelines detailing what types of projects are permitted and those not permitted based on safety concerns. Projects should be assigned with primary consideration given to the age, maturity, and mental capacity of the students involved. An approved list of projects should be made available to students and parents so that they are aware that dangerous projects will not be allowed, particularly since many parents assist their children in designing and completing science fair projects at home.

If projects are constructed during the school day, teachers must provide adequate instruction and supervision for students to ensure that they are following proper directions. It is foreseeable that science fair projects, depending on their nature, may present safety challenges for students. Quality instruction and supervision will greatly reduce safety threats to students.

130. Can a Teacher Be Held Liable for a Teacher Aide's Conduct That Results in Injury to a Student?

Maybe. It depends on the facts and circumstances surrounding the situation. The key issue is whether the teacher exercised care in providing the aide proper instruction and reasonable supervision. If the teacher did so and the aide's action resulted in injury to a student regardless, the aide would be liable. However, if the teacher did not exercise due care in providing proper instruction and supervision where it is clearly foreseeable that an absence of such could result in injury to students, the teacher may also be held liable. Conversely, if the student's injury was not foreseeable by either the teacher or the aide and not directly related to the aide's conduct, then there would likely be no successful liability charges against either. In all cases, the particular facts and circumstances surrounding the injury would be a major factor in assessing liability charges.

Teacher aides are normally responsible for their own tortious acts. Aides must meet the same standard of care as the regular teacher under the same or similar circumstances.

Not all accidents or injuries in school form a basis for negligent liability, as illustrated by the *Fagan v. Summers* case in which a lawsuit for damages was filed on behalf of a seven-year-old student against Summers, a teacher aide. During a noon recess, a fellow student threw a small rock, which hit a larger rock on the ground and then bounced up and struck Fagan, causing him to lose the sight in his left eye. Defendants Summers and the school district moved for summary judgment, which was granted by the trial court. Prior to the accident, Summers had walked past the plaintiff and five or six other boys twice while they were sitting on the ground near the school building. The boys were laughing and talking, and she saw nothing out of the ordinary. After Summers strolled by this group of youngsters, she heard an outcry from the plaintiff. The accident had occurred during that interval. There was no evidence that Summers's explanation of the incident was not true. Summers was also considered to be reliable, conscientious, and capable in her work as a good playground supervisor.

In holding for Summers and the school district, the court stated, "It is apparent from all we have said that the proximate cause of George Fagan's injury was the act of his fellow student in throwing a rock. It was not the failure of the Park County School District No. 1 to maintain the playground in a safe condition. Appellant has made no effort to show that supervision of the playground was inadequate or that the accident would have been prevented if more supervisors had been present. We need not discuss counsel's casual suggestion that there may have been negligence in this regard. Summary judgment for Summers and for the school district was justified and proper."[10]

131. Are School Officials and Teachers Liable for Injuries Based on Defective Conditions of School Buildings and Grounds?

It depends on the nature of the defect and if school officials or teachers knew or should have known about the defective condition. If the conditions pose a serious problem such that any reasonable school official or teacher should have been aware of it, such as broken glass in windowpanes, defective playground equipment, or loose railings on the stairway, it is probable that liability will be imposed for negligence if injury occurs. School officials must inspect buildings and grounds to foresee potential harm to students. Once harm has been foreseen by school officials or teachers, decisive action must be taken to warn students of the danger and to initiate corrective measures to alleviate the dangerous condition. However, if the defect is minor and occurred without school officials' or teachers' knowledge, they cannot incur liability. School officials and teachers are not expected to anticipate every possible danger as soon as it occurs. They simply must respond prudently when harm is foreseeable.

132. What Responsibilities Do Teachers Have to Students Who Arrive on Campus Before the School Day Begins or Remain on Campus After School Hours?

School personnel have a degree of responsibility for students who arrive early and for those picked up after the normal school day ends. The level of supervision depends on the age, maturity, and mental capacity of students and their arrival and departure time. The courts do not expect school personnel to be available during unreasonable times either before or after school. However, once it is determined that students are arriving very early and departing late, reasonable rules should be formulated and communicated to students and parents regarding the behavior expected of students during these times and the consequences for not adhering to those rules. Additionally, school personnel should be assigned to periodically monitor students to ensure they are following the prescribed rules. Parents should be informed in writing that school personnel are not available for student supervision during the early morning hours and late after-school hours. The principal has the overall responsibility for developing a plan to protect students before and after school. The courts tend to take the view that students have no choice but to arrive on campus or depart late based on their parents' decisions; therefore, some form of reasonable supervision is expected that does not create undue hardship for school personnel yet provides a measure of safety for students.

In a California case, a school opened its campus at 7:00 a.m., but trouble occurred in areas such as unsupervised restrooms before 7:45 a.m.

School administrators were aware that one eighth-grade special education student usually arrived at 7:15 a.m. A classmate who also had disabilities teased and ridiculed the student daily before classes began. The student who was teased sometimes went to the office to escape. He also complained to the staff. The student was instructed to stay away from his classmate, even after he informed the vice principal that this avoidance did not work. The classmate twice isolated the student and sexually assaulted him. The district learned of the incidents and expelled the classmate, who was also arrested.

The California Court of Appeals observed that schools have a special relationship with students that imposes a duty on school districts to initiate all reasonable steps to protect students. The duty arises from both the compulsory nature of education and a state constitutional declaration of each student's inalienable right to attend safe, secure, and peaceful campuses. School districts have an established duty to supervise students at all times while on school grounds and to enforce necessary rules and regulations for their protection. This duty includes supervision during recess and before or after school. The district was liable for injuries resulting from the failure of the school staff to use ordinary care to protect students. The district unlocked its gates at 7:00 a.m. each day but did not provide supervision until 7:30 a.m. It could have simply precluded students from arriving early or kept them in particular areas of the school. The district's claim to immunity failed because there was no exercise of discretion by the principal and evidence that he knew of the classmate's violent behavior. The damage award was not excessive, and the court affirmed the judgment.[11]

Summary of Legal Cases Involving Liability

- A sixteen-year-old student who weighed 327 pounds collapsed, experienced seizures, and died during a P.E. class in a 90°F gymnasium that was not air-conditioned. Parents sued the district for wrongful death and were awarded $500,000 based on a breach of duty to exercise reasonable care and supervision.[12]

- A second-grade student was bullied and sexually assaulted in his classroom while the teacher sat at her desk when students were supposedly working independently. The court held for the student based on negligent supervision. The teacher and the school board were held jointly responsible for the assault. Damages were apportioned among the parties.[13]

- A thirteen-year-old child was killed while walking home from school at an intersection with no crossing guard. A suit was filed by parents claiming negligence against the school for scheduling school from 9:00 a.m. to 4:00 p.m. during which time students are exposed to rush hour traffic. The court held for the school board, stating that no hidden dangers were created by the board and that school hours established by the board deserved immunity.[14]

- A student drove his parents' car during a field trip and was involved in a serious accident when he struck another vehicle. The parents sued, claiming that the student was acting as the board's agent because he was under school control. The field trip allowed students to drive their own vehicles or ride with others to a store to purchase health uniforms. The appellate court held for the school board as there was no basis for finding the school board liable since the student was not a board employee.[15]

Summary Guides

1. Most tort liability cases involve civil wrong; however, some cases may involve criminal charges.

2. Liability charges, assessed by the courts, compensate the injured party for his or her injuries; however, punitive damages may be assessed by the courts for willful and wanton negligence.

3. Teachers and administrators have a legal duty to supervise and protect student safety while students are under the school's supervision.

4. Foreseeability is critical in determining liability. School personnel are expected to anticipate that certain situations may prove harmful to students. When this determination is made, school personnel must act responsibly to prevent harm to the student.

5. Each teacher and administrator is expected to exercise the same degree of prudence in supervising students as any other professional would under the same or similar circumstances.

6. Teachers and administrators may be charged with assault and battery during the administration of corporal punishment if evidence reveals that the punishment was excessive or administered with malice.

7. All persons, including students, have a right to protect their reputation against defamation.

8. Teachers and administrators should refrain from disciplinary practices that create mental distress for students.

(Continued)

(Continued)

9. Teachers and administrators should adhere to school or district policy regarding detention of students after school hours.

10. Negligent behavior by teachers will usually result in liability charges if the facts reveal that they breached a legal duty that resulted in injury to students.

11. Defenses against liability are only valid in the absence of negligence. Negligent behavior by teachers mitigates liability defenses.

NOTES

1. *Rock v. School Central Square School District*, 494 N.Y.S.2d 579 (N.Y. App. Div. 1985).

2. *Collette v. Tolleson Unified School Dist. No 214*, 54 P.3d 828 (Ariz. Ct. App. 2001).

3. *Katz v. St. John the Baptist Parish School Board*, 860 So. 2d 98 (La. Ct. App. 2003).

4. *Penn Harris Madison School Corp. v. Howard*, 832 N.E.2d 1013 (Ind. Ct. App. 2005).

5. *Edelson v. Uniondale Union Free School Dist.*, 631 N.Y.S.2d 391 (N.Y. App. Div. 1995).

6. *Batson v. Pinckneyville Elementary School Dist. No. 50*, 690 N.E.2d 1077 (Ill. App. Ct. 1998).

7. *Doe v. Archbishop Stepinac High School*, 729 N.Y.S. 2d 538 (App. Div. 2001).

8. *Rollins v. Concordia Parish School Board*, 465 So. 2d 213 (La. App. 1985).

9. *Nix v. Franklin County School Dist.*, 311 F.3d 1373 (11th Cir. 2002).

10. *Fagan v. Summers*, 498 P.2d 1227 (Wyo. 1972).

11. *M. W. v. Panama Buena Union School Dist.*, 1 Cal. Rptr. 3d 673 (Cal. Ct. App. 2003).

12. *James v. Jackson*, 898 So. 2d 596 (La. App. 4th Cir. 2005).

13. *Vaughn v. Orleans Parish School Board*, 802 So. 2d 967 (La. Ct. App. 2001).

14. *Orlando v. Broward County, Florida No.0 4-3445*, 2005 WL 3478364 (Fla. Dist. Ct. App. 2005).

15. *Louis v. Skipper*, 851 So. 2d 895 (Fla. Dist. Ct. App. 2003).

9

School Attendance and Instructional Programs

⚜ INTRODUCTION ⚜

Public schools are agents of the state. Since education is a state function, courts are reluctant to intrude on curriculum decisions and instructional matters. The prevailing view of the courts is that educators are better able to execute curriculum and instructional decisions than the courts.

The state legislature has the authority to define the curriculum of public schools within each state. The legislature may, based on statute, delegate curriculum matters to the state board of education. The courts provide legislatures with broad discretion in prescribing basic courses of study, testing, and graduation requirements. The legislature may also prescribe compulsory attendance and health requirements to be satisfied by students and can determine consequences for students and parents who fail to abide by the standards prescribed. The state's police powers allow the legislature to formulate and implement regulations designed to protect the health, safety, and welfare of all citizens, including children.

133. Are Children Required to Attend Public Schools Under Compulsory Attendance Laws?

No. They may attend private schools or parochial schools or receive home schooling as long as those alternative forms of schooling meet prescribed state law regarding curriculum, teacher qualifications, and health and safety standards. The concept of compulsory attendance emerged in Massachusetts in the mid-nineteenth century and was based on the view that the state's interest supersedes parental rights to exercise control over a child's educational welfare. According to this view, the state has a legal right to require compulsory school attendance based on the principle that the state is the guardian of all citizens who reside in the state, including children, and has a responsibility to provide for their welfare. As guardian, the state can prescribe laws designed to protect children, who are not capable of making decisions considered to be in their best interest. Through the state's police powers, state legislatures are also empowered to pass laws that serve the best interest of the state. An educated citizenry serves a compelling interest of the state.

It is important that state attendance laws be clearly stated for ease of interpretation so that they are not ambiguous and subject to varied interpretations. The courts have consistently supported state officials when challenges emerge regarding compulsory attendance requirements. The only exception has been based on compulsory attendance laws that conflicted with parents' religious rights, as illustrated by the following cases in Oregon and Wisconsin.

In *Pierce v. Society of Sisters*, the U.S. Supreme Court held in 1925 that Oregon's compulsory act requiring attendance at public schools only was unconstitutional under the due process clause of the Fourteenth Amendment.[1] Similarly, in 1972, the U.S. Supreme Court held that the Wisconsin compulsory school attendance law violated the free exercise clause of the First Amendment because it required attendance beyond the eighth grade, which interfered with the right of Amish parents to direct the religious upbringing of their children. The parents in each of these cases had been fined for violating the state's compulsory law.[2]

134. What Latitude Can States Exercise in Matters Regarding Health, Safety, and Residency Requirements in Public Schools?

States in their efforts to protect the health and general welfare of students can promulgate laws requiring mandatory immunizations and health exams as a condition of school attendance. The state's police power was defined by a court in the late 1800s when it stated that the concept encompassed all elements vested in state sovereignty, including those powers necessary to preserve the peace, morals, good order, and well-being of society.[3]

Most courts have consistently supported immunization requirements. Some states enact provisions for exempting students from immunizations based on religious grounds, but others do not allow exemptions. Immunizations are required as a method to protect students from communicable diseases. Most challenges to immunization requirements have centered on religious objections involving First Amendment claims. In those cases, parents have alleged that immunization requirements conflict with their religious beliefs and consequently violate their free exercise rights. While the courts support the free exercise of religious rights, they also support the state's power to establish certain health standards for the general welfare of its citizens. As conditions to public school enrollment, courts tend to support the view that the state's interest in health and safety outweigh individual parents' interests. However, a different decision was reached in an immunization case in New York.

In that case, a student's mother who was a member of the congregation of Universal Wisdom objected to the introduction of any foreign material into the body based on religious grounds. The mother notified school district officials of her religious objections to the New York public health law that required immunizations prior to admission to public schools. The district determined that the congregation was not a genuine religion and denied the mother's objection. The district claimed that the mother's objection was based on personal philosophy rather than on a legitimate religion. The mother filed a lawsuit. The district court allowed the student to attend school pending the outcome of the case. Although the court found the mother's religious affiliation questionable, the court indicated that the mother was likely to prevail on the merits of the case because her objection was apparently based on religion, not a philosophical or scientific basis. The board's request for summary judgment was denied.[4]

135. How Do Residency Requirements Apply to School Attendance?

In addition to compulsory attendance laws, there are also residency requirements governing public school attendance. In general, public schools are expected to educate children who reside within the district and who intend to remain domiciled in the area. The courts have been fairly consistent in supporting this expectation, even if the students' parents are illegal aliens. The basic premise underlying a free public school education is that children must not be deprived of an educational opportunity based on the citizenship status of their parents, over which they have no control. Residency also covers children who are housed in state-owned facilities as wards of the state. These children are also entitled to an equal educational opportunity.

The recent views regarding residency and public school attendance has changed from previous years due in part to the large influx of illegal aliens migrating to the United States. A leading case involving the residency of illegal aliens arose in Texas when the legislature revised its education laws to withhold state funds from local school districts that were educating children not legally admitted to the United States. It also authorized local school districts to deny enrollment in public schools to children not legally admitted into the country. These laws were challenged by numerous groups, one of which filed a class-action lawsuit on behalf of school-aged children of Mexican origin. The group claimed that their children were being excluded from public schools. A federal district court enjoined the district from denying a free education to those children. The U.S. Court of Appeals for the Fifth Circuit upheld the decision, ruling that the law violated the equal protection clause of the Fourteenth Amendment. On appeal to the U.S. Supreme Court, the state claimed that undocumented aliens are not persons within the jurisdiction of its laws. The High Court rejected this argument, stating that, whatever an alien's status under the immigration laws, an alien is a person. The High Court noted that the Texas statute imposed a lifetime hardship on a discrete class of children who were not accountable for their disabling status.[5] These factors were pivotal to the U.S. Supreme Court's ruling:

1. The discrimination contained in the statute could not be supported unless Texas could demonstrate that the statute rationally advanced a substantial goal of the state.

2. Children have no choice regarding their status or where their parents choose to reside.

3. Any child who resides in a district with a degree of permanency is entitled to a free public education.

4. There was no evidence to demonstrate that the exclusion of the children would improve the overall quality of education in the state.

It is certainly in the country's and children's best interest that they receive a public school education.

In the past, common law dictated that a student's domicile was the same as his or her father's, even though the child might be living in another state with the mother; regardless, the child would still be domiciled in the state where the father resides. Currently, the child's domicile is associated with the location in which his or her legal guardian resides and represents where the child intends to live indefinitely. Therefore, if a student is living within a district with a level of permanency, the child must be educated in the district wherein he or she resides.

136. What Are Home Schools?

Home schools provide instruction by parents or professional tutors for children at home. Parents who wish to offer a different learning environment can choose the home school option. Minimum standards for home schools are established in each state. Although there are variations, most laws require compulsory attendance, specify curricular and instructional standards, and stipulate the length of instructional time and the number of required days in which instruction should be offered. Failure to meet these minimum requirements might result in legal action against parents who are not in compliance with state law. The burden of proof rests with parents to demonstrate that the instruction offered at home is equivalent to the instruction offered in public schools. One challenge faced by students who are home schooled is the absence of formal transcripts such as those found in public schools. This issue becomes very important when home-schooled students apply for college. Some states permit parents to issue a high school transcript for their child. Detailed records and student portfolios are important means of documenting home-schooled students' performance.

137. What Is a Charter School?

Charter schools emerged as a component of the educational reform movement, which arose due to general dissatisfaction with the quality of public schools. Charter schools are funded as public schools. In fact, they are viewed as innovative public schools that are governed in many cases by both public and private entities. These schools are provided considerable latitude in school design, curriculum design, and overall planning in exchange for high-quality educational outcomes, as established by the charter. Charter schools are essentially free to formulate their own policies, rules, and regulations regarding day-to-day school operations. They are free from most rules that govern traditional public schools. Their charter establishes the ground rules that govern the school. Conceptually, charter schools are thought to be educationally sound due to their freedom from traditional bureaucratic barriers that can stifle innovative and creative programming. Even though charter schools are provided considerable flexibility regarding their operations, they are required to meet certain state guidelines in expending funds, maintaining records, and ensuring school accountability. Results to date appear to be mixed. Some charter schools are achieving based on measurable outcomes, whereas others are not meeting expected outcomes. At any rate, many parents and teachers find these innovative schools to be appealing because of their goals of meeting the individual needs of children.

138. What Latitude Are Teachers Provided in Assigning Grades?

Teachers have a responsibility to assess student progress and fairly assign grades based on supporting documentation. Courts are increasingly reluctant to interfere with teachers' decisions regarding grades and other academic matters based on the view that educators are trained and prepared to render academic decisions. Since there is no student constitutional right associated with the academic prerogatives of teachers, courts tend not to be actively involved in conflicts over grading. The fact that courts rarely concern themselves in grading matters does not suggest that teachers are free to arbitrarily assign grades without a justification. Students expect to be assigned grades fairly. While grading is not a high priority of the courts, they have been called upon to render decisions.

The Arkansas Supreme Court held that two teachers and a middle school principal had discretion to deny a reading credit to a student who claimed to have read four Harry Potter books in less than one week. No law entitled the student to the relief he sought in court. The student had participated in his school's accelerated reader program, in which students could win prizes or awards by reading books and passing tests based on them. He stated that he read four of five books in the Harry Potter series because of the high points assigned to the books. After the student scored 100 percent on each of the tests, his reading teacher accused him of cheating, stating that it was impossible to read all of the books in the required one-week period. The student's classroom teacher agreed and confronted him about cheating. The student's mother sought reinstatement of the scores. The school principal permitted only one to be reinstated, finding no obligation to reinstate the others under program incentive rules.

The student petitioned a state court for an order requiring the principal and teachers to reinstate the cancelled scores and apologize publicly and by letter, and preventing them from "further humiliating and using coercive tactics." The court dismissed the case and awarded the school district $1,500 in attorneys' fees. The student appealed to the state supreme court, which held he was not entitled to relief; no law compelled school officials to reinstate scores in voluntary reading programs. The court found "a general policy against intervention by the courts in matters best left to school authorities." Reinstatement of test scores was left to the discretion of school officials. As the student had no legal remedy available, the court affirmed the judgment, including the award of attorneys' fees.[6] Although the courts have shown reluctance to intervene in grading conflicts, they have rendered decisions in the following areas: grade reductions for absences, unexcused absences, and academic misconduct.

139. Can Schools Impose Academic Sanctions for Excessive Student Absences?

Yes. Student absenteeism represents a major challenge for many school districts. Most school boards have formulated policies that include academic penalties to address excessive absenteeism. Courts have been fairly supportive of academic sanctions for excessive absenteeism when those sanctions have been reasonably related to the state's interest in educating students. Students who challenge grade reductions have cited substantive and procedural due process concerns; therefore, school officials must ensure that a valid objective is reached when imposing academic sanctions. Students who are penalized academically must be provided an opportunity to present their side of the issues and be heard by an impartial school official.

---

140. Can Academic Sanctions Be Imposed on Students for Unexcused Absences?

Yes. Unexcused absences are oftentimes more challenging than excused absences because students are away from school illegally. Unexcused absences are not only a detriment to students; they also affect many school districts' funding formulas based on average daily attendance. School districts thus receive less funding to operate schools when they experience excessive unexcused student absences, many times resulting in the loss of teachers and other school personnel. Courts have been supportive of academic sanctions designed to reduce unexcused absences. In all cases, whether absences are excused or unexcused, there should be written policies that inform students and parents of the penalties that will be imposed and under what conditions they will be imposed. Due process provisions must always be associated with student penalties. The following is an example of a policy that addresses unexcused absences:

- Absence from school or class without approval of the school officials and permission of parents will be considered an unexcused absence.
- Each unexcused absence shall be recorded on the student's record.
- The parents or guardian of the student receiving an unexcused absence shall be notified in writing by the school.
- Unexcused absences will result in appropriate consequences for the student, including disciplinary measures such as school suspension and/or the imposition of academic sanctions for classes missed.
- Persistent unexcused absenteeism by a student may, in the judgment of the teacher and school administration, result in a failing grade.
- Necessary legal action may be initiated by school officials to enforce school attendance requirements.
- The maximum number of unexcused absences a student may incur before judicial proceedings are initiated to enforce compulsory attendance is three days in one month or ten days in one year.

---

141. Can Academic Sanctions Be Imposed on Students for School Suspension?

Probably so. Students can be reasonably penalized for work missed while on school suspension. It is within the school's discretion to allow or disallow makeup work. School district policy must provide guidance regarding makeup provisions. While the courts have been supportive of credit denial for work missed during suspension, they have been less supportive of additional sanctions.

For example, some districts formulated policies that denied academic credit for suspension unrelated to academic performance, as illustrated in the *Smith v. School Dist. of Hobart* case. An Indiana student was suspended for an alcohol-related offense. The high school then implemented a policy that required an automatic four-point reduction as punishment for his offense. The student's parents brought suit claiming Fourteenth Amendment substantive due process rights violations. The parents requested summary judgment on behalf of their son. The court held for the student in stating that such a rule was invalid based on an arbitrary policy and was a violation of the student's substantive due process rights. The court stated further that school officials failed to demonstrate a reasonable relationship between the use of alcohol during school hours and a grade reduction.[7]

142. Can a Student's Grade Be Reduced for Academic Dishonesty or Misconduct?

Yes. School officials can invoke academic sanctions for academic dishonesty or cheating that occurs during an academic exercise. Courts are quite reluctant to involve themselves in academic matters based on the view that educators are better suited to render academic decisions; consequently, considerable discretion is provided educators in assigning grades. District policies should inform students and parents that grade reductions can be imposed for academic misconduct. When academic misconduct policies are clearly established and communicated, the courts tend to have minimal concern with the enforcement of such policies. For example, a California court of appeals upheld a teacher's right to assign poor conduct grades to several students, which resulted in making them ineligible for the honor society. The court ruled that the teacher's grades were final and could only be changed in limited circumstances involving clerical or mechanical errors.[8]

143. Can a Student Be Physically Punished for Poor Academic Performance?

No. Physical punishment for failure or inability to achieve certain academic requirements is not viewed as an acceptable practice by the courts. Courts have consistently ruled against educators who have used physical punishment when the behavior by the student did not involve improper conduct. For example, one court in a very early decision ruled against physical punishment of a student who failed to perform athletically at a desired level, even though the coach considered the punishment to be instructive and a source of encouragement to the student.[9] Courts have consistently held that public school students should not be physically punished for conduct not related to disciplinary infractions. Teachers and school officials run the risk of inviting lawsuits based on assault and battery in cases where corporal punishment or other forms of punishment are employed for poor academic performance.

144. Can Schools Legally Test Students and Place Them in Academic Tracks?

Generally yes. Public schools can test students and place them in academic tracks if testing and placement are reasonably related to educational purposes and assignments are not discriminatory. Providing optimal opportunity for students to learn would satisfy a legitimate educational purpose. Tracking is usually supported by the courts in the absence of discriminatory intent. Title VI of the Civil Rights Act of 1964, however, prohibits discrimination in assigning students to school classes or courses in programs and activities receiving federal assistance. The concept of ability groups is legally permissible as long as accurate measures are used to place students appropriately. If students are misclassified and placed in inappropriate groupings, however, they might not receive the maximum benefits of an education, which may trigger educational malpractice challenges.

School officials must also be mindful of and sensitive to the impact of placing students in academic tracks, especially where larger numbers of minorities fall in lower academic tracks, thus leading to racial segregation. Courts are reluctant to interfere with academic matters based on the ability of school personnel to render discretionary decisions regarding student placement; educators are better prepared to render these decisions than are the courts. However, when challenges arise regarding equal protection issues, the courts have shown a willingness to confront the issue.

A court intervened in a highly publicized case in Washington, D.C., where school officials grouped students based on standardized intelligence test scores. The court found that these tests measured intellect gained through cultural experiences rather than innate intelligence. Children were erroneously placed in lower tracks with minimal opportunities to advance to higher tracks because of limited curriculum and a lack of remedial instruction. The court held that the methods used by school officials discriminated against minority children. The entire testing system was consequently held to be unconstitutional.[10]

In *Moses v. Washington Parish School Board* in Louisiana, the courts permitted school officials to continue to track students if the following safeguards were met:

- School officials must demonstrate that a valid educational objective is served by grouping students.
- There must be evidence to demonstrate that groupings are based on actual ability.

- External factors must be considered such as the cultural environment to which students are exposed.
- Remedial instruction must be provided that allows students in lower tracks to move into higher ones.
- Reevaluation procedures must be employed to allow mobility between tracks and to facilitate the movement of students to higher tracks based on remediation results.[11]

145. Can a Student's Diploma Be Withheld for Misconduct?

Probably not. When a student has met prescribed academic requirements for graduation, he or she has earned a diploma, which must be awarded. A student may, however, be denied participation in the graduation ceremony if he or she fails to meet acceptable standards of behavior. There is no direct relationship between earning a diploma and participation in the graduation ceremony itself. There have been instances in which a student has been denied the diploma for nonacademic reasons—primarily misconduct. The courts have been very consistent in ruling that the student must be granted his or her diploma if all academic requirements have been met.

An early court case, *Valentine v. Independent School District of Casey*,[12] arose when a number of students refused to wear the caps and gowns required for participation in the graduation ceremony. These students indicated that the gowns smelled, even though they had been cleaned. They were denied diplomas based on their refusal to wear the prescribed dress. The court in holding for the students stated that these particular students had earned their diploma based on their academic performance; consequently, participation in the actual ceremony was not a prerequisite to receiving a diploma.

However, in a case with a different twist, the Michigan Court of Appeals supported the school for withholding a diploma when a high school senior was found guilty of forging excuse notes for missing classes on six occasions. The fact that she forged the notes and lost course credit was pivotal to the court's decision.[13]

146. What Do Teachers Need to Know About Using Copyrighted Materials in Their Classrooms?

The Copyright Act prohibits unauthorized use of copyrighted material for profit or public display without appropriate payment to or permission from the copyright proprietor. Under the act, the owner of a copyright has the exclusive rights to authorize any of the following:

1. Reproducing the copyrighted work in copies or phonorecords.

2. Preparing derivative works based upon the copyrighted work.

3. Distributing copies or phonorecords of the copyrighted work to the public by sale or other transfer of ownership, or by rental, lease, or lending.

4. In the case of literary, musical, dramatic, and choreographic works; pantomimes; and motion pictures and other audiovisual works, performing the copyrighted work publicly.

5. In the case of literary, musical, dramatic, and choreographic works; pantomimes; and pictorial, graphic, or sculptural works, including the individual images of a motion picture or other audiovisual work, displaying the copyrighted work publicly.

   a. The act permits educators and libraries to make "fair use" of copyrighted material. Section 107 specifically permits "reproduction in copies or phonorecords . . . for purposes such as . . . teaching (including multiple copies for classroom use, scholarship or research)."[14]

The guidelines are fairly liberal with respect to producing single copies for teaching or research purposes but fairly restrictive regarding the reproduction of multiple copies. For example, reproduction of a poem should not exceed 1,000 words or 10 percent of the work, whichever is less. Additionally, copies should be reproduced by the specific teacher who intends to use the materials for teaching purposes. These guidelines are not based on law but, rather, are widely accepted as meeting the legal intent of the Copyright Act.

The Copyright Act specifies four factors that constitute fair use:

1. The purpose or use relative to whether use is commercial in nature or for nonprofit, educational purposes.

2. The nature of the work.

3. The amount of material extracted from the work in relation to the work as a whole.

4. The impact of the use on the potential market in relation to the value of the copyrighted work.[15]

147. What Is the Impact of Educational Malpractice on Public Schools, and How Might It Affect Teachers?

To date, educational malpractice has had little impact on public schools based on a variety of factors. One of the primary challenges facing the courts is to determine precisely where the actual fault lies in cases involving alleged academic injury. Educational malpractice is considered to be unprofessional conduct or a lack of skill in the performance of professional duties that results in academic injury to students. Most litigation involving malpractice centers on negligence in teaching performance or inappropriate diagnosis of students resulting in student misplacement. Most claims involve students who have reached graduation and lack the basic or rudimentary skills to function in society.

In perhaps the earliest malpractice case, *Peter W. v. San Francisco Unified School District*, "plaintiffs brought suit alleging that the school district negligently failed to provide an effective education, and in doing so, violated its professional duty to educate, at least to a minimum standard."[16] The California court, in refusing to recognize educational malpractice as an appropriate cause of action, stated that the issue was a "novel and troublesome question." The *Peter W.* suit was originally filed in 1973 but not decided until 1976. The parents filed suit against the San Francisco Unified School District, its agents, and its employees. The suit alleged intentional misrepresentation, negligence, and a violation of statutory and constitutional duties owed students and parents. The defendant school district was charged with negligently failing to use reasonable care in the discharge of its duties and failing to exercise that degree of professional skill required for an ordinary, prudent education.

After high school graduation, Peter W. was unable to read above a fifth-grade level. Teachers had systematically promoted him each year and informed the parents that he was performing at or near grade level. The court of appeals refused to recognize a legal duty of care and decided in favor of the school district on public policy grounds. The court held that it could not establish standards of care for classroom instruction and that California's education code had been "structured to afford optimum educational results, not to guard against risk of injury."

In one of the most provocative cases, *Hoffman v. Board of Education of New York City*, the court held for the student, stating that he had experienced diminished intellectual development and psychological injury as a result of inappropriate placement. At age six, Danny Hoffman had a speech defect. He was given a verbal abilities test by his school to determine placement. He scored 74, one point below normal. That one point resulted in his being placed, for eleven years, in programs for the mentally retarded. An intelligence test required by the Social Security Administration was administered to Danny at age seventeen. He scored an IQ of 94 and then sued the schools. The trial court held for Hoffman:

> Had the plaintiff been improperly diagnosed or treated by medical or psychological personnel in a municipal hospital, the municipality would be liable for the ensuing injuries. There is no reason for any different rule here because the personnel were employed by a government entity other than a hospital. Negligence is negligence,

even if a defendant . . . prefer(s) semantically to call it educational malpractice.[17]

This case was significant in that the district court ruled on the merits of the case rather than on public policy grounds. The lower court in this case refused to grant an exception because a governmental entity was involved or because a new theory of educational malpractice would be created. The appellate court upheld the lower court's decision but lowered the damages to $500,000. The New York Court of Appeals, however, reached the same decision as the appellate court had in California. It stated that the plaintiff had failed to establish that the school board had breached its duty and that such a cause of action must not, as a matter of public policy, be entertained by the courts of New York.

The courts to date, with the *Hoffman* exception, have not been willing to address educational malpractice as a liability issue due in part to their lack of awareness regarding the teaching and learning process. As educational malpractice continues to be addressed by the courts, it is conceivable that some of these cases will eventually be won on merit rather than lost on public policy grounds.

Summary of Cases Involving School Attendance

• The Arkansas Supreme Court held that schools' immunization requirement for children supersedes parents' religious practices when those practices are inconsistent with the peace, health, and safety of children within the state.[18]

• The New Jersey Supreme Court held that education offered outside of the school requires parents to provide evidence of educational equivalencies.[19]

• The U.S. Supreme Court held that a state-derived residency requirement is constitutionally permissible.[20]

• A New Mexico court held that the state is permitted to ban home schooling to promote the goal of ensuring that children are brought into contact with others besides their parents to expose them to at least one additional set of values, lifestyles, and intellectual abilities.[21]

Summary Guides

1. The courts are reluctant to intrude on curriculum and instructional decisions that are best left to educators.

2. State legislatures have the responsibility to define public school curricula but may delegate that responsibility to the state board of education.

3. The state's police powers provide broad discretion to the legislature to formulate rules and regulations designed to protect the health, safety, and welfare of all citizens within the state.

4. Students may attend private schools or receive home schooling as long as prescribed state laws regarding curricula, teacher qualifications, and health and safety standards are followed.

5. Compulsory attendance is required by the state in its role as guardian of all students residing within the state.

6. The courts tend to support school districts in requiring immunizations over religious objections in support of the view that the health and safety of students outweigh the religious objections of parents.

7. Courts have ruled fairly consistently in supporting schools that educate children who reside within a district and intend to remain there.

8. Teachers have a leading responsibility to assign grades in a fair and defensible manner based on students' academic performance without interference by the courts.

9. Schools may impose academic penalties for excessive absenteeism.

10. Courts have been supportive of academic sanctions designed to reduce unexcused absences.

11. Students may be penalized for work missed during school suspension but may not be penalized academically for receiving the actual suspension.

12. Students may be tested and placed in academic tracks as long as the placement serves educational purposes and does not result in segregating students.

NOTES

1. *Pierce v. Society of Sisters of the Holy Names of Jesus and Mary,* 268 U.S. 510; 45 S.Ct. 571; 69 L.Ed. 1070; 39 A.L.R. 468 (1925).
2. *Wisconsin v. Yoder,* 406 US 205, 215, 92 S Ct 1526, 32 L Ed 2d 15 (1972).
3. *Leeper v. State,* 103 Tenn. 500, 53 S.W. 962 (1899).
4. *Turner v. Liverpool Central School,* 186 F. Supp. 2d 187 (N.D. N.Y. 2002).

5. *Plyler v. Doe*, 457 U.S. 202, 102 S.Ct. 2383, 72 L. Ed. 2d 786 (1982).

6. *T. J. v. Hargrove*, No. 04-1055, 2005 WL 1406332 (Ark. 2005).

7. *Smith v. School Dist. of Hobart*, 811 F. Supp., 391 80 Ed Law Rept. 839 (Ind. 1993).

8. *Las Virgenes Educators Ass'n v. Las Virgenes Unified School Dist.*, 02 Cal. Rptr. 2d 901 (Cal. Ct. App 200).

9. *Hogenson v. Williams*, 542 S.W. 2d 256 (Tex. App. 1976).

10. *Hobson v. Hansen*, 267 F. Supp. 401 (D.D.C. 1967) affd 408 F.2d 175 (1969).

11. *Moses v. Washington Parish School Board*, 330 F. Supp 1340 (U.S. Dist. Ct. La. 1971).

12. *Valentine v. Independent School District of Casey*, 191 Iowa 1100, 183 N.W. 434 (1921).

13. *Isbell v. Brighton Area Schools*, 500 N.W. 2d 748 Mich. App. (1993).

14. 17 U.S.C. § 101 et. seq. (1996).

15. Ibid.

16. *Peter W. v. San Francisco Unified School District*, 131 Cal. Rptr. 854 (1976).

17. *Hoffman v. Board of Education of New York City*, 64 A.D. 2d, 369 N.Y.S. (1978).

18. *Cude v. Arkansas*, 337 S. W. 2d 816 (Ark. 1964).

19. *New Jersey v. Massa*, 231 A. 2d 252 (N.J. Sup. Ct. 1967).

20. *Martinez v. Bynum*, 461 U.S. 321 (1983).

21. *State v. Eddington*, 663 P. 2d 374, 378 (N.M. Ct. App.) cert. denied 104 S.Ct. 354 (1983).

10

Religious Freedoms and Restrictions in Public Schools

⊞ INTRODUCTION ⊞

Conflicts regarding religion evoke deep emotional responses because religious views and beliefs are highly personal. There has been and continues to be tension regarding the separation of church and state as evidenced by the volume of court cases pertaining to religious conflicts, particularly in public schools. The First Amendment to the U.S. Constitution stipulates that "Congress shall make no laws respecting an establishment of religion or prohibiting the free exercise thereof." The First Amendment initially focused on the federal government's prohibitions regarding religion; however, the federal government's proscriptions were applied to the states by virtue of a landmark ruling in *Cantwell v. Connecticut* in which the U.S. Supreme Court held that the same rules applied to the states.[1] Practically speaking, schools as agents of the state must adhere to the tenets of the First Amendment. Public school officials and employees must maintain a neutral position in matters involving religion. They can neither support nor endorse religion, show preference of one over the other, or prevent students from exercising their religious rights as long as doing so does not infringe upon the rights of others.

The First Amendment pertaining to religion contains two important clauses—the *establishment clause* and the *free exercise clause*. The establishment clause prohibits states from passing laws that aid a religion or show preference of one religion over another. The free exercise clause prohibits the state from interfering with individual religious freedoms. These two clauses represent the focus of litigation surrounding church-state conflicts.

Students possess religious rights and freedoms in public schools. As with any right, reasonable restrictions can be imposed by school personnel if there is a justifiable basis for doing so. Students may, under special conditions, offer student-initiated voluntary prayer at graduation ceremonies, participate in student-initiated devotional exercises, distribute religious literature, and refuse to participate in Pledge of Allegiance ceremonies.

148. May Students Legally Initiate Prayer and Devotional Meetings in Public Schools?

Probably so. If student prayer is initiated *solely* by students with no coercion or involvement by school personnel, it is permissible and does not violate the separation of church-state provisions in the First Amendment. In fact, denial of students' right to initiate prayer would result in a violation of their rights to freedom of expression and free exercise of their religious freedoms. Student-initiated prayer is legal as long as the school does not advocate for it or actively participate in the prayer ceremony. School officials can prescribe the time and place of an organized student-initiated prayer activity to minimize disruption in their schools; however, schools are not permitted to develop or implement policies or practices requiring student prayer or any school-sponsored events.

Two leading cases affirmed students' rights to initiate voluntary prayer in public schools. In the *Jones v. Clear Creek*[2] case, a three-judge panel of the U.S. Court of Appeals for the Fifth Circuit ruled that Clear Creek Independent School District's practice of allowing graduating seniors to decide whether or not to include invocation and benedictions in graduation ceremonies did not violate the First Amendment ban on the government's establishment of religion. While this decision only affected the states of Texas, Louisiana, and Mississippi, it was significant. More important, the U.S. Supreme Court declined to review this case. In yet another student-initiated prayer case, *Adler v. Duval*[3] in Florida, the school board provided discretion to graduating seniors by allowing them to select opening and closing remarks not to exceed two minutes by a student of their choice. This practice allowed the chosen student to prepare a message without supervision or review by school officials. A suit was filed challenging this practice as a church-state violation under the First Amendment. The court ruled that the policy did not have the primary effect of advancing religion. It had a secular purpose and was thereby permissible.

In a totally different case, *Santa Fe Independent School District v. Jane Doe*,[4] the U.S. Supreme Court struck down a high school's policy that expressly allowed the school's student council chaplain to deliver a prayer over the public address system before each home varsity game. The policy was challenged as a church-state violation. Because of the challenge, the policy was revised to authorize two student elections to determine whether invocations would be offered at home games and to elect a spokesperson to deliver the prayer. The Supreme Court ruled that the school's policy represented an impermissible act that violated the establishment clause of the First Amendment. The obvious concern focused on a school policy requiring invocation that was supervised by school officials. School officials are protected as long as they do not endorse prayer in their schools and if the prayer is strictly student initiated with no involvement or approval by school personnel. School officials were not supported by the Supreme Court in this case because the prayer was school initiated rather than student initiated.

149. Can Students Hold Devotional Gatherings on School Grounds?

It depends on when they are held. Students may gather on school grounds during noninstructional times to hold religious meetings that are initiated solely by students, provided the school has a limited open forum. A forum is simply a place where speech can be determined based on the nature of the environment in which the speech occurs. A limited open forum exists when school officials allow noncurricular clubs or groups to meet during noninstructional times. Once a limited open forum is established, school officials cannot restrict access based on the content of the expression during these meetings. They must remain viewpoint neutral. It is within the discretion of the school district to determine whether it will offer a limited open forum. There is no legal requirement to do so. However, if a limited open forum is provided to student groups, they cannot be discriminated against based on ideology or philosophy. Such an action would constitute viewpoint discrimination.

The Equal Access Act was enacted in 1984 for the purpose of allowing student religious clubs an equal opportunity to utilize school facilities as do nonreligious clubs. Schools that receive federal support and provide a limited open forum thus cannot deny student religious clubs access to school facilities based on the religious content of their meeting. As with any student club, school advisors must be assigned to ensure that proper order and decorum are established. They may be physically present but may not participate in any of the club's activities. To do so would constitute an establishment clause violation.

150. How Do the Courts View the Distribution of Religious Literature on School Property?

The courts are not altogether consistent in their rulings regarding the distribution of religious material in public schools by outside religious groups. As early as 1953 in *Tudor v. Board of Education*, the New Jersey Supreme Court struck down the distribution of the Gideon Bible by Gideon's International on the grounds that it showed preference of one religion over others in violation of the establishment clause of the First Amendment.[5] However, court rulings in West Virginia and Illinois supported distribution by outside groups as unrelated to the school itself and therefore not triggering establishment clause concerns. One distribution had occurred in the school, while the other had occurred on the sidewalk in front of the school. Student distribution of religious material typically pits freedom of speech protection against establishment clause limitations. The prevailing view among the courts regarding distribution of religious material by students centers on the freedom of expression rights of students, in the absence of significant disruption.

Since the U.S. Supreme Court has not agreed to hear a religious distribution case involving viewpoint discrimination in public schools, the lower courts have been fairly consistent in their rulings with a few exceptions. For example, in *Johnston-Loehner v. O'Brien*, the federal district court ruled that a ban on all student religious speech clearly inhibits religion.[6] A school policy that required an elementary school principal to grant prior approval to nonschool material, which allowed the principal to screen out and prohibit religious materials, was found to be unconstitutional. The principal's action in this case amounted to viewpoint discrimination because the prohibition was based strictly on the religious content of the literature the student wished to distribute. Even though the policy purported to cover religious and nonreligious materials, only after reviewing the content would the school decide whether particular materials could be distributed. Prior restraint of speech based on content is impermissible without a showing that the speech in question materially and substantially interferes with school operations.

Speech restrictions based on viewpoint in any type of forum trigger the most demanding judicial scrutiny under the free speech clause. Flagrant acts involving viewpoint discrimination abridge the First Amendment, as held in *Walz v. Egg Harbor Township Board of Education*.[7] Courts in the Ninth Circuit, *San Diego v. Grossmont*,[8] and Eleventh Circuit, *Searcey v. Harris*,[9] have held that restrictions on speech must be viewpoint neutral even in a nonpublic forum. In *Rivera v. East Otero School District*, a federal district court in Colorado ruled that high school students had a freedom of expression right to distribute a religious newsletter as long as the distribution did not create a disturbance.[10] The court held further that the distribution of religious material was protected speech. A restriction by school officials constitutes viewpoint discrimination and must not be allowed.

In a related case, *Rusk v. Crestview Local School District*, the Sixth Circuit Court held that a school could distribute third-party fliers as long as students were not allowed to participate in the advertised activity without parental permission.[11] A similar decision was reached by the Fourth Circuit Court in *Child Evangelism Fellowship of Md., Inc. v. Montgomery County Public Schools*.[12] In these cases, the courts ruled that it is the school's responsibility to ensure that parents and students understand that the school does not endorse any religious or nonreligious group but distributes its materials neutrally.

The courts have also held that schools may exercise limited discretion in determining which fliers can be sent home with students. The Ninth Circuit Court ruled in *Hills v. Scottsdale Unified School District* that a school may not refuse to distribute literature advertising a program with underlying religious content when it distributed quite similar literature for secular summer programs.[13] Such restrictions constitute viewpoint discrimination. School officials may, however, refuse to distribute literature that contains proselytizing language.

A federal district court in *Slotterback v. Interboro School District* rejected the argument that a ban on religious or political material is necessary to preserve an educational environment in secondary schools.[14] Such a ban constitutes viewpoint discrimination. Courts, however, will generally support reasonable time, place, and manner of distribution as long as those restrictions are applied equally to all written material.

151. May Students Refuse to Recite the Pledge of Allegiance?

Yes. As referenced in Chapter 2, public school students cannot be coerced to recite the Pledge of Allegiance. While a number of student objections are based on religious grounds, others may object based on their freedom of conscience. Public school students may thus object to participation based on religious or personal grounds (see *West Virginia v. Barnette* in Chapter 2). The courts have fundamentally held the view that public school officials cannot legislate patriotism. In other words, students cannot be coerced to be patriotic. Patriotism comes from free minds inspired by willing hearts rather than through coercion. "To sustain the compulsory flag salute, we are required to say that a Bill of Rights which guards the individual's right to speak his own mind, left it open to public school authorities to compel him to utter what is not in his mind."[15] Students may thus refuse to participate in patriotic ceremonies; however, they may not create disruption or interfere with other students who elect to participate in those ceremonies.

152. Is Teaching the Bible in Public Schools Legal?

Yes. The Bible may be taught in public schools as a part of the school's curriculum if it is not associated with any form of worship and is taught objectively as a part of a secular program. In fact, the U.S. Supreme Court ruled in *Stone v. Graham* that the Bible may be used constitutionally as an appropriate study of history, civilization, ethics, or comparative religion.[16] If the Bible is used strictly in this context, there is no First Amendment conflict with the separation of church and state. When it is used to enhance students' understanding of modern and classical works, public sentiment appears strongly in support of the Bible as a part of the curriculum in public schools. In fact, a national council on Bible curriculum in public schools was formed by congressmen, legislators, and attorneys across the nation to ensure that reliable information and legal support of schools' right to teach the Bible as an elective is assured.

The Supreme Court in the landmark *Schempp* case stated that "one's education is not complete without a study of comparative religion or the history of religion and its relationship to the advancement of civilization."[17] The position by the High Court thus supports the view that the Bible can be taught in a secular context. The American Association of School Administrators (AASA) has also endorsed teaching the Bible in public schools.

In spite of support for teaching the Bible in public schools, many school officials remain skeptical regarding a Bible curriculum for fear they will invite legal challenges based on the separation of church and state. In fact, the tension between church and state does persist, as reflected by ongoing litigation involving the use of the Bible in public schools. For example, in *Gibson v. Lee County Board of Education,* plaintiffs challenged the practice of teaching the Bible in public schools by contending that the specific curricula adopted by the school board did not present the Bible objectively as part of a secular program in education.[18] They argued further that the school district's intent in officially offering and preparing to offer courses on Bible history (Bible History: Old Testament and Bible History: New Testament) was designed to promote religion generally and Christianity specifically, resulting in excessive entanglement. The court, in citing the *Lemon* test, noted that no government act or practice can be upheld under the establishment clause unless it (1) was adopted for a secular purpose, (2) has a primary effect that neither advances nor inhibits religion, and (3) does not foster an excessive government entanglement with religion.[19] Plaintiffs argued that the Bible history curricula failed all three tests.

In reviewing this case, the court held for the school district, stating that the district had satisfied the secular purpose requirement by adopting a curriculum that was modified based on the advice of the school board's legal counsel. The court also noted that the teachers for the proposed Bible history classes had been properly instructed on how and what to teach and what not to teach. The court concluded that it could not evaluate the second and third *Lemon* requirements without some record of classroom instruction. The court ruled that plaintiffs had not demonstrated a substantial likelihood of success on the merits regarding the Bible history curriculum.

However, in a contrasting case, *Wiley v. Franklin*, a federal district court held that the account of the resurrection of Jesus Christ as presented in the New Testament constitutes the central statement of the Christian religious faith. The court thus ruled that the only reasonable interpretation of the resurrection is a religious interpretation and that it was difficult to conceive how the resurrection could be taught as secular literature and history. The court noted that counsel for the defendants recommended the deletion of references to the resurrection as well as many other modifications to the proposed Bible History II curriculum. The court found that plaintiffs had established a substantial likelihood of success on the merits regarding the Bible History II curriculum adopted by the school board.[20]

Issues surrounding the use of the Bible continue to be an emotional one for those who support its use as well as those who oppose it. The line between teaching the Bible and instilling religious belief among students is not always clearly distinguished. The public school's focus when using the Bible must be strictly academic in nature. School officials must proceed cautiously by observing the following guidelines that distinguish teaching religion from religious indoctrination:

- The school's approach to religion must be academic, not devotional.
- The school may strive for student awareness of religions but must not demand student acceptance of any religion.
- The school may sponsor study regarding religion but may not sponsor the practice of religion.
- The school may expose students to diverse religious views but may not impose, discourage, or encourage any particular view.
- The school may educate students about all religions but may not promote or denigrate any religion.
- The school may inform the student about various beliefs but must not seek to conform him or her to any particular belief.*

153. Can Public Schools Hold Holiday Concerts and Display Holiday Decorations?

Yes. Public schools may offer various holiday concerts and activities as long as they serve a secular purpose. The First Amendment prohibits teachers from offering any programs that show a preference for one religion over another. If the concert or activity does not create a devotional atmosphere and serves a nonreligious purpose, it can be offered. For example, the band and choir may perform at holiday concerts and include a wide array of musical selections, including those involving religious content. If these

---

*Used by permission, First Amendment Center, 2009.

diverse selections are offered for purposes of entertainment, they are permissible because they are included with other secular arrangements.

154. Can Holiday Decorations Be Displayed by Teachers in Their Classrooms?

It depends. Teachers can decorate bulletin boards in their classrooms as long as the boards include only secular decorations. For example, it is permissible to feature snowmen, reindeer, eggs, rabbits, and other secular items simply as a reminder of the joy and merriment associated with various holiday seasons. If there is a clear separation of secular items from religious items, these displays do not conflict with or offend the establishment clause of the First Amendment. In fact, one court in New Jersey upheld a school district's calendar that included Christmas and Hanukkah when the district referenced these holidays as a means of broadening students' sensitivity toward religious awareness. Their inclusion of these holidays served a secular purpose, did not promote or inhibit religion, and did not create excessive entanglement between religion and the school.[21]

155. May Teachers Be Provided Religious Leaves of Absence?

Yes. Teachers possess religious freedoms that are not lost as a condition of employment in public schools. Title VII provides protection against religious discrimination. The act addresses religious observances, practices, and beliefs. Reasonable accommodation must be afforded by school boards to allow school personnel to use personal leave to attend religious conventions or to observe religious holidays. If these leave requests are not excessive in nature and do not create significant disruption in the teaching and learning process, teachers should be supported. The district may, however, require evidence that the requested leave serves a religious purpose, as reflected in a case that arose in New York.

The collective bargaining agreement between a New York teachers' association and a school district provided for three paid absences per year based on five days' prior approval. No reason was required for two days of the paid leave, but applicants needed to explain the reason for the third day, which had to be for specific reasons, including Title VII accommodation. Two teachers who professed to be devout, practicing Catholics filed a successful grievance against the district challenging their denial of days off for "Title VII accommodation" on Catholic Holy Days of Obligation. The arbitrator held that the district had violated the collective bargaining agreement by denying leave. After losing in arbitration, the district eliminated the requirement that teachers demonstrate that an absence from work was mandated by religion. Under a new policy, the district reserved its right to interview applicants to determine whether they held genuine personal religious beliefs requiring absence from work. The district processed requests from Catholic, Episcopal, and Buddhist teachers for days off based on their answers to inquiries from district administrators.

Even though they were not denied permission to take days off for religious purposes, the teachers sued the district, its superintendent, and other administrators in a federal district court, seeking a declaration that the district could not inquire into their religious practices and beliefs to determine whether a conflict existed between the practices and work hours. The district and administrators moved for summary judgment, asserting the teachers had no legal standing to bring the action since they had never been adversely affected by the new policy. The court explained that Article III of the U.S. Constitution limits federal court jurisdiction to cases and controversies, an essential component of the right to file a lawsuit. Even though the teachers claimed to be injured by the district's pre-arbitration policy, none of them could demonstrate that the district's existing policy was likely to cause them recurring injury. The Constitution permitted the district to inquire about the sincerity of employee religious beliefs and to determine whether teachers had a good-faith belief in the need to take a day off for religious observance. The district could not be precluded from questioning teachers about their religious requirements, and the teachers were unable to show that the new policy injured them. The district and administrators were entitled to summary judgment.[22]

156. Can School Personnel Offer Prayer, a Period of Silence, or Bible Reading in Public School?

No. Any prayer that is sanctioned by a school is illegal. The establishment clause of the First Amendment prohibits school officials as agents of the state from creating a devotional atmosphere in public school. The First Amendment to the Constitution expressly forbids Congress from creating laws in respect to an establishment of religion or prohibiting the free exercise thereof. In addition, through the Fourteenth Amendment to the U.S. Constitution, the U.S. Supreme Court in *Cantwell v. Connecticut*,[23] referenced earlier in this chapter, ruled that this same prohibition applied to the states. Consequently, any actions initiated by school officials to offer prayer in schools are illegal and violate the establishment clause. In the landmark case *Engel v. Vitale*[24] in 1962, the U.S. Supreme Court ruled that prayer was unconstitutional and offensive to the First Amendment.

157. Can Teachers Initiate a Period of Silence in Their Classrooms?

No. School personnel cannot request a period of silence; however, in the past a number of state laws requiring silent meditation were passed under the assumption that such a practice was legal. The courts have been unwilling to accept this presumption. The most notable case, *Wallace v. Jaffree*, occurred in Alabama in 1981. The U.S. Supreme Court ruled that a period of silence mandated by the state for meditation is in violation of the First Amendment. The overriding issue involved a state-endorsed practice due to a statute enacted by the legislature. Students, however, may elect, based on their own decision, to engage in silent meditation at any time as long as the practice is not endorsed by the school or does not negatively impact the school's instructional program.

The U.S. Supreme Court's decision in *Wallace v. Jaffree* was a significant decision regarding religion because it ruled on three separate state-sanctioned religious practices prescribed for public schools in Alabama.[25] The case arose in Mobile, Alabama, when Jaffree, a parent, challenged the constitutionality of the three state statutes. The first statute authorized a one-minute period of silence in public schools within the state for meditation. The second statute allowed a period of silence for meditation or voluntary prayers. The third statute authorized teachers to lead "willing" students in a state-prescribed prayer. Interestingly, the district court concluded that the establishment clause of the First Amendment does not prohibit a state from creating a religion; consequently, Jaffree's challenge was dismissed on the grounds that it failed to state a claim on which relief could be granted.

The court of appeals reversed the district court's ruling, however, charging that the lower court misapplied its decision by concluding that statutes requiring meditation or voluntary prayer and teacher-led prayer did not advance religion in the schools. The legislative intent of these statutes was to convey a clear message of endorsement for state-approved religious activities in schools. The case was appealed to the U.S. Supreme Court, which ruled against the state of Alabama by concluding that all three statutes were invalid and violated the establishment clause of the First Amendment. It reaffirmed the appellate court's ruling that the legislature's intent was to establish prayer in the public schools—an obvious violation of the separation of church and state as required by the U.S. Constitution.

Based on establishment clause restrictions, school personnel are prohibited from exercising the following practices in public schools: *offering prayer, designating a period of silence or meditation, reading the Bible over the public address system, proselytizing in the classroom, creating religious displays,* and *wearing religious dress.*

158. Can Public Schools Offer Bible Reading Over the School's Intercom?

No. Bible reading as a school-sponsored practice is illegal and violates the establishment clause of the First Amendment. This issue was addressed by the U.S. Supreme Court in a landmark case in 1963. Pennsylvania law required that at least ten verses from the Holy Bible would be read, without comment, at the opening of each public school on each school day. "Any child shall be excused from such Bible reading, or attending such

Bible reading, upon written request of his parents or guardian."[26] A family sued to enjoin enforcement of the statute as a violation of the First Amendment. A three-judge district court panel held that the statutes violated the establishment clause and granted injunctive relief.

Similarly, the school commissioner of Baltimore adopted a rule that mandated that at the opening of the school day a chapter of the Bible or the Lord's Prayer would be read without comment. The rule was challenged in the Maryland state court system, which eventually reached the conclusion that the rule did not offend the First Amendment. On appeal, the Supreme Court held that both rules violated the establishment clause. The High Court reiterated the premise of *Engel v. Vitale* that neither the state nor the federal government may constitutionally force a person to profess a belief or disbelief in any religion. Nor may it pass laws that aid one religion or all religions or prefer one over another. The High Court used a test, later to become the first two prongs of the *Lemon* test. The High Court stated that the primary purpose of the state requirement that the Bible be read was religious. The court also noted that it was intended by the state to be a religious ceremony. The compulsory nature of the ceremony was not mitigated by the fact that students could absent themselves from the ceremony, for that fact provides no defense to a claim of unconstitutionality under the establishment clause.

159. Can Teachers Engage Students in Religious Discussions in Their Classrooms?

No. Teachers cannot use their classrooms as a forum to discuss religion. Such a practice would constitute an establishment clause violation. Teachers must at all times be sensitive to the impact of their behavior on young, impressionable children. Teachers must refrain from espousing their religious views or philosophy and must refrain from being drawn into religious discussions by students. However, teachers may use the Bible as a literary, historical, or philosophical document if the focus of the discussion is clearly secular in nature.

160. Can Teachers Refuse to Teach the Prescribed Curriculum Based on Religious Objections?

No. Teachers cannot refuse to teach required curricula based on religious objections. They are obligated to follow the school- or district-approved curriculum, irrespective of their personal religious views. Failure to do so may result in charges of insubordination and neglect of duty, which constitute grounds for dismissal.

A case arose in Maine that addressed conflicts regarding religious content in the classroom. A teacher taught a seventh-grade social studies course that included Eastern history, culture, and religion. After he taught the course for several years without incident, an angry parent confronted him about the religious aspects of his curriculum. She believed "every word of the Bible is true" and that "the earth is probably 8,000 to 10,000 years old." A few days later, the district curriculum coordinator stated that the teacher's "whole program was incorrect." The teacher complied with her instructions. The district superintendent met with him and acknowledged the influence of the parent and her family, who attended the same church as a former school board chair. A principal later reprimanded the teacher in writing for teaching major study units on Sumaria, Ancient Egypt, and Israel.

The teacher sued the district in federal court for First Amendment violations. The court held that school officials have broad discretion to design the curriculum and select textbooks. On the other hand, public school students are "particularly vulnerable to the inculcation of orthodoxy in the guise of pedagogy." The court found that the teacher drew "a straight line of causation" from his first encounter with the parents, the complaints to the school, and the district's responses. His evidence warranted further consideration of whether the curricular restrictions were motivated by a desire to eliminate references to non-Christian religions. The teacher's evidence, if believed, would permit the court to find a First Amendment violation. He showed "adverse employment action" by alleging retaliation in the form of poor evaluations, a reprimand letter, and the threat of discharge if he disobeyed curricular directives. The court denied the district's motion for summary judgment.[27]

161. Can Teachers Use Religious Symbols and Displays in Their Classrooms?

No. Teachers may not use religious symbols and displays. Religious symbols and displays are illegal if sponsored by teachers and violate the separation of church and state as well as the principle of neutrality. It would be difficult to defend religious symbols and displays as having a secular practice, as is demonstrated by a Kentucky case.

A state statute required that the Ten Commandments, purchased with private contributions, be posted on the wall of each public classroom in the state. A group of citizens sought an injunction against the statute's enforcement claiming that it violated the First Amendment's establishment and free exercise clauses. The Kentucky state courts upheld the statute, finding that its purpose was secular, not religious, and that the statute neither advanced nor inhibited any religion or involved the state excessively in religious matters.

Utilizing the three-part test first announced in *Lemon v. Kurtzman*, the U.S. Supreme Court struck down the statute. The High Court concluded that the posting of the Ten Commandments had no secular purpose. Kentucky state education officials had insisted that the statute in question served the secular purpose of teaching students the foundation of Western Civilization and the Common Law. The High Court stated, however, that the preeminent purpose was plainly religious in nature. The Ten Commandments undeniably is derived from a religious text, despite the legislative recitation of a secular purpose. The High Court stated that the text was not integrated into a course or study of history, civilization, ethics, or comparative religion but simply posted to induce children to read, meditate upon, and perhaps venerate and obey it. The High Court also stated that it made no difference that the expense of posting the Commandments was remunerated through private funds and that they were not read aloud.[28]

162. Can Teachers Wear Religious Dress in Public Schools?

It depends on where the teacher is employed. Teachers cannot wear dress that creates a devotional atmosphere in most states. At issue is freedom of expression rights of school personnel versus First Amendment establishment clause violations. Religious dress has the potential of producing a proselytizing influence on students because it emphasizes the teacher's religious convictions. Additionally, religious dress may lead students and parents to believe that such dress is endorsed by the school, thus triggering establishment clause conflicts. Many states have passed legislation banning religious dress by school personnel while attending official school functions. School personnel are free to exercise their freedom of religion away from school anytime they wish.

The court noted in *McGlothin* that the district is required under the First Amendment and Title VII to make some accommodation for the practice of religious belief when it pursues an end that incidentally burdens religious practices.[29] Despite this statement in the *McGlothlin* case, a number of courts have rejected claims that state statutes restricting teachers from wearing religious clothing are unconstitutional. In *United States v. Board of Education*, for example, the Third Circuit rejected a Title VII religious discrimination claim against a school board for prohibiting a Muslim substitute teacher from wearing her religious clothing. The case originated with a Pennsylvania statute called the "Garb Statute," which provided that "no teacher in any public school shall wear . . . or while engaged in the performance of his duty as such teacher, any dress, mark, emblem or insignia indicating the fact that such teacher is a member or adherent of any religious order, sect or denomination." In its ruling, the Third Circuit determined that it would impose an "undue hardship" on the school to require it to accommodate the Muslim teacher's request to wear her religious clothing. Such an accommodation, according to the court, would represent a "significant threat to the maintenance of religious neutrality in the public school system."[30] However, this court was careful to emphasize that it would not be permissible to dismiss a teacher for wearing an unobtrusive religious symbol such as a cross or necklace.

Similarly, the Oregon Supreme Court rejected a free exercise challenge under the First Amendment and a provision of the state constitution to an Oregon statute prohibiting teachers from wearing religious clothing. The teacher, who was an adherent to the Sikh religion, argued against the constitutionality of a state law that indicated that "no teacher in any public school shall wear any religious dress while engaged in the performance of duties as a teacher." The Oregon high court upheld the statute, writing that "the aim of maintaining the religious neutrality of the public schools furthers a constitutional obligation beyond an ordinary policy preference for the legislature."[31]

It must be noted that, although these decisions permit states and school districts to restrict the wearing of religious garb, they do not require such restrictions. To date, two states, Arkansas and Tennessee, have statutes explicitly allowing teachers to wear religious garb in public schools. In states without such laws, the vast majority of state courts have held that public schools may allow teachers to wear religious clothing.

Summary of Cases Involving Religious Freedoms

• The Fifth Circuit Court of Appeals invalidated a Louisiana law that allowed schools to observe a brief silent prayer or meditation period at the beginning of each day. The court held that such a purpose was motivated by the wholly religious purpose of restoring verbal prayer to Louisiana schools.[32]

• The U.S. Supreme Court held in a Pledge of Allegiance case that state law did not authorize a father to dictate what others could say or not say to his daughter regarding religion. It was improper for federal courts to accept a claim by a person whose standing was based on family law rights that were in dispute when the lawsuit might adversely affect the person who was the very source of the claim to standing.[33]

• The U.S. Supreme Court held that school officials are not permitted to exclude a student religious club from facilities solely because of its religious viewpoint. Such action is unconstitutional viewpoint discrimination.[34]

• The Sixth Circuit Court of Appeals held that a display of the Ten Commandments donated to an Ohio school had no secular purpose. Even though the display was modified, it remained overly religious.[35]

Summary Guides

1. School personnel possess First Amendment rights to freedom of religion but may not exercise those rights in public schools. Such an exercise would violate the establishment clause of the First Amendment.

2. School personnel are free to fully exercise their religious rights away from public schools.

3. Students possess religious rights and freedoms that must not be restricted unless the exercise of their rights creates material disruption or infringes upon the rights of others.

4. Students may offer student prayer and devotionals if it is solely initiated by students and without any coercion or involvement by school personnel.

5. Students may distribute religious materials under their freedom of expression rights as long as the distribution does not create significant disruption.

6. Students may not be coerced to recite the Pledge of Allegiance or participate in any patriotic ceremonies based on religious beliefs and/or freedom of expression guarantees. These students must not be ostracized for failure to participate.

7. Public schools may offer holiday concerts and display holiday decorations as long as they serve a secular purpose and do not create a devotional atmosphere.

8. Teachers, based on their First Amendment freedom of religion rights, may be granted religious leaves of absence as long as they are not excessive and do not create significant disruption to the teaching and learning process.

9. School-sanctioned prayer and periods of silence are illegal and violate the establishment clause of the First Amendment.

10. School-sponsored Bible reading is illegal and constitutes an establishment clause violation. However, the Bible can be used as a literary, historical, or philosophical document if its utilization serves a secular purpose.

11. Teachers may not use classrooms to discuss religion or to espouse their religious views or beliefs. They may not display religious symbols or displays.

12. School personnel may not wear religious apparel in public schools. Religious dress worn by school personnel might be interpreted by parents and students as a school endorsement of a certain religion or might demonstrate preference of one religion over another in violation of the principle of neutrality.

NOTES

1. *Cantwell v. Connecticut*, 310 U.S. 296 (1940).

2. *Jones v. Clear Creek Independent School District*, 977, F.2d 963 (5th Cir. 1992).

3. *Adler v. Duval County School Board*, 851 F.Supp. 446 (M.D. Fla. 1994).

4. *Santa Fe Independent School District v. Jane Doe*, 120 S.Ct. 2266; 147 L.Ed. 2d 295 (2000).

5. *Tudor v. Board of Education of Borough of Rutherford*, 14 N.J. 31, 100 A. 2d 857 (1953) cert. den., 348 U.S. 816, 75 S.Ct. 25, 99 L. Ed. 664 9 (1954).

6. *Johnston-Loehner v. O'Brien*, 859 F. Supp. 575 (M.D. Fla. 1994).

7. *Walz v. Egg Harbor Township Board of Education*, 342 F.3d 271 (3d Cir. 2003).

8. *San Diego Community Against Registration and the Draft v. Governing Board of Grossmont Union High School District*, 790 F.2d 1471 (9th Cir. 1986).

9. *Searcey v. Harris*, 888 F.2d 1314 (11th Cir.1989).

10. *Rivera v. East Otero Sch. Dist. R-1*, 721 F. Supp. 1189 (D. Colo. 1989).

11. *Rusk v. Crestview Local School District*, 379 F.3d 418 (2004).

12. *Child Evangelism Fellowship of Md., Inc. v. Montgomery County Public School*, 373 F.3d 589 (2004).

13. *Hills v. Scottsdale Unified School District*, 329 F.3d 1044 (2003).

14. *Slotterback by Slotterback v. Interboro School District*, 766 F. Supp. 280 (1991).

15. *West Virginia State Bd. of Education v. Barnette*, 319 U.S. 624, 63 S.Ct. 1178, 87 L.Ed. 1628 (1943).

16. *Stone v. Graham*, 599 S.W. 2d 157 (KY 1980).

17. *School District of Abington v. Schempp; Murray v. Curlett*, 374 U.S. 203, 835 S.Ct. 1650 (1965).

18. *Gibson v. Lee County Board of Education*, F. Supp. 2d 1426; 1998 U.S.

19. *Lemon v. Kurtzman*, 403 U.S. 602, 612-613, 29 L.Ed. 2d 745, 91 S.Ct. 2105 (1971).

20. *Wiley v. Franklin*, 468 F. Supp. 133, 150 (E.D. Tenn. 1979).

21. *Clever v. Cherry Hill Township Board of Education*, 838 F. Supp. 929 (D.N.J. 1993).

22. *Burns v. Warwick Valley Cent. School Dist.*, 166 F. Supp. 2d 881 (S.D.N.Y. 2001).

23. *Cantwell v. Connecticut*, 310 U.S. 296 (1940).

24. *Engel v. Vitale*, 370 U.S. 421, 82 S.Ct. 1261 (1962).

25. *Wallace v. Jaffree*, 472 U.S. 38, 105 S.Ct. 2479 (1985).

26. *Abington School District v. Schempp*, 374 U.S. 203, 83 S.Ct. 1560, 10 L.Ed.2d 844 (1963).

27. *Cole v. Maine School Administrative Dist. No. 1*, 350 F. Supp. 2d 143 (D. Me. 2004).

28. *Stone v. Graham*, 449 U.S. 39, 101 S.Ct. 192, 66 L. Ed. 2d 199 (1981).

29. *McGlothin v. Jackson Municipal Separate School District*, 829 F. Supp. 853 (S.D. Miss. 1993).

30. *U.S. v. Bd. of Education*, 911 F.2d 882 (3rd Cir. 1990).

31. *Cooper v. Eugene Sch. Dist. No. 41*, 301 Ore. 358 (1986), app. dismissed, 480 U.S. 942 (1987).

32. *Doe v. School Board of Ouachita Parish,* 274 F.3d 289 (5th Cir. 2001).

33. *Elk Grove Unified School Dist. v. Newdow,* 542 U.S. 124 S.Ct. 2301, 159 L.Ed. 2d 151, (2001).

34. *Good News Club v. Milford Cent. School,* 533 U.S. 98, 121 S.Ct. 2093, 150 L.Ed. 2d 151 (2001).

35. *Baker v. Adams County Ohio Valley School Board,* Nos. 02-3776, 02-3777 86 Fed. Appx. 164, WL 68523 (6th Cir. 2004).

11

Teacher Dismissal and Due Process

⚏ INTRODUCTION ⚏

Teacher dismissal is governed by state statute in most cases. State laws define specific causes for dismissal, including a general category upon which school boards may rely if dismissal does not fall into other specific categories. Central to any dismissal proceeding is the requirement that all provisions of due process be met to ensure fundamental fairness. As emphasized in Chapter 2, both aspects of due process, namely *procedural* and *substantive*, must be fulfilled to succeed in a dismissal case. The burden of proof rests with school officials to demonstrate that dismissal recommendations are based on valid grounds and that all procedural requirements are satisfied. Teachers who face dismissal charges must be provided an opportunity to respond to the charges and refute any evidence presented against them. It is critical that all due process requirements be fully met because tenured and nontenured teachers under contract have a property interest in their employment position. Due process assures that school personnel will not be deprived of life, liberty, or property without full compliance with Fourteenth Amendment provisions.

163. What Does Dismissal for Cause Really Mean for Teachers?

Dismissal for cause means that a statutory reason has been established to terminate the employment of a teacher. Dismissal requirements differ from state to state. The school board cannot base termination on any grounds other than what is specified by state statute. As referenced in the overview, most state laws include a generic phrase usually referred to as "other good and just cause" that allows the school board to pursue termination proceedings on causes not specified in the statute. Dismissal always involves a property interest, that is, a legitimate claim of entitlement to the employment position held by the individual. In the dismissal proceedings, all aspects of Fourteenth Amendment due process must be applied. Other good and just cause may vary from state to state, providing wide latitude for school boards in some instances and more limited flexibility for other school boards.

164. How Is Incompetency Defined by the Courts?

Incompetency can encompass a wide range of issues regarding teacher performance. It is typically identified as

- unprofessional conduct or conduct unbecoming of a teacher;
- lack of knowledge and skill;
- inefficiency;
- inadequate command of subject matters;
- inability or unwillingness to teach the prescribed curriculum;
- lack of effective classroom management skills;
- inability or unwillingness to work effectively with parents, colleagues, and supervisors; or
- attitudinal deficiencies.

Incompetency charges normally occur over a period of time during which a discernable pattern of behavior is observed. Very rarely is it based on a single incident, although it is possible. Because of the wide range of behaviors associated with incompetency, it tends to be used more frequently by school boards as grounds for dismissal. A North Dakota court reinforced this view when it defined incompetency as

> a habitual failure to perform work with a degree of skill or accuracy displayed by other persons. . . . Nevertheless, there are times when only one incident may be of such magnitude or for such reaching consequences that a teacher's ability to perform his or her duties will be permanently impaired and a finding of "incompetency" would be proper.[1]

When specific teaching deficiencies are cited by school officials, they must be documented and communicated to the affected teacher(s).

Additionally, guidance and support must be provided to facilitate an improvement in the teacher's performance. Sufficient time must then be granted to assist the teacher in improving performance. It is difficult for school boards to sustain charges of incompetency involving classroom teaching in the absence of these components, as revealed in the following case.

The Ohio Supreme Court decided not to review lower court decisions ordering a school board to rehire a teacher. Her evaluations did not give her specific recommendations for improvement or a procedure to obtain assistance. The state court of appeals held that comments such as "see me before next observation" did not satisfy state statute. The principal had argued that the teacher lost control of her class and noted that many of her students wandered around, slept, or otherwise failed to participate in class. The court of appeals held that the board had to rehire her. Recommendations in teacher evaluations must be specific enough to alert a reasonable person to the need for change.[2]

Conversely, courts do not support teachers when there is documented evidence of incompetency, as is demonstrated in the following case. A Michigan teacher received unsatisfactory performance ratings and was transferred to a new school. When her performance was again rated unsatisfactory, she sought assistance from her teachers' union. The union declined the teacher's request to process her grievances against the school board. The board advised her that it would not proceed on its charges with the intent of terminating her employment, but she appealed its finding of unsatisfactory instructional performance to the state tenure commission. A hearing officer found that the teacher failed to plan, prepare, develop, and provide appropriate lessons and educational activities for students and did not effectively control them or maintain a proper learning atmosphere. The board discharged the teacher, and the state court of appeals affirmed the decision. She filed unfair labor practice charges against the union and board with the Michigan Employment Relations Commission (MERC). A MERC hearing officer recommended dismissing the charge against the union and the school board because the tenure commission's finding of just cause for discharge was a complete defense against claims that the union had violated its duty of fair representation. The court of appeals affirmed the MERC decision, and both the Michigan Supreme Court and the U.S. Supreme Court refused to review it.[3]

165. Does Insubordination Involve a Pattern of Nonconforming Behavior, or Can a Single Nonconforming Act Constitute Insubordination?

It can involve both. Insubordination is generally viewed as willful failure or refusal to conform to a reasonable administrative directive or school rule. School officials who issue the directive must possess the legal authority to do so. In most instances, there is a discernable pattern of behavior that falls into the category of insubordination. In all cases, school officials must provide defensible evidence to sustain charges of insubordination. Stronger cases of insubordination are those in which warnings have been issued to the teacher regarding undesirable actions, with specific directives the teacher is expected to follow to remedy the problem. Insubordination charges related to academic performance tend to achieve greater support by the courts. In all cases, fundamental fairness must be applied to ensure that the teacher's equal protection rights are protected.

It is important to note that valid insubordination charges can also involve a single act of misconduct, as was the case involving a teacher in Tennessee. The Tennessee teacher did not meet the requirements of an improvement plan while teaching a kindergarten class. She was transferred to another school and assigned to a classroom of third graders needing remedial education. A few weeks into the school year, a student reported that the teacher had smacked her on the face. The principal and assistant principal met with the teacher, stressed the importance of being positive with children, and admonished her that she was not, under any circumstances, to place her hands on the students. Later in the school year, parents of another student reported that the teacher had slapped their child. The district conducted an investigation. Students told administrators that the teacher had placed her hands on their faces when she was angry and pinched and hit them with a soft-cover textbook. When administrators questioned the teacher about the report, she admitted placing her hands on students to get their attention. She admitted slapping five of seven students in the class when she was angry and when the children were being disrespectful. The district immediately suspended the teacher for complete insubordination.

The school board upheld the recommendation to discharge the teacher for insubordination, incompetency, and inefficiency. A state trial court upheld the decision, and the teacher appealed. The Court of Appeals of Tennessee held that insubordination includes the refusal to carry out specific assignments made by the principal. The principal and assistant principal had instructed the teacher to refrain from placing her hands on students. The court found that she had refused to follow a specific directive. It expressed shock that a teacher with over ten years of experience felt the need to grab and hit students. Teachers were required to provide leadership and direction for others by setting an appropriate example. The court stated that "a teacher with that much experience must be capable of controlling her anger and handling her students in a more professional and safe manner." As there was evidence of unfitness, as well as inefficiency and insubordination, the judgment was affirmed.[4]

---

166. Does It Matter if Neglect of Duty Is Intentional or Unintentional as a Cause for Dismissal?

No, it does not matter whether neglect of duty is intentional or unintentional to sustain valid charges. Neglect of duty normally occurs when a teacher fails to execute assigned duties. Failure to execute duties can be intentional or based on an omission that results in nonexecution. Neglect of duty is commonly associated with classroom and other school-related activities. An example of neglect of duty can be illustrated by a Texas case.

A Texas teacher signed out a district vehicle to drive to a soccer clinic. Before calling on a colleague who was also attending the clinic, the teacher stopped at a dry cleaner and then a grocery store where he purchased beer and other items. A witness reported seeing him leaving the store with beer and getting into the vehicle. The teacher admitted buying beer while using the vehicle when the school principal confronted him about it. He submitted his resignation after being formally reprimanded, but he later changed his mind and rescinded it. The superintendent recommended not renewing his contract, and the school board voted for nonrenewal after a hearing. The state education commissioner affirmed the decision, finding substantial evidence that the teacher was in the course and scope of his employment while he was in possession of alcohol.

A Texas district court affirmed the decision, and the teacher appealed to the state court of appeals, arguing that he was on a purely personal side trip to run errands at the time of the beer purchase. The court held that the commissioner's decision had to be affirmed unless it was arbitrary and capricious. A court could not substitute its judgment for the commissioner's and could only review it to determine if it was supported by substantial evidence. The teacher admitted his error and stated that buying beer was a "dumb thing to do." He also stated to the board that he was acting within the scope of his duties to attend the soccer clinic. The teacher agreed that it was reasonable to assume he was acting for the school when the school day began. As the commissioner's decision was supported by substantial evidence, the court affirmed it.[5]

167. Can Immorality Charges Involve In-School Behavior as well as Out-of-School Behavior?

Yes, immorality is often cited as grounds for dismissal. It is a term that lacks preciseness. Most legislatures have been reluctant to identify specific behaviors that can lead to dismissal for immorality; however, it is generally viewed as conduct that offends the ethics of a particular community that renders the teacher unfit to teach. One of the difficulties facing the courts is the link between the teacher's conduct and the ethics or morals of a particular neighborhood. A teacher's behavior may offend the morals of one community but be acceptable in another. Based on the variations in community standards, the courts tend to view unprofessional acts as those that adversely affect the teacher's ability or fitness to teach. One court stated that "the teacher served as a role model for students, exerting a subtle but important influence over their perceptions and values."[6] The California Supreme Court, in *Morrison v. State Board of Education*, identified a number of factors for determining if teachers' behavior rendered them unfit to teach:

- The likelihood that the conduct will adversely affect students or fellow teachers
- The degree of adversity anticipated
- The proximity or remoteness in time of the conduct
- The type of teaching certificate held
- The extenuating circumstances, if any, that surround teachers' conduct
- The extent to which disciplinary action may have an adverse impact upon the constitutional rights of teachers involved[7]

Immoral conduct can occur on or off school grounds. An example of an immoral act that occurred in school arose in Connecticut in regard to a tenured Connecticut teacher, who at the time was actively seeking a promotion after twenty years of teaching. She was accused of filling in answers to questions her students left blank on the Connecticut Mastery Test, a state-required student achievement exam. Ninety-six percent of the teacher's class had exceeded the state achievement goal on the test. All those students were placed in advanced English classes the following year, but when they were retested, only 15 percent exceeded the state goal. A hearing panel held that the teacher's actions constituted moral misconduct.

The school board discharged the teacher for moral conduct and other due and sufficient cause, and a Connecticut trial court upheld the decision. The Court of Appeals of Connecticut rejected her argument that she was improperly denied the opportunity to supplement the trial transcript on appeal. It agreed with the board that substantial evidence supported the finding that the teacher had tampered with her students' state proficiency examinations. Her assertion that students had tampered with the tests was implausible, and the hearing panel had reached a reasonable conclusion. As there was due and sufficient cause to discharge the teacher, the court affirmed the judgment.[8]

An example of an immoral act occurring out of school can be illustrated by a South Carolina case. A South Carolina teacher was arrested for possessing crack cocaine in 1988, but authorities dismissed his case. In 2000, the teacher was arrested in his car in a well-known drug area while his passenger attempted to buy crack. Charges against the teacher were dropped when the passenger pled guilty. After the 2000 incident, the teacher was placed on administrative leave, pending an investigation into the arrest and similar behavior in the past. The superintendent advised him by letter that his contract was being terminated under state code. At the teacher's school board hearing, the superintendent indicated that termination was based solely on the teacher's unfitness.

The superintendent later testified that he did not consider negative publicity in rendering the decision. The board upheld the discharge based on substantial, compelling evidence justifying immediate employment termination and evident unfitness as manifested by his conduct, which, after a reasonable time for improvement—twelve years—did not show that improvement had been made. A state circuit court held that an arrest without a conviction for two criminal charges was not substantial evidence of unfitness to teach. The court reversed the board's decision, and the board appealed. The state court of appeals reinstated the board's action. It found substantial evidence of the teacher's unfitness to teach based on the arrests, his dishonesty, the publicity surrounding the arrest in 2000, and the negative response it caused in the community.

The teacher petitioned the South Carolina Supreme Court to review his case. That court ruled that the appeals court committed an error by failing to confine its decision to the grounds stated in the order terminating the employment. The appeals court had instead searched the record and made independent factual findings supporting the action. The supreme court found that two drug arrests twelve years apart that did not result in charges failed to support a finding of unfitness to teach. This was especially true when the district did not contend that the teacher ever used, possessed, or sold illegal drugs. The teacher was entitled to reinstatement with back pay and benefits from the date of his suspension.[9]

Any act that substantially interferes with the education of children and directly affects the teacher's fitness to teach, however, can form the basis for charges of immorality.

168. What Essential Requirements Must Be Met in Abolishing School Personnel Positions?

Reduction in force occurs when there is a decrease in the number of tenured and probationary teachers employed by a school district arising from a decline in enrollment, district reorganization, or significant program changes. Grounds for a reduction in force are generally established when one or more of the following conditions exist:

1. *Declining enrollment:* When enrollment or projected enrollment for the succeeding school year is reduced and the established state funding formulas for certified personnel allow for less than the number currently employed.

2. *Financial exigency:* When the sum of estimated revenues and appropriate funds is less than the estimated expenditures to maintain the current number of certified tenured and probationary teachers.

3. *District reorganization:* The closing or consolidation of departments or services or reorganization of a school or schools within a system because of declining enrollment, financial exigency, or budget constraints.

4. *Program change:* The reduction, elimination, or consolidation of pro-grams or services offered by the school system, which is affected by declining enrollment, financial exigency, or district reorganization.

Reduction in force must be supported with evidence of a bona fide financial crisis arising from the factors listed above. Additionally, there must be a rational connection between the benefits derived from person-nel dismissal and the alleviation of the financial crisis. Most districts have developed reduction in force (RIF) plans that identify specific criteria to be used in rendering reduction decisions, some of which might encompass subject matter needs, length of experience (seniority), highest degree earned, areas of certification, length of time a teacher has held degrees and certificates, and teaching performance.

The courts tend to place a high priority on teacher seniority in assess-ing reduction plans. In cases involving reduction in personnel, all due process standards must be met, as is illustrated in an Arkansas case. The Arkansas Supreme Court held that a full-time nonprobationary cook whose position was being eliminated was entitled to a notice and a hearing as mandated by the state Public School Employee Fair Hearing Act, despite her employer's claim that her position was being eliminated due to budget constraints. The court held that, although this employment relationship could be terminated at the will of either party, Arkansas employees remain entitled to the notice provisions of state law. In other words, even though the board could terminate the cook's employment for any reason, she was still entitled to adequate notice and hearing protections prior to the action.[10]

A different type of reduction in force case arose in Kentucky. A Kentucky school board reduced the extended employment days for forty-six of its six hundred certified employees based on a "budget allocation" that allowed for the funding of an alternative learning center. Several of the teachers sued the school board in a state circuit court for violations of state law. The court held that the reduction in extended employment days had been accomplished according to a uniform plan, in compliance with the law, and that there had been no violation of the state open meetings law. The teachers appealed to the state appellate court, which held that teacher salaries cannot be lowered unless the reduction is part of a uniform plan affecting all teachers in the entire district and there is evidence of a reduc-tion in responsibilities. The reduction in extended employment days was, in fact, a reduction of responsibilities under the law.

The court further noted that the board's records indicated that the plan included only forty-six of six hundred certified employees and that spe-cific teachers were targeted for reductions. While a school board is per-mitted to adjust its budget to meet district needs, the legislature had mandated uniformity when making such adjustments so that no teacher or class of teachers is sacrificed. All teachers are to be encompassed in such a plan, even though not all are affected by its implementation, to prevent arbitrary salary reductions of a targeted class. Because the circuit court did not decide the issue of whether the teachers received a reduction in responsibility or proper notice as required by the law, the court remanded the case for further proceedings. The determination that no violation of the open meetings law occurred was upheld.

169. How Does Other Good and Just Cause Affect Teacher Dismissal?

Again, other good and just cause is prescribed by statute in many states to provide a means for school boards to dismiss school personnel for reasons not specifically identified, as long as a valid reason is established and all procedural requirements are met. School boards, where statutorily permitted, can dismiss personnel for other good cause, as illustrated by a case that arose in Texas. A Texas teacher found an icon labeled "Teacher Evaluations" on a classroom computer. Some of his students later discovered documents involving employee reprimands on the computer's hard drive. The teacher recognized some of the information as confidential and inappropriate for students, but he read it with them. A student saved the personnel documents on floppy disks, and the teacher gave them to his attorney without telling school administrators of the discovery. The district discharged the teacher, and a Texas trial court later affirmed the state commissioner of education's decision upholding the discharge. The teacher appealed to the Texas Court of Appeals, which dismissed several procedural claims before advancing to the question of whether the discharge was supported by "good cause"—a term undefined in the Texas Education Code. The commissioner defined "good cause" as an employee's failure to perform employment duties that a person of ordinary prudence would have done under the same or similar circumstances. The court upheld the commissioner's finding of good cause under any definition. The commissioner did not commit error in finding that the teacher's dissemination of teacher reprimands could cause a loss of confidence in the district. The teacher did not dispute that he had discovered confidential records and allowed students to review and download them for future use. The court affirmed the commissioner's decision upholding the discharge.[11]

170. Can a Teacher Be Dismissed for Improper Personal Use of School Computers?

Yes. School districts have the right to determine how school-owned computers may be used. For example, teachers have been dismissed for using school computers for personal use involving pornography, betting on sporting events, shopping, and other nonschool-related activities. These situations have become more critical when these impermissible activities occur during times when teachers should be instructing their students.

Summary of Cases Involving Dismissal

- A Washington high school math teacher was dismissed for soliciting sex when a seductive note written to a student was intercepted by school officials.[12]

- The school board was upheld when it dismissed a teacher whose classroom was consistently filthy, who failed to develop lesson plans, and who was unable to maintain order.[13]

- A district court held that teachers can be dismissed for unprofessional conduct when they use the classroom for purposes other than teaching and incorporate sexually graphic or otherwise inappropriate materials.[14]

- A district upheld the dismissal of a teacher who was convicted of theft, welfare fraud, income tax evasion, and shoplifting.[15]

Summary Guides

1. Boards of education may dismiss school personnel for almost any reason as long as the reasons are valid and consistent with state statute and all due process requirements are met.

2. All school personnel, whether tenured or nontenured, are entitled to procedural due process if dismissal occurs during the contract year.

3. Even though there are variations, most states identify incompetency, insubordination, immorality, neglect of duty, justifiable decrease in the number of teaching positions, and other good and just cause as grounds for dismissal.

4. Incompetency generally includes skill deficiencies, inefficiency, lack of knowledge of subject matter, inability or unwillingness to teach the curriculum, not working well with coworkers or parents, and attitudinal deficiencies.

5. Insubordination involves the willful failure to obey a reasonable and valid directive. It may involve a pattern of behavior or a single incident that is significant enough to warrant dismissal.

6. Immorality is constitutionally vague and varies with the morals of a community. Courts tend to link immoral behavior with general unfitness to teach.

7. Neglect of duty occurs when a teacher fails to execute assigned duties normally associated with the classroom and related activities. It may be intentional or unintentional but does establish grounds for dismissal.

8. Justifiable decreases in teaching positions occur when there is a bona fide financial crisis that can be alleviated by reducing the workforce. Due process requirements must be an integral component of reduction in force proceedings.

9. The phrase *other good and just cause* allows school boards to dismiss personnel for valid reasons that may not be specifically identified in state statutes.

10. School officials may face liability charges for wrongful dismissal of school personnel.

NOTES

1. *Collins v. Faith Sch. Dist. No. 46-2*, 574 N.W. 2d 889 (1998).
2. *Cox v. Zanesville City School Dist. Board of Educ.*, 105 Ohio St. 3d 1466, 824 N.E. 2d 93, Table No. 2004-1605 (Ohio 2005).
3. *Knubbe v. Detroit Bd. of Ed. No. 240076*, 2003 WL 22681553 (Mich. Ct. App. 2003).
4. *Ketchersid v. Rhea County Board of Educ.*, 174 S. W. 2d 163 (Tenn. Ct. App. 2005).
5. *Simpson v. Alanis*, No. 08-03-00110-CV, 2004 WL 309297 (Tex. Ct. App. 2004).
6. *Ambach v. Norwich*, 441 U.S. 68, 99 S.Ct. 1589, 60 L. Ed. 2d 49 (1979).
7. *Morrison v. State Board of Education*, 461 P. 2d 375, 386-387 (Cal. 1969).
8. *Hanes v. Board of Educ. of City of Bridgeport*, 783 A.2d 1 (Conn. App. Ct. 2001).
9. *Shell v. Richland County School Dist. One*, 362 S.C. 408, 608 S.E. 2d 428 (S.C. 2005).
10. *Gould Public Schools v. Dobbs*, 338 Ark. 28, 993 S.W. 2d 500 (Ark. 1999).
11. *Tave v. Alanis*, 109 S.W. 3d 890 (Tex. Ct. App. 2003).
12. *Sauter v. Mount Vernon School District No. 320*, 58 Wn. App. 121, 128, 791 P.2d 549 (1990).
13. *Board of Education of the School District of Philadelphia v. Kushner*, 109 Pa Commw. 120, 530 A.2d 541 (1987).
14. *Forest Hill School District v. Forest Hill Education Association*, 2004 WL 243586 (Pa. Cmwlth 2004).
15. *Board of Directors of Lawton-Bronson v. Davies*, 489 N.W. 2d 19 (Iowa, 1992).

12

Discrimination in Employment

🌐 INTRODUCTION 🌐

The equal protection provision of the Fourteenth Amendment provides protection against group discrimination in general. The Fourteenth Amendment states in part that "the state shall not deny any person within its jurisdiction equal protection under the laws." Since the Fourteenth Amendment has been applied to the states, schools as state agencies are subject to Fourteenth Amendment restrictions. In addition to the U.S. Constitution, a number of federal statutes provide safeguards against employment discrimination based on race, color, national origin, gender, religion, and age to ensure that individuals in these protected classes are not subject to discrimination. Almost all forms of employment discrimination are subject to federal and state laws. These laws are not designed to promote affirmative action but rather to ensure that individuals in protected classifications are insulated against unfair treatment. Courts have not been reluctant to hear cases involving constitutional due process claims regarding employment discrimination. Additionally, protection was strengthened with the passage of one of the most significant federal statutes addressing employment discrimination, Title VII of the Civil Rights Act of 1964.

171. How Does Title VII Affect the Operation and Management of Public Schools?

Title VII is perhaps the most extensive federal employment law passed by Congress. It states, in part, the following:

a. It shall be an unlawful employment practice for an employer

   (1) to fail or refuse to hire or to discharge any individual, or otherwise to discriminate against any individual with respect to his compensation, terms, conditions, or privileges of employment, because of such individual's race, color, religion, sex, or national origin; or

   (2) to limit, segregate, or classify his employees or applicants for employment in any way which would deprive or tend to deprive any individual of employment opportunities or otherwise adversely affect his status as an employee, because of such individual's race, color, religion, sex, or national origin.

b. It shall be an unlawful employment practice for an employment agency to fail or refuse to refer for employment, or otherwise to discriminate against, any individual because of his race, color, religion, sex, or national origin, or to classify or refer for employment any individual on the basis of his race, color, religion, sex, or national origin.

Title VII affects public schools by prohibiting school officials from discriminating in their employment decisions based on race, color, religion, gender, or national origin. Title VII essentially calls for discrimination-free decision making. The statute also prohibits discrimination based on the classifications listed above regarding employment promotion, compensation, and fringe benefits. The initial burden falls on an employee or prospective employee to establish a bona fide case of discrimination. See Table 12.1 for the number of Title VII charges from 1997 to 2006.

In a leading nonpublic school case, *McDonnell Douglas Corp. v. Green*, the U.S. Supreme Court developed a three-step process regarding Title VII challenges. For example, if a teacher or prospective teacher challenges an employment decision, the initial burden rests with him or her to establish a prima facie case of employment discrimination. The burden then shifts to the school board to refute the prima facie claim of discrimination by demonstrating that a legitimate nondiscriminatory purpose supported its decision. If the school board succeeds in convincing the court that discrimination was not a factor in its decision, the burden then reverts to the teacher to prove that the school board's action was simply a pretext for discrimination. This task is sometimes difficult because there has to be proof of intent to discriminate. In assessing discrimination cases, the court may consider past employment practices to determine if a pattern of discrimination is evident. A case in South Dakota illustrates such discrimination.

Table 12.1 Title VII of the Civil Rights Act of 1964 Charges, Fiscal Years 1997–2006

The following chart represents the total number of charge receipts filed and resolved under Title VII.

Receipts include all charges filed under Title VII as well as those filed concurrently under the ADA, ADEA, and/or EPA. The sum of receipts for all statutes will therefore exceed total charges received.

The data have been compiled by the Office of Research, Information, and Planning from EEOC's Charge Data System—quarterly reconciled data summary reports.

	FY 1997	FY 1998	FY 1999	FY 2000	FY 2001	FY 2002	FY 2003	FY 2004	FY 2005	FY 2006
Receipts	58,615	58,124	57,582	59,588	59,631	61,459	59,075	58,328	55,976	56,155
Resolutions	62,533	60,888	59,085	57,136	54,549	56,392	52,227	51,355	46,885	44,228
Resolutions by type										
Settlements	2,272	2,657	3,748	4,828	4,493	5,362	5,215	5,365	4,991	5,165
	3.6%	4.4%	6.3%	8.5%	8.2%	9.5%	10.0%	10.4%	10.6%	11.7%
Withdrawals w/benefits	1,924	1,767	2,084	2,251	2,201	2,188	2,188	2,151	2,405	2,373
	3.1%	2.9%	3.5%	3.9%	4.0%	3.9%	4.2%	4.2%	5.1%	5.4%
Administrative closures	17,405	16,114	14,265	11,439	10,766	9,791	9,225	8,563	7,255	7,143
	27.8%	26.5%	24.1%	20.0%	19.7%	17.4%	17.7%	16.7%	15.5%	16.2%
No reasonable cause	38,731	37,792	35,614	33,822	32,075	34,671	32,418	32,646	29,344	27,178
	61.9%	62.1%	60.3%	59.2%	58.8%	61.5%	62.1%	63.6%	62.6%	61.4%

(Continued)

Table 12.1 (Continued)

	FY 1997	FY 1998	FY 1999	FY 2000	FY 2001	FY 2002	FY 2003	FY 2004	FY 2005	FY 2006
Reasonable cause	2,201	2,558	3,374	4,796	5,014	4,380	3,181	2,630	2,890	2,426
	3.5%	4.2%	5.7%	8.4%	9.2%	7.8%	6.1%	5.1%	6.2%	5.5%
Successful conciliations	568	671	859	1,091	1,177	1,060	747	697	788	618
	0.9%	1.1%	1.5%	1.9%	2.2%	1.9%	1.4%	1.4%	1.7%	1.4%
Unsuccessful conciliations	1,633	1,887	2,515	3,705	3,837	3,320	2,434	1,933	2,102	1,808
	2.6%	3.1%	4.3%	6.5%	7.0%	5.9%	4.7%	3.8%	4.5%	4.1%
Merit resolutions	6,397	6,982	9,206	11,875	11,708	11,930	10,584	10,146	10,286	9,964
	10.2%	11.5%	15.6%	20.8%	21.5%	21.2%	20.3%	19.8%	21.9%	22.5%
Monetary benefits (millions)*	$88.7	$78.0	$113.1	$142.4	$141.1	$141.7	$138.7	$128.6	$146.0	$126.5

Source: The U.S. Equal Employment Opportunity Commission.

* Does not include monetary benefits obtained through litigation.

The total of individual percentages might not always sum to 100 percent due to rounding.

EEOC total workload includes charges carried over from previous fiscal years, new charge receipts, and charges transferred to EEOC from Fair Employment Practice Agencies (FEPAs). Resolution of charges each year may therefore exceed receipts for that year because the workload being resolved is drawn from a combination of pending, new receipts, and FEPA transfer charges rather than from new charges only.

A female South Dakota physical education teacher applied for a full-time middle school physical education teaching position. She had previously supervised both male and female students and had assisted a physically challenged male student change into a swimsuit for an adaptive physical education course. The job notice for the full-time position did not specify a gender preference, but the school district did not consider the female teacher's application. It hired a male who was not currently teaching, did not have a valid teaching certificate, and was not certified to teach swimming, perform CPR, or administer first aid. The female teacher had the certification and qualifications the male teacher lacked. She sued the school district in a federal district court for violating Title VII of the Civil Rights Act of 1964 and Title IX of the Education Amendments of 1972.

The court agreed with the district that gender-based discrimination is permitted if it is reasonably necessary to the normal operation of a school. However, an employer must have some basis in fact for believing that members of one sex cannot perform the job. The employer was required to establish that it could not reasonably arrange job responsibilities to minimize the clash between the privacy interests of students and the nondiscrimination rule of Title VII. The court noted a factual dispute over whether locker-room supervision made gender a bona fide occupational qualification of the full-time physical education teaching position. The job description was silent concerning gender, and the district admitted it did not communicate a male-only job requirement until after it employed a male. The court held that there was a factual dispute concerning the district's ability to rearrange job duties if it hired a female physical education teacher. As the evidence indicated, a balance of male and female physical education teachers was necessary, and opposite-sex staff occasionally supervised locker rooms. The court denied the district's motion for pretrial judgment.[1]

Teachers cannot be discriminated against for having filed a discrimination claim. They cannot be demoted or assigned difficult work assignments or placed in undesirable working environments based on having made discrimination claims. The courts are keenly concerned about decisions that affect school personnel subsequent to their having filed a discrimination suit.

Two other types of discrimination claims may be made by school personnel currently employed in a school district—*disparate treatment* and *disparate impact*. For example, an employee may claim disparate treatment if evidence reveals that he or she was treated differently based on race, color, religion, gender, or national origin than his or her colleagues regarding promotional opportunities, work conditions, or employment. For example, if there is a discernable trend toward promoting men over qualified women for certain leadership positions, an employee can claim gender discrimination. Disparate impact is a bit different. In impact allegations, the claim is made that employment policies or practices are racially neutral but have a disproportionate impact on certain groups. The policy or actions may not be outwardly discriminatory, but the effect results in discrimination against a group of employees (with respect to the protected categories referenced previously). The most common example might be the use of standardized examinations that negatively affect minorities more so than others. The burden rests with those who make a claim of discriminatory impact to prove that there is an intent to discriminate.

172. What Standard Must Be Met in Hiring Practices for Public Schools?

Hiring practices implemented by school officials must meet the standard of fundamental fairness, meaning that decisions should be unbiased and based on a thorough assessment of each candidate's qualifications for a particular position. Although the courts allow school officials to use observable subjective measures in assessing candidates, such as personal skills, speech, poise, and writing samples, districts should attempt to implement a system that relies as much as possible on objective measures, such as relevant degrees and certificates, years of experience, and undergraduate grade-point averages if applicable.

Issues should not be raised regarding age, birthplace, national origin, religious preference, marital status, number of children, preference for creating a family, spouse's profession, home ownership, or type of military discharge, as these issues should have no bearing on the employment decision. Questions should be standardized and specifically related to the position for which an applicant is applying, and they should be asked of all candidates. All prospective candidates have a right to expect fair treatment—a fair interview and assessment process—as employment decisions are reached. All efforts should be made to attract and maintain the most diverse and talented faculty and staff based on the most objective criteria that support the district's mission and values. Hiring standards should adhere not only to the equal protection provisions of the Fourteenth Amendment but also to federal statutes designed to protect individuals against discriminatory practices, namely Title VII, Title IX, the Age Discrimination Act, the Americans With Disabilities Act, the Rehabilitation Act, Section 504, the Equal Pay Act, the Pregnancy Discrimination Act, and other applicable federal and state statutes. Any measures used, such as standardized tests, should be thoroughly researched for evidence of culture or gender bias to ensure that they do not have a disparate impact on protected groups.

173. What Areas of Public School Operations Are Affected by Title IX?

Title IX defines and protects against gender-based discrimination. Title IX of the Education Amendments Act was passed in 1972 as a comprehensive federal law that prohibits discrimination on the basis of sex in any federally funded program or activity. The primary objective of Title IX is to ensure that federal funds are not used to support sexually discriminatory practices in education programs. Examples of sexually discriminatory practices include sexual harassment and employment discrimination. One component of the law states that "no person in the United States shall, on the basis of sex be excluded from participating in, be denied the benefits of, or be subjected to discrimination under any educational program or activity receiving federal assistance." The Office of Civil Rights (OCR) is the enforcement arm in the Department of Education. Since public schools are deemed educational institutions under the act and receive federal funds, they are subject to the requirements of the act.

Gender discrimination occurs in public schools when school boards only employ individuals of a certain gender to specific positions. For example, a common practice in the past was to employ only males in high school principalship positions, even though there were qualified female applicants. These actions were discriminatory and violated Title IX stipulations because women were summarily excluded from serious consideration for these secondary school leadership positions. School boards must ensure that personnel decisions are gender neutral and based on qualifications for specific employment positions rather than on the gender of each application. Title IX protects all individuals—males or females—against gender discrimination in employment decisions.

174. How Are Public Schools Affected by Racial Discrimination?

School personnel, as with other citizens of the United States, are protected against discriminatory practices based on race. The Fourteenth Amendment and civil rights statutes and regulations provide protection for racial minorities. Title VII is one of the leading statutes providing protection against discrimination based on race. School districts guilty of employment discrimination or unlawful employment practices will face challenges from the affected individuals.

Many plaintiffs file complaints with the Equal Employment Opportunity Commission (EEOC), which was established by Congress. The EEOC views discrimination broadly and addresses blatant acts of discrimination as well as more subtle forms that result in disparate impact. School districts run the risk of facing expensive lawsuits if the complaint is not resolved satisfactorily. An individual who claims racial discrimination under Title VII must file a complaint within 180 days following the alleged unlawful act by school boards or within 300 days if the individual has filed a claim with a state agency. It is important that these timetables are met, or the individual loses the legal standing to challenge the alleged act. (See Table 12.2 for statistical information relating to employment discrimination.)

Table 12.2 Race-Based Charges, Fiscal Years 1997–2006

The following chart represents the total number of charge receipts filed and resolved under Title VII alleging race-based discrimination.

The data have been compiled by the Office of Research, Information, and Planning from EEOC's Charge Data System—a national database.

	FY 1997	FY 1998	FY 1999	FY 2000	FY 2001	FY 2002	FY 2003	FY 2004	FY 2005	FY 2006
Receipts	29,199	28,820	28,819	28,945	28,912	29,910	28,526	27,696	26,740	27,238
Resolutions	36,419	35,716	35,094	33,188	32,077	33,199	30,702	29,631	27,411	25,992
Resolutions by type										
Settlements	1,206	1,460	2,138	2,802	2,549	3,059	2,890	2,927	2,801	3,039
	3.3%	4.1%	6.1%	8.4%	7.9%	9.2%	9.4%	9.9%	10.2%	11.7%
Withdrawals w/benefits	912	823	1,036	1,150	1,203	1,200	1,125	1,088	1,167	1,177
	2.5%	2.3%	3.0%	3.5%	3.8%	3.6%	3.7%	3.7%	4.3%	4.5%
Administrative closures	8,395	7,871	7,213	5,727	5,626	5,043	4,759	4,261	3,674	3,436
	23.1%	22.0%	20.6%	17.3%	17.5%	15.2%	15.5%	14.4%	13.4%	13.2%
No reasonable cause	24,988	24,515	23,148	21,319	20,302	21,853	20,506	20,166	18,608	17,324
	68.6%	68.6%	66.0%	64.2%	63.3%	65.8%	66.8%	68.1%	67.9%	66.7%
Reasonable cause	918	1,047	1,559	2,190	2,397	2,044	1,422	1,189	1,161	1,016
	2.5%	2.9%	4.4%	6.6%	7.5%	6.2%	4.6%	4.0%	4.2%	3.9%

	FY 1997	FY 1998	FY 1999	FY 2000	FY 2001	FY 2002	FY 2003	FY 2004	FY 2005	FY 2006
Successful conciliations	248	287	382	529	691	580	392	330	377	292
	0.7%	0.8%	1.1%	1.6%	2.2%	1.7%	1.3%	1.1%	1.4%	1.1%
Unsuccessful conciliations	670	760	1,177	1,661	1,706	1,464	1,030	859	784	724
	1.8%	2.1%	3.4%	5.0%	5.3%	4.4%	3.4%	2.9%	2.9%	2.8%
Merit resolutions	3,036	3,330	4,733	6,142	6,149	6,303	5,437	5,204	5,129	5,232
	8.3%	9.3%	13.5%	18.5%	19.2%	19.0%	17.7%	17.6%	18.7%	20.1%
Monetary benefits (millions)*	$41.8	$32.2	$53.2	$61.7	$86.5	$81.1	$69.6	$61.1	$76.5	$61.4

Source: The U.S. Equal Employment Opportunity Commission.

* Does not include monetary benefits obtained through litigation.

The total of individual percentages may not always sum to 100 percent due to rounding.

EEOC total workload includes charges carried over from previous fiscal years, new charge receipts, and charges transferred to EEOC from Fair Employment Practice Agencies (FEPAs). Resolution of charges each year may therefore exceed receipts for that year because the workload being resolved is drawn from a combination of pending, new receipts, and FEPA transfer charges rather than from new charges only.

Remedies for disparate treatment discrimination available under Title VII include compensatory damages, punitive damages, front pay, back pay, and reinstatement, as well as injunctive relief for attorneys' fees in certain circumstances. EEOC also has the prerogative to issue a "right to sue" order if a reasonable solution is not reached based on the allegation of racial discrimination. EEOC complaints resulting in lawsuits are expensive and time consuming. Additionally, they have the potential of casting a negative light on the district for wrongful or unlawful acts against minorities that might adversely affect the image the district wishes to convey to the public. However, racial discrimination is not a valid claim in the absence of acceptable performance, as was illustrated in a Missouri case.

For six years, an African American teacher received acceptable evaluations as a marketing education teacher at a Missouri alternative high school. An assistant principal then expressed concerns about her teaching, communications, and classroom management skills. The following year, he reprimanded the teacher for swearing at a student and using a person's income tax form for instructional purposes without consent. The teacher was placed on an improvement plan designed to address her deficiencies. She was again reprimanded for denigrating students and using profanity. The teacher received another performance improvement plan and was transferred to a newly created business education teaching position. The school board hired a white employee to fill her former position. The teacher filed a grievance challenging the action, followed by a race discrimination complaint. The assistant principal reprimanded the teacher again for cursing in class and for tape-recording her class after being instructed not to do so. The board issued her a notice of deficiency, alleging incompetency, inefficiency, and insubordination. The notice also indicated that the teacher's conduct reflected a mental condition that rendered her unfit to instruct or associate with children. The board allowed the teacher five months to correct her deficiencies. At her request, a three-member team evaluated her performance. The evaluators all expressed strong concerns, and each recommended discharge. After a hearing, the board discharged the teacher. She sued the district and school officials in a federal district court for employment discrimination and retaliation.

The court awarded summary judgment to the district and officials. The teacher appealed. The U.S. Court of Appeals, Eighth Circuit, held that the teacher's case quickly unraveled because she failed to demonstrate that the board's legitimate expectations were met. While she claimed her teaching ability far exceeded that of any other teacher at her school, there was no evidence presented to support the claim. Instead, there was evidence of poor evaluations and failure to cure serious and repeated deficiencies. Even under known scrutiny and with five additional months to improve, the teacher's performance was unacceptable. Evaluators had found serious deficiencies in her relationships with students and an inability to structure lessons. They found that the teacher's instruction was harming students due to her negativity. One evaluator indicated that she was probably the worst teacher he had ever observed. The teacher's denial of this evidence was insufficient to allow her to proceed with legal claims. The board had legitimate, nondiscriminatory reasons for discharging her, and the judgment for the district was affirmed.[2]

175. What Safeguards Are Provided to Teachers Regarding Religious Discrimination?

Teachers receive religious discrimination coverage under Title VII. They cannot be discriminated against in employment decisions, compensation, and fringe benefits for religious reasons. Admittedly, it may be difficult for teachers to prove discrimination charges based on religion because very rarely, if ever, will there be direct evidence of discrimination. Since employment decisions are generally reached based on who is considered to be most qualified, it is difficult to prove that religion was a factor in not being offered a position. Additionally, other subjective factors are often relied upon in addition to an individual's credentials. It is unlawful to seek information regarding an applicant's religious beliefs or affiliations. The burden of proof for religious discrimination resides with the individual who brings the charge. In most cases, it is a difficult task; however, challenges do occur, as illustrated in Table 12.3.

Once individuals are employed, school officials must determine reasonable accommodations for their religious affiliations. Personal leave should be granted for religious observances or to attend conferences as long as leaves are not excessive, create minimal disruption to the teaching and learning process, and result in minimal hardship to school officials. The burden of proof rests with school boards to demonstrate that an undue hardship exists. Flexibility is required to accommodate the religious rights of personnel such as making adjustments in class scheduling, allowing school personnel sufficient time to support their religious activities, identifying qualified substitutes, and employing other measures that do not create an undue hardship for either the teacher or school officials.

A religious conflict arose in Connecticut. A Connecticut high school teacher belonged to a church that required members to refrain from secular employment during designated holy days, requiring him to miss approximately six school days each year for religious purposes. The district's collective bargaining agreement allowed only three days of paid leave for religious observation. The agreement also allowed three days paid leave for necessary personal business, which, the district said, could not be used for religious purposes. The teacher repeatedly requested permission to use three days of his necessary personal business leave for religious purposes. He also offered to reimburse the salary of a substitute teacher if the school board would compensate him for the extra days he

Table 12.3   Religion-Based Charges, Fiscal Years 1997–2006

The following chart represents the total number of charge receipts filed and resolved under Title VII alleging religion-based discrimination.

The data have been compiled by the Office of Research, Information, and Planning from EEOC's Charge Data System—a national database.

	FY 1997	FY 1998	FY 1999	FY 2000	FY 2001	FY 2002	FY 2003	FY 2004	FY 2005	FY 2006
Receipts	1,709	1,786	1,811	1,939	2,127	2,572	2,532	2,466	2,340	2,541
Resolutions	2,137	2,247	2,187	2,230	2,217	2,729	2,690	2,676	2,352	2,387
Resolutions by type										
Settlements	89	97	144	156	182	237	221	241	227	244
	4.2%	4.3%	6.6%	7.0%	8.2%	8.7%	8.2%	9.0%	9.7%	10.2%
Withdrawals w/benefits	74	81	87	94	77	100	86	101	98	118
	3.5%	3.6%	4.0%	4.2%	3.5%	3.7%	3.2%	3.8%	4.2%	4.9%
Administrative closures	614	559	532	429	382	451	434	490	384	364
	28.7%	24.9%	24.3%	19.2%	17.2%	16.5%	16.1%	18.3%	16.3%	15.2%
No reasonable cause	1,265	1,363	1,269	1,343	1,349	1,729	1,744	1,672	1,442	1,524
	59.2%	60.7%	58.0%	60.2%	60.8%	63.4%	64.8%	62.5%	61.3%	63.8%
Reasonable cause	95	147	155	208	227	212	205	172	201	137
	4.4%	6.5%	7.1%	9.3%	10.2%	7.8%	7.6%	6.4%	8.5%	5.7%

	FY 1997	FY 1998	FY 1999	FY 2000	FY 2001	FY 2002	FY 2003	FY 2004	FY 2005	FY 2006
Successful conciliations	32	42	42	56	43	54	67	38	36	38
	1.5%	1.9%	1.9%	2.5%	1.9%	2.0%	2.5%	1.4%	1.5%	1.6%
Unsuccessful conciliations	63	105	113	152	184	158	138	134	165	99
	2.9%	4.7%	5.2%	6.8%	8.3%	5.8%	5.1%	5.0%	7.0%	4.1%
Merit resolutions	258	325	386	458	486	549	512	514	526	499
	12.1%	14.5%	17.7%	20.5%	21.9%	20.1%	19.0%	19.2%	22.4%	20.9%
Monetary benefits (millions)*	$2.2	$2.6	$3.1	$5.5	$14.1	$4.3	$6.6	$6.0	$6.1	$5.7

Source: The U.S. Equal Employment Opportunity Commission.

* Does not include monetary benefits obtained through litigation.

The total of individual percentages may not always sum to 100 percent due to rounding.

EEOC total workload includes charges carried over from previous fiscal years, new charge receipts, and charges transferred to EEOC from Fair Employment Practice Agencies (FEPAs). Resolution of charges each year may therefore exceed receipts for that year because the workload being resolved is drawn from a combination of pending, new receipts, and FEPA transfer charges rather than from new charges only.

missed. The board rejected his offer, and the teacher filed a lawsuit alleging that the board's policy regarding necessary personal business leave was discriminatory on the basis of religion.

The Second Circuit held that the board was required to accept one of the teacher's proposed solutions unless that accommodation created undue hardship on the employer's conduct of business. On appeal, the U.S. Supreme Court modified the decision. It held that the district did not need to accept the teacher's proposals, even if acceptance would not result in undue hardship. The board was only bound to offer a fair and reasonable accommodation for the teacher's religious needs. However, the collective bargaining agreement regarding the additional days of necessary personal business leave would not be reasonable if that paid leave provided for all purposes except religious ones. Because the lower courts had not decided whether the necessary personal business leave policy had been administered fairly, the Supreme Court remanded the case for resolution of that question.[3] On remand, the Second Circuit held that the accommodation was reasonable.[4]

176. What Protections Do Female Teachers Have Regarding Childbirth and Employment?

The Pregnancy Discrimination Act of 1978 (P.L. 95-555) is an amendment to Title VII and protects pregnant employees from any form of discrimination due to pregnancy. Prior to the enactment of P.L. 95-555, school officials exercised complete authority over pregnancy leave and determined when the teacher could return to her position. Female employees were sometimes forced to accept assignments in a different school. They were also required to provide notice as soon as pregnancy was established and required to accept leave at an arbitrary time determined by the school board, irrespective of the teacher's physical abilities.

This practice changed with the passage of the Pregnancy Discrimination Act. The authority shifted from the school board to the attending physician in determining when the teacher should leave her position and when she is physically able to return. The physician also prescribes the activities the teacher can engage in during pregnancy and those she should not perform. The Pregnancy Act prohibits female employees from being denied employment, being dismissed, or being denied promotions based on pregnancy. Female employees must be allowed to utilize sick leave just as other employees do for medical reasons. Thus, pregnancy under the statute must be treated as a temporary condition that allows female employees to receive sick leave and insurance coverage just as other employees do with temporary illnesses. The act covers pregnancy, childbirth, and other related medical conditions. The courts have been quite consistent in supporting female employees.

Unlawful practices regarding pregnancy can be illustrated by a case that arose in Maine. A Maine school district employed a teacher on a probationary basis after she served as a long-term substitute for most of one year. Although she experienced classroom management issues, her performance improved during the year, and she received a second probationary contract. When the teacher received the second contract, she was pregnant. She missed the first weeks of her second probationary year due to her pregnancy. Upon resuming her duties, she received a poor evaluation due to her messy and disorganized classroom. The teacher demonstrated improvement during the year and eventually received recommendations for a continuing contract. She had become pregnant again during her second probationary year, asserting that she was visibly pregnant when the school board voted not to award her a continuing contract. Without explanation, the board replaced her with a teacher who was not pregnant.

The teacher sued the district in a state court. The case was removed to a federal district court, which applied the same legal standard to the Maine Human Rights Act and pregnancy discrimination claims under Title VII. Title VII prevents an employer from discharging an employee on the categorical fact of her pregnancy or in retaliation for taking an authorized maternity leave. The board asserted, however, that the teacher was not effective enough to deserve tenure, even though the principal and superintendent had given her good evaluations when her case was presented for review. Two of the board members who had voted against tenure alleged that they were unaware of her pregnancy; however, one of them had had contact with her frequently at a time when the signs of her advancing pregnancy were unmistakable. In tenure denial cases involving alleged poor performance, employees can avoid summary judgment by demonstrating that an employer's stated reason for denying tenure is only a pretext. The teacher pointed out inconsistencies and weaknesses in the statements of four board members and established a financial motive for her termination. The court denied summary judgment to the board, finding that the teacher had produced sufficient evidence of false justifications for denying her tenure to make a trial necessary.[5]

177. Must Public School Teachers Retire at a Mandatory Age?

No, school personnel are not required to retire at a designated age and may continue in their employment position as long as their performance meets prescribed standards. Prior to the passage of the Age Discrimination in Employment Act (ADEA), teachers were forced to retire when they reached the retirement age specified by their state. Courts were inconsistent in their rulings regarding mandatory retirements prior to the passage of the act, with some courts supporting mandatory retirement and others opposing it. The passage of the act brought clarity to issues regarding retirement. The courts will, however, support mandatory retirement for positions where rigorous physical demands are required and public safety is jeopardized, such as police officers, airline pilots, and firefighters.

ADEA was passed in 1967 and amended in 1978. It essentially prohibits forced retirements by providing protection against discriminatory practices against employees over forty years old. The act includes hiring, dismissal, compensation, and other terms and conditions of employment. The amended law in 1978 raised the retirement limit to age seventy. An amended act in 1986 removed the limit altogether with the exception of certain public safety positions. Teachers, administrators, and other public school employees are covered under the act. Teachers' contracts may not be terminated based solely on age.

An age discrimination disparate impact case arose in Mississippi when a city increased all employee salaries in 1999. Those with less than five years of experience received comparatively higher raises than did more seasoned employees. The city justified the action as a means to remain competitive and ensure equitable compensation to all employees. A group of veteran police officers, most over forty years old, claimed that the city's action constituted discrimination on the basis of age. The officers sued the city in a federal district court for ADEA violations, alleging disparate treatment and disparate impact. The court held for the city. The U.S. Court of Appeals, Fifth Circuit, affirmed the judgment, finding that ADEA does not recognize disparate impact claims; however, the officers could proceed with intentional discrimination claims. The Supreme Court agreed to review the disparate impact claim. It compared ADEA with Title VII of the Civil Rights Act of 1964. Except for the substitution of the word "age" for "race, color, religion, sex or national origin," ADEA and Title VII language is identical. Title VII disparate impact claims have long been recognized by the High Court.

The High Court stated that ADEA authorizes potential recovery for disparate impact cases in a manner comparable with Title VII disparate impact claims for race, religion, or sex discrimination. Employees alleging that an employer practice has a disparate impact on a class of employees need not demonstrate that the practice is intentional. Although the High Court held that the officers were entitled to submit a disparate impact claim under ADEA, they could not demonstrate that the city violated ADEA in this case. The High Court noted ADEA's coverage for disparate impact is narrower than that for Title VII. Under ADEA, an employer can treat workers differently if the employer is motivated by reasonable factors other than age. The High Court found that Congress had narrowed ADEA's scope because there is often a connection between age and ability to perform a job. The High Court agreed with the city that the decision to make itself competitive in the job market was based on a reasonable factor other than age. Because the city's goal was to raise employee salaries to be competitive, the employees could not prove that the increase had a disparate impact. The High Court affirmed the judgment for the city.[6]

178. What Should Teachers Know About Sexual Harassment?

Sexual harassment was not included in Title VII of the Civil Rights Act of 1964 until 1980. Harassment is considered to be a form of sexual discrimination. It may be present in many forms, from verbal statements and gestures to overt behavior. The victim, as well as the harasser, may be male or female and not necessarily of the opposite sex. Economic injury is not required to file a successful case of harassment against a supervisor.

There are various levels of verbal harassment behavior, including making personal inquiries of a sexual nature, offering sexual comments regarding a person's anatomy or clothing, and repeatedly requesting dates and refusing to accept "no" as an answer. Nonverbal harassment includes prolonged staring at another person, presenting personal gifts without cause, throwing kisses, making various sexual gestures, or posting sexually suggestive cartoons or pictures.

EEOC guidelines address two types of sexual harassment: *quid pro quo* and *non–quid pro quo*. In *quid pro quo* harassment, an employee exchanges sexual favors for job benefits, promotion, or continued employment. In *non–quid pro quo* or hostile environments, the employee is subjected to a sexually hostile work environment that may affect the employee's well-being and has a negative impact on job performance.

The more serious levels of harassment involve sexual coercion or unwanted physical relations. When this behavior is *quid pro quo*, it is most commonly associated with superior-subordinate relationships in which the victim, for fear of reprisal, unwillingly participates. The supervisor has the capacity to refuse to hire, promote, or grant certain privileges based on his or her position. In some cases, the promise of some job-related benefit is offered in exchange for sexual favors.

A different level of harassment involves unwanted touching of another's hair, clothing, or body. Undesirable acts involving hugging, kissing, stroking, patting, and massaging one's neck or shoulders are examples of physical harassment that contribute to a hostile work environment. Verbal harassment may include off-the-cuff comments such as referring to a female as babe, honey, or sweetheart or turning work discussions into sexual discussions.

Each of these levels represents a serious form of sexual discrimination for which the victim may recover damages. The burden resides with the victim, however, to convey to the abuser that the harassment is unwanted. Once established, the harasser has an obligation to discontinue the undesirable behavior immediately. Failure to do so may create a hostile work environment resulting in sexual harassment charges by the victim. Sexual harassment claims are sometimes difficult for the victim to prove. In many instances, embarrassing and graphic details must be revealed that are often denied by the person(s) against whom charges are being made.

Victims of various forms of discrimination have been awarded monetary damages that have increased significantly in recent years.

The definition of harassment, under the act, is sufficiently broad to allow coverage of most forms of unacceptable behavior. Any type of sexual behavior that is unwanted or unwelcomed is considered covered under the act. The regulation defines sexual harassment in the following manner:

> Unwelcomed sexual advances, requests for sexual favors and other verbal or physical contact of a sexual nature constitute sexual harassment when (1) submission to such conduct is made either explicitly or implicitly as a term or condition of an individual's employment, (2) submission to or rejection of such conduct by an individual is used as the basis for employment decisions affecting such individuals, or (3) such conduct has the purpose or effect of unreasonably interfering with an individual's work performance or creating an intimidating, hostile or offensive working environment.[7]

Legally, employees cannot be denied promotions or other benefits for unwillingness to accept sexual advances by their superiors. They also cannot be subjected to hostile, unfriendly working environments by superiors or peers. Under the Civil Rights Act, every person is entitled to an environment free from unwelcomed sexual conduct.

A landmark case involving sexual harassment arose in the private sector when a female bank employee filed action against the bank and her supervisor. The employee alleged that she had been subjected to sexual harassment by her supervisor during her employment, in violation of Title VII. The supervisor's contention was that the sexual relationship was consensual and had no bearing on the employee's continued employment. The bank indicated that it had no knowledge or notification about the allegation and therefore could not be held liable.

The Supreme Court in a landmark ruling on the case, *Meritor Savings Bank v. Vinson*, held that unwelcomed sexual advances that create an offensive or hostile work environment violate Title VII.[8] It further held that, although employers are not automatically liable for sexual harassment committed by their employees, lack of awareness does not automatically protect the employers from liability charges.

This ruling was significant because it set the stage for sexual harassment cases by defining the specific acts that fall within harassment. The U.S. Supreme Court held that Title VII guidelines are not limited to economic or tangible injuries. Harassment that leads to noneconomic injury can also violate Title VII. The High Court considered the claim that sexual activity was voluntary to be without merit. The litmus test, according to the High Court, was whether such advances were unwelcomed.

The implications derived from this case suggest that employers can be held liable for acts of sexual harassment by employees when the employer knew or should have known about the undesirable conduct. Failure to take decisive action can thus result in liability charges against the employer in known or suspected cases of harassment.

179. How Does the Americans with Disabilities Act and the Rehabilitation Act, Section 504, Affect Public Schools?

The Americans with Disabilities Act (ADA) and the Rehabilitation Act, Section 504, impact the operation of public schools because both federal statutes prohibit disability-based discrimination. A person is disabled under ADA who has a physical or mental impairment that substantially limits a major life activity, has a past record of such an impairment, or is regarded by others as having such an impairment.[9]

An employee is qualified under ADA if, with or without reasonable accommodations, he or she can perform the essential functions of the employment position. The act prohibits individuals with disabilities from being denied an employment position because of tasks not essential to the core function of the position sought. If necessary, reasonable accommodations should be made by the employer to enable an employee with disabilities to perform his or her job responsibilities. Accommodations may include ready access to the facility, job restructuring, modified schedules, and acquisition of equipment or devices. An employer may be exempt if an undue hardship exists involving the overall financial resources of the entity, the type of operation, the size of the business and number of employees, the type and location of facilities, and the effect on the resources of the facility. The burden of proof to demonstrate undue hardship resides with the employer. The ADA Amendments Act of 2008 made important changes to the definition of the term "disability." The amended act became effective January 1, 2009.

Section 504 protects disabled individuals of all ages against discrimination in numerous programs and activities that receive federal financial assistance. Section 504 requires an absence of discrimination and is not an affirmative action act. The law states that no "otherwise qualified individual with a disability . . . shall . . . be excluded from participation in, denied the benefits of or subjected to discrimination under any program or activity receiving federal financial assistance." School districts are subject to the requirements of this act since they are the recipients of federal funds. The Office of Civil Rights is the agency with which complaints of this nature are filed.

180. Does the Family and Medical Leave Act (FMLA) Apply to Public Schools?

Yes. The Family and Medical Leave Act (FMLA) was passed by Congress in 1993. It is designed to allow eligible employees up to a total of twelve work weeks of unpaid leave during any twelve-month period for one or more of the following reasons:

- Birth and care of the newborn child of the employee
- Placement with the employee of a son or daughter for adoption or foster care
- Care for an immediate family member (spouse, child, or parent) with a serious health condition
- When the employee is unable to work because of a serious health condition

Employers with fifty or more employees are covered by this act. An eligible employee is one who has been employed for at least twelve months or for at least 1,250 hours over the previous twelve months. The law permits the employee to choose to use accrued paid leave or the employer to require the employee to use accrued paid leave, such as vacation or sick leave, for some or all of the FLMA leave period. When paid leave is substituted for unpaid FMLA leave, it can be counted against the twelve-week FMLA leave entitlement if the employer is properly notified of the designation when the leave begins.

An employer can ask the employee questions to confirm whether the leave qualifies for FMLA purposes. Periodic reports regarding the employee's status and intent to return to work after leave are also permissible under the act. If an employer wishes to obtain another opinion, the affected employee may be required to secure additional medical certification at the employer's expense.

Summary of Relevant Court Cases Involving Discrimination

- The U.S. Court of Appeals, Fifth Circuit, held that a Mississippi school board did not discriminate against a fifty-seven-year-old African American female applicant by hiring a "young white female" for a principal's position. The applicant did not perform well in her interview, and she did not prove that the board's use of the interview was discriminatory. The board used standardized questions for the interviews and selected the candidate who received the highest score. The court held that the board's decision was based on a legitimate, nondiscriminatory reason. It rejected the applicant's claim that the board ignored all her objective qualifications and relied instead on a subjective interview.[10]

- In 1998, the Supreme Court held that Title VII is violated if an employee is exposed to disadvantageous terms or conditions of employment to which members of the other sex are not exposed. In *Burlington Industries, Inc. v. Ellerth*[11] and *Faragher v. City of Boca Raton*,[12] the court held that Title VII may impose vicarious liability on employers for sexual harassment committed by their supervisors. However, where no adverse employment action (such as discharge or demotion) occurs, an affirmative defense is available. In other words, the employer may be able to avoid liability by demonstrating that reasonable care was taken to prevent and promptly correct any sexual harassment and that the employee unreasonably failed to avail himself or herself of any employer remedies or to otherwise avoid harm.

- The Seventh Circuit stated that homosexuals do not enjoy a heightened level of constitutional protection. Title VII does not provide a private right of action based on sexual orientation discrimination, and there is no remedy under 42 U.S.C. § 1983 for sexual orientation discrimination based on rights created under Title VII.[13]

Summary Guides

1. Employees can rely on the U.S. Constitution and various civil rights laws for protection against discrimination based on race, color, national origin, gender, age, religion, and disability.

2. Title VII is one of the most significant and comprehensive statutes that affects employment discrimination.

3. The U.S. Supreme Court developed a three-step procedure for Title VII challenges.
   a. The plaintiff carries the initial burden of establishing discrimination.
   b. The defendant refutes the claim of discrimination by demonstrating that a legitimate nondiscriminatory purpose existed for the action.
   c. The burden reverts to the plaintiff to prove that the defendant's explanation was only a pretext for discrimination.

4. Valid and reliable standardized tests can be used if it is demonstrated that they serve a legitimate employment purpose.

5. Disparate impact is an unintentional employment practice that affects a protected class of employees, even though the practice was facially neutral and not intended to be discriminatory.

(Continued)

(Continued)

6. Disparate treatment involves facial discrimination claims where it is alleged that an employee was treated differently than other employees based on any of the protected categories included in Title VII.

7. Employers guilty of employment discrimination can be assessed compensatory damages or punitive damages and can be required to discontinue certain practices deemed to be discriminatory.

8. Pregnancy-related conditions must be treated as any other temporary disability.

9. Pregnant employees cannot be required to take leaves of absence at a time determined by the board or return at a designated time. Only the employee's physician is allowed to make this determination.

10. No female can be discriminated against based on pregnancy with respect to employment, promotion, leave, or other terms and conditions of employment.

11. With the exception of certain employment positions that require a level of skill and agility related to public safety, no employee can be required to take mandatory retirement. If the employee continues to perform job duties responsibly, he or she may continue employment.

12. Age discrimination claims are available for employees who are forty years old or older based on the Age Discrimination in Employment Act.

13. Reasonable religious accommodations must be provided as long as they do not create significant disruption to the teaching and learning process.

14. Sexual harassment is discrimination and is defined as unwelcomed sexual behavior that creates a hostile working environment. Remedies are available under Title VII for employees who exercise a loss of tangible benefits.

15. The Americans with Disabilities Act and the Rehabilitation Act, Section 504, prohibit disability-based discrimination. Reasonable accommodations must be made to meet the needs of employees with disabilities. Injunctive relief and monetary damages are available for victims of disability-based discrimination.

NOTES

1. *McCardle v. Mitchell School Dist.*, No. Civ. 03-4092-KES, 2005 WL 1118154 (D.S.D. 2005).

2. *Shanklin v. Fitzgerald*, 397 F.3d 596 (8th Cir. 2005).

3. *Ansonia Board of Educ. v. Philbrook*, 479 U.S. 60, 107 S.Ct. 367, 93 L. Ed. 2d 305 9 (1986).

4. *Philbrook v. Ansonia Board of Educ.*, 925 F.2d 47 (2d Cir. 1991).

5. *Johnson v. School Union No. 107,* 295 F. Supp. 2d 106 (D. Me. 2003).

6. *Smith v. City of Jackson,* 544 U.S. 228 (U.S. 2005).

7. 29 C.F.R. § 1604.11(a) (1991).

8. *Meritor Savings Bank v. Vinson,* 106 S.Ct. 2399 (1986).

9. § 111. A. 1.

10. *Todd v. Natchez-Adams School Dist.,* No. 05-60239, 2005 WL 3525596, 160 Fed. Appx. 377 (5th Cir. 2005).

11. *Burlington Industries, Inc. v. Ellerth,* 524 U.S. 742 (1998).

12. *Faragher v. City of Boca Raton,* 524 U.S. 775 (1998).

13. *Schroeder v. Hamilton School District,* 282 F.3d 946 (7th Cir. 2002).

13

Collective Negotiations

⚏ INTRODUCTION ⚏

Collective bargaining, despite its controversial nature, has become increasingly popular in public education. It has not always enjoyed the popularity it does today. In the early mid-twentieth century, collective bargaining, for the most part, was viewed as an illegal activity, with very few state statutes supporting it. It slowly gained support during the last century. The courts were hesitant to become involved in matters regarding negotiations and virtually relegated it to the states by suggesting that school boards could engage in collective bargaining. Visibly absent was any requirement that school boards actually do so. As teachers' rights became more prevalent, teachers desired a greater role in the administration of schools through consultation on major decisions affecting the management and operation of schools. Additionally, teachers became increasingly concerned with the terms and conditions of employment as well as compensation issues. These factors along with others provided impetus for the introduction of collective bargaining into public schools. Currently, most states have adopted some form of negotiation, ranging from meet-and-confer provisions to full-fledged bargaining.

The range of negotiable items varies among the states according to state law. In addition, some states require arbitration, whereas others prohibit it. A number of states have passed laws supporting union membership for teachers and prohibiting school boards from initiating arbitrary and capricious actions, such as demotions, unwarranted transfers, and even dismissals, against teachers who participate in union activities. Central to all state statutes is the requirement that school boards bargain in good faith with recognized unions. Good faith, as applied to collective negotiations, infers that school boards enter into the bargaining process with a genuine intent to reach a reasonable agreement within the parameters in which the board operates.

181. Do Public School Teachers Have Advantages in Public Sector Bargaining Over Individuals Involved in Private Sector Bargaining?

Probably not. There are advantages and disadvantages associated with both. On the private side, employees are protected by the National Labor Relations Act (NLRA) or the Wagner Act, which defined the right of private employees to organize and bargain collectively. Additionally, employees' rights are safeguarded to ensure that unfair labor practices cannot be employed. NLRA also makes sure that, to the greatest degree possible, negotiations meet good faith requirements. Private-sector bargaining is not constrained by state laws that do not permit bargaining per se but allow for some type of meet-and-confer requirement, as is the case for public schools. In the public sector, one major advantage enjoyed by public school employees is possessing constitutional rights not found in the private sector. Public school employees can readily seek court intervention after exhausting district remedies if there is a view that constitutional rights have been violated.

Private employees by and large are able to initiate strikes, whereas public school employees in thirty-seven states cannot do so. Many proponents of strikes view the inability to strike as a major limitation that limits the scope of public-sector negotiations. School personnel, based on state law, can be terminated for participating in an illegal strike. School districts also rely on the state for funding purposes; therefore, negotiations involving compensation are restricted based on the ability of school officials to generate desired compensation. Teachers possess a constitutional right to join a union under freedom of association rights; however, they may or may not be permitted to engage in collective bargaining based on state law. Last, some states do not permit school leadership personnel to participate in a union in which their supervised personnel hold membership.

182. Can Teachers Be Assessed Union Fees Even if They Are Not Members of a Recognized Union?

Yes. Many states, in fact, have laws that support the agency shop concept. Under an agency shop, teachers must be union members in good standing, meaning that they must pay dues as a condition of employment. In a leading U.S. Supreme Court decision in Michigan, the court held in *Abood v. Detroit Board of Education*[1] that an agency shop does not violate nonunion employees' constitutional rights unless their fees are used to support objectionable political activities.

In that case, two months prior to the effective date of the agency shop clause in Michigan, a group of teachers filed a class-action lawsuit in a state court against the school board, the union, and its officials. They stated that they had refused to pay dues based on their opposition to public-sector collective bargaining and the union's political activities unrelated to collective bargaining. They further challenged the constitutionality of the agency shop requirement. Michigan state law was requiring every teacher who was not affiliated within sixty days of employment to remit to the union an amount equivalent to regular dues or to face termination. The teachers petitioned the court to declare the agency shop requirement unconstitutional based on their freedom of association rights guaranteed by the First and Fourteenth amendments. The U.S. Supreme Court held for the state and its officers in stating that such a requirement was constitutional, acknowledging that this same practice had been upheld previously in private-sector labor relations. The theory supporting the ruling stated that all employees benefited from the union's advocacy and therefore should defray union expenses related to negotiations.

In a later case, *Chicago Teachers Union Local No. 1 v. Hudson,*[2] the court addressed fair procedures regarding the collection of agency fees from nonmembers. The court held that an explanation must be provided regarding the basis for the union fees and that nonmembers should have an opportunity to challenge the amount of the fees assessed and an escrow for the disputed amounts while the challenge is pending.

183. Do Teachers Have a Constitutional Right to Join a Union and Engage in Collective Bargaining?

Yes and no. Yes, teachers have the right to join a union. Courts have been fairly consistent in supporting teachers' right to organize. In an early case, *Atkins v. City of Charlotte,*[3] a court held that a state law prohibiting public employees from joining a union violated the First and Fourteenth amendments to the

U.S. Constitution. In *McLaughlin v. Tilendis*, the Seventh Circuit held that the First Amendment prohibits any state from disallowing its teachers from joining a union or dismissing those who join. The court stated:

> It is settled that teachers have the right of free association, and unjustified interference with teachers' associational freedom violates their constitutional rights. Public employment may not be subjected to unreasonable conditions, and the assertion of First Amendment rights by teachers will usually not warrant their dismissal. Unless there is some illegal intent, an individual's right to form and join a union is protected by the First Amendment.[4]

However, teachers have no inherent constitutional right to engage in bargaining, unless it is permitted by state law. The right to bargain is thus a state function. Most states have passed legislation providing for some form of bargaining for teachers, ranging from meet-and-confer conferencing to full-fledged bargaining. However, in the absence of state statute, teachers are not allowed to bargain collectively, a situation first established in *Commonwealth v. County Board of Arlington County*.[5] Any negotiated contest between a teacher's organization and a school board is consequently without merit in the absence of permissive legislation.

184. How Does the Scope of Collective Bargaining in Public Schools Impact the Negotiations Process?

The scope of collective bargaining refers to the range of negotiable issues determined by state laws. In other words, these laws essentially determine what items are negotiable. There are typically three categories of negotiations that affect public schools:

1. *Mandatory:* These generally include items such as compensation, teaching load, extra-duty assignments, fringe benefits, and other terms/conditions of employment. There are often conflicts regarding what items are mandatory, which ultimately can reach the courts for resolution. Both parties must bargain in good faith regarding mandatory items.

   A challenge arose in South Dakota regarding items that constituted mandatory bargaining. The court held that the school calendar could not be converted into a negotiable item. The state supreme court held that the calendar was a matter of general public interest that affected the community and was an inherently managerial subject that could not be bargained over. The court observed that the state law mandated that all parties involved in a collective bargaining agreement negotiate over wages, hours of employment, and other conditions of employment. To determine whether an issue could be the subject of mandatory negotiation in public employment, the court was required to balance competing interests by considering the extent to which collective bargaining would impair the determination of government policy.

The court held that requiring the board to negotiate the school calendar would significantly interfere with the exercise of its inherent management prerogatives. Most other jurisdictions that had addressed the issue had held that the school calendar is an inherently managerial subject and not a mandatory topic of negotiation. The school calendar affects teachers, other school employees, students, parents, taxpayers, other school districts, and entire communities. The calendar is thus a matter of general public interest that requires basic judgments regarding how government can best educate students. If the employee association was allowed to bargain the issue, none of the other community interests would be represented.[6]

2. *Permissive:* These generally include items resulting from a common agreement between both parties. Because these items are based on common agreement, there is no breach if there is disagreement between the two parties. There is also no suggestion that there is a failure to bargain in good faith based on the nature of the mutual agreement. Permissive items can include but are not limited to personnel recruitment, selection, and induction.

3. *Illegal subjects:* These items are those that exceed the school board's power to negotiate. For example, school boards are policymaking bodies; therefore, they cannot legally delegate their primary responsibility to others. Decisions involving teacher evaluation, dismissal, and transfer also cannot be delegated.

185. Are Teachers Allowed to Strike if Negotiations Reach an Impasse?

It depends on where they teach. Teachers in thirty-seven states are provided a statutorily limited right to strike provided that they have followed their state's procedures for resolving an impasse. They must also inform their school board of the intent to strike. The following thirteen states permit strikes: Alaska, California, Colorado, Hawaii, Illinois, Louisiana, Minnesota, Montana, Ohio, Oregon, Pennsylvania, Vermont, and Wisconsin. There are statutory conditions that must be met in these thirteen states prior to initiating a strike. The conditions normally include the steps involved when negotiations reach an impasse. In the thirty-seven states, when no-strike laws were challenged, courts have been quite consistent in upholding them. For example, serious penalties have been imposed in states like Georgia, Tennessee, and North Carolina. Even though not legally sanctioned, districts in states like Indiana, Michigan, and Massachusetts have initiated illegal strikes.

An impasse is reached when there is a breakdown in negotiations resulting in failure to reach an agreement and neither party is willing to compromise. When parties reach an impasse, a dispute resolution process is often employed. It includes the following:

- *Mediation:* involves a neutral person who will attempt to assist both parties reach a resolution. The mediator is generally chosen by mutual agreement between both parties involved in the negotiation process. If mediation does not achieve resolution, the second option is to engage a fact finder.
- *Fact Finder:* also a third, neutral party who has the responsibility of investigating the courses of the dispute and generating proposed solutions. These proposed solutions are not binding. If fact finding fails to resolve the impasse, the third option is to engage an arbitrator.
- *Arbitrator:* performs similar functions as those associated with the fact finder. The essential difference between fact finding and arbitration is that in many instances the arbitration is binding, which means that both parties are obligated to execute the agreement.

Summary of Court Rulings Regarding Collective Negotiations

- The Supreme Court of Rhode Island upheld a lower court contempt order against a teacher for failure to obey an order to report to class.[7]

- The Michigan Supreme Court held that early retirement benefits are not considered to be wages or salaries; therefore, the school board has the authority to include retirements in the collective bargaining agreement.[8]

- A New York court upheld a school board authority to impose economic sanctions against teachers who go on strike.[9]

- The North Dakota Supreme Court identified five mandatory subjects that include salary, hours, a binding arbitration agreement, formulating an agreement, and an interpretation of an existing agreement.[10]

Summary Guides

1. State statutes determine the scope of public-sector bargaining.

2. School boards are required to bargain in good faith with teacher unions regarding terms and conditions of employment.

3. Public school employees have constitutional rights regarding collective bargaining that are not afforded private-sector employees.

4. The National Labor Relations Board (NLRA) defines the rights of private-sector employees.

5. Private-sector employees can initiate strikes that may or may not be initiated by public school employees.

6. Compensation issues are somewhat restricted in public school bargaining based on the funding provided by the states.

7. Teachers possess a constitutional right to join a union.

8. School leadership personnel typically cannot affiliate with the same union to which their teachers belong.

9. An agency shop is legal as defined by most courts.

10. The right to bargain is a function of state laws and does not carry a constitutional privilege.

11. Collective bargaining usually entails mandatory, permissive, and illegal subject matter.

12. Failure to reach an agreement usually results in mediation, fact finding, and arbitration that may be binding.

NOTES

1. *Abood v. Detroit Board of Education*, 431, U.S. 209, 97 S.Ct. 1782 (1977).
2. *Chicago Teachers Union Local No. 1 v. Hudson*, 475, U.S. 292 (1986).
3. *Atkins v. City of Charlotte*, 297 F. Supp. 1068 (W.D.N.C.) (1970).
4. *McLaughlin v. Tilendis*, 398, F.2d 287, 289 (7th Cir. 1968).
5. *Commonwealth v. County Board of Arlington County*, 558, 232, S.E. 2d 30 (1977).
6. *West Cent. Educ. Ass'n v. West Cent. School Dist. 49-4*, 655 N. W. 2d 916 (S.D. 2002).
7. *Warwick School Committee v. Warwick Teacher's Union*, 637 A. 2d 777 (R.I. 1994).
8. *Perry Educ. Ass'n. v. Perry Local Educ. Ass'n*, 460 U.S. 37 (1983).
9. *Lawson v. Bd. of Educ.*, 307 N.Y. S. 2d 333 (N.Y. Sup. Ct. 1970).
10. *Fargo Educ. Ass'n. v. Fargo Pub. Sch. Dist.*, 291 N.W. 2d 267 (N.D. 1980).

14

No Child Left Behind

186. Why Was No Child Left Behind Passed?

The No Child Left Behind (NCLB) Act was passed to close the achievement gap among schools and to ensure that all children have a fair, equal, and significant opportunity to obtain a high-quality education. At a minimum, all students are expected to achieve proficiency on state academic standards and state academic assessments.[1] As stated by the act, this purpose can be accomplished by the following:

- Ensuring that high-quality academic assessments, accountability systems, teacher preparation and training, curriculum, and instructional materials are aligned with challenging state academic standards so that students, teachers, parents, and administrators can measure progress against common expectations for student academic achievement
- Meeting the educational needs of low-achieving children in our nation's highest-poverty schools, limited English proficient children, migratory children, children with disabilities, [American] Indian children, neglected or delinquent children, and young children in need of reading assistance
- Closing the achievement gap between high- and low-performing children, especially the achievement gaps between minority and non-minority students, and between disadvantaged children and their more advantaged peers

- Holding schools, local educational agencies, and states accountable for improving the academic achievement of all students and identifying and turning around low-performing schools that have failed to provide a high-quality education to their students, while providing alternatives to students in such schools to enable the students to receive a high-quality education
- Distributing and targeting resources sufficiently to make a difference to local educational agencies and schools where needs are greatest
- Improving and strengthening accountability, teaching, and learning by using state assessment systems designed to ensure that students are meeting challenging state academic achievement and content standards and increasing achievement overall, but especially for the disadvantaged
- Providing greater decision-making authority and flexibility to schools and teachers in exchange for greater responsibility for student performance
- Providing children an enriched and accelerated educational program, including the use of schoolwide programs or additional services that increase the amount and quality of instructional time
- Promoting schoolwide reform and ensuring the access of children to effective, scientifically based instructional strategies and challenging academic content
- Elevating significantly the quality of instruction by providing staff in participating schools with substantial opportunities for professional development
- Coordinating services under all sections of this title with each other, with other educational services, and, to the extent feasible, with other agencies providing services to youth, children, and families
- Affording parents substantial and meaningful opportunities to participate in the education of their children.[2]

With passage of NCLB, Congress reauthorized the Elementary and Secondary Education Act (ESEA) of 1965—the principal federal law affecting education from kindergarten through high school. In amending ESEA, the new law represented a sweeping overhaul of federal efforts to support elementary and secondary education in the United States. It is built on four commonsense pillars: accountability for results, an emphasis on doing what works based on scientific research, expanded parental options, and expanded local control and flexibility.

187. What Are the Basic Provisions of NCLB?

States were required to develop plans with annual measurable objectives that would ensure that all teachers providing instruction in core academic subjects were highly qualified by the end of the 2005–2006 school year.

States were also required to implement corrective active to strengthen low-achieving schools. Corrective action must be taken if school improvement efforts have failed after two years and should include adjustments more likely to generate meaningful change at the school, such as replacing school staff responsible for the continued failure to make adequate yearly progress, implementing a new curriculum, and reorganizing the school entirely.

188. How May Title I Funds for Educational Practices Be Used?

Title I funds should be used only for effective educational practices. Title I schoolwide and targeted assistance programs are required to use effective methods and instructional strategies grounded in scientifically based research. School improvement plans, professional development activities, and technical assistance that districts provide to low-performing schools must be based on strategies that have a proven record of effectiveness. Local school districts must have ensured that all Title I teachers in core academic subjects hired after the first day of the 2002–2003 school year were "highly qualified." For new teachers, that meant being certified by the state (including alternative routes to state certification), holding at least a bachelor's degree, and demonstrating subject area competency. Fundamental restructuring of any school that fails to improve over an extended period of time must be initiated. Restructuring may include reopening the school as a charter school or turning over school operations either to the state or to a private company with a demonstrated record of effectiveness. Paraprofessionals must earn two years of postsecondary education or an applicant with a high school diploma must demonstrate the necessary skills on a formal state or local academic assessment. All new hires must meet these requirements, and existing paraprofessionals had four years to comply with them. Paraprofessionals may not provide instructional support services and cannot offer instruction except under the direct supervision of a teacher. Eligibility for schoolwide programs financed by Title I funds is expanded under the act. The poverty threshold for these programs, which raise the achievement of at-risk students by improving the quality of instruction, has been lowered from having 50 percent to 40 percent of the total student body from low-income families.

189. What Is Required Through Annual Assessment?

NCLB requires annual assessments in grades 3–8 that include all students. It also calls for state and local report cards on student academic achievement and requires states to implement a single, statewide accountability system. States are to assess basic skills for all students in certain grades if they desire to continue receiving federal funding for their schools. NCLB reinforces provisions concerning adequate yearly progress. States were required to specify annual measurable objectives to ensure that all groups of students, disaggregated by poverty, race, and ethnicity as well as by those with disabilities and with limited English proficiency, would reach proficiency in reading and math within twelve years.

NCLB substantially increased funding for state and local support for school improvement. Funding increased from .5 percent of Title I funds under the 1994 Elementary and the Secondary Education Act reauthorization to 2 percent under the act, rising to 4 percent in 2004. It also established a separate $500 million authorization for local school improvement grants.

190. How Does the Act Empower Parents?

The act requires local school districts to offer public school choice to the parents of students in schools identified for improvement, corrective action, or restructuring. This provision ensures that no student is trapped in an underperforming school. School districts must provide transportation for eligible students, subject to the 20 percent rule described below. It also requires school districts to permit low-income students attending chronically underperforming schools to obtain supplemental educational services from a public- or private-sector provider. Providers must have been approved by the state. Faith-based organizations are eligible to apply for approval to provide supplemental educational services. The act requires school districts to spend an amount equal to 20 percent of their Part A Title I funds for transportation of students who exercise a choice option or for supplemental educational services. This amount is required unless a lesser amount is needed to meet all requests. These funds may not necessarily be taken from Title I allocations but may be provided from other allowable federal, state, local, or private sources. Parents must be notified of school choice and supplemental educational services options. This provision requires districts to promptly notify parents of students attending schools that have been identified for improvement, corrective action, or restructuring of their option to transfer their child to a better public school or to obtain supplemental educational services. Finally, the act establishes a parents' "right to know" provision. This provision requires local school districts to annually notify parents of their right to request information on the professional qualifications of their children's teachers.

191. What Is the Impact of NCLB on Teachers and Other School Professionals?

NCLB outlines the minimum qualifications needed by teachers: a bachelor's degree, full state certification, and demonstration of subject-matter competency for each subject taught. States were to achieve the goal that all teachers of core academic subjects be highly qualified by the end of the

2005–2006 school year. States must have included in their plans annual, measurable objectives that each local school district and school would meet in moving toward the goal. They were also required to report their progress on annual report cards.

Student test results will affect everyone employed by the school district. K–3 teachers must teach all children to read. These teachers must learn how to assess children and how to use assessment results to plan effective instruction. If a child is not making progress with one method of instruction, the teacher must identify a different, more appropriate method. Teachers must use research-based methods of teaching and be knowledgeable regarding phonemic awareness and phonics, even though they may not have been exposed to research based on teaching methods in their preparation programs. Many teacher-training programs do not require students to learn about research-based teaching methods or phonemes in order to graduate, and many states do not require this knowledge for certification or licensure of elementary school teachers. Under NCLB, however, elementary school teachers must meet this new, "highly qualified" standard.

Teachers of upper elementary grades must provide instruction in math, reading, and science at higher skill levels. These teachers must possess the skills to instruct many levels of students. Annual testing will indicate gains made by students taught by individual teachers. Schools will not be able to retain ineffective teachers. The stakes are simply too high.

Middle school and high school teachers must meet the new "highly qualified" standard in the subjects they teach. Teachers in higher grades are responsible for the gains made by their students. These teachers are also responsible for educating students who transfer into their schools without the level of instruction they should have received.

Music teachers, physical education teachers, computer teachers, and foreign language teachers are not immune from this law. If their school is determined to be underperforming and must offer school choice, many of their students may leave. It may be necessary that they follow the students to a better school and teach the rising population there.

Speech pathologists, occupational therapists, physical therapists, and guidance counselors may be required to integrate academics into their therapies to compensate for pulling the child out of the classroom. When children exercise their school choice options and leave unsuccessful schools, there may not be a need for as many related service providers.

Special education teachers must elevate students to the appropriate level of proficiency. If a special education teacher provides instruction in a core subject, he or she must meet the standard of a highly qualified teacher in that subject. Special education teachers must collaborate more closely with regular educators. A student can pursue an alternative assessment if his or her disabilities prevent him or her from taking the regular state assessment, but alternative assessments must test grade-level knowledge.

192. Are There Controversies Surrounding NCLB, and When Will It Be Reauthorized?

Yes. The act has and continues to be hotly contested. For example, there is great skepticism among some educators and policymakers that the law actually has the capacity to improve educational experiences for children, especially for minorities and those in poverty. There is also skepticism that the law will actually provide students in low-performing schools a genuine opportunity to transfer to better schools. Since standards are determined by each state, some believe that certain states are enhancing student achievement statistics to present their districts in a more positive light. Additionally, there are differences among states regarding quality standards, which produce uneven measures of quality. There is a strong view among school and district officials that Congress has not appropriated sufficient funding to effectively implement the act. It is viewed by many as an unfunded mandate. There is also a view that the law gives Washington, D.C., too much power over local school district decisions regarding education and threatens state and local control as provided by the Tenth Amendment to the U.S. Constitution. Some lawmakers feel that the name of the act is too tarnished to gain bipartisan support and advocate a name change.

A funding challenge involving NCLB arose in California when a coalition of school districts, bilingual education advocates, civil rights organizations, parents, teachers, and students filed suit through a *writ of mandamus* challenging the state to allow limited English proficiency (LEP) students to take standardized tests in their native languages.[3] (A *writ of mandamus* is an order from a court directing a court, officer, or body to perform a certain act.) NCLB requires that states establish and administer valid and reliable tests in core academic subjects. The California Supreme Court noted that the plaintiffs could only succeed if NCLB created a ministerial or mandatory duty for the state. Participating states are required to submit a locally developed plan for approval by the U.S. Department of Education. Once approved, the focus of the program is on local administration, with significant flexibility and discretion regarding how the assessment, reporting, accountability, and remediation objectives are met. The court determined that California's general authority under NCLB is not merely ministerial in nature. The court concluded that NCLB established the goal of valid and reliable testing but did not prescribe how that goal was to be achieved. Therefore, the state of California was not required to provide standardized assessment tests in the native languages of limited English proficiency students in order to comply with the law.

In a NCLB challenge, a federal district court in Ohio ruled that the act does not create a private right of action for private providers of supplemental education services (SES) to sue local school districts over the NCLB requirement that schools failing to make adequate yearly progress must offer students their services. Under NCLB, school districts are required to allocate a certain percentage of their federal funds to provide SES. School districts must provide parents with a list of state-approved SES providers, from which parents can choose. Fresh Start Academy, a private SES provider, filed suit against Toledo Public Schools, alleging that the district violated its rights under NCLB by depriving it of a fair opportunity to obtain SES funds. The school district filed a motion to dismiss Fresh Start's claim, arguing that NCLB does not confer on private SES providers a right of action to enforce NCLB's SES provisions. Relying on the U.S. Supreme Court's decision in *Gonzaga University v. Doe*, the district court concluded that Congress did not intend to imply any such right of action. Like the Family Education Rights and Privacy Act (FERPA) at issue in *Gonzaga*, the court found, NCLB focuses on the entity regulated rather than on the individual benefited. The court concluded that (1) NCLB lacks the sort of "rights-creating language" required to demonstrate that Congress clearly intended to create a private right to sue; (2) NCLB has an "aggregate focus" rather than being concerned with whether the needs of particular individuals are met; and (3) NCLB's primary enforcement tool—permitting the U.S. Department of Education to withhold funds from noncompliant states—indicates that "Congress did not intend to provide for piecemeal enforcement by individuals."[4]

NCLB REAUTHORIZATION

NCLB was scheduled to be reauthorized in 2007. A revised version was subsequently scheduled for reauthorization in early 2008. Because of the controversy, the partisan views regarding the act, and the presidential election in 2008, it was difficult to gain the support needed to pass legislation of its magnitude. Although reauthorization is not expected in 2009, all major national education organizations have or are in the process of revising their NCLB recommendations.

193. How Does NCLB Affect Students?

As a provision of the accountability requirement established by the law, NCLB has set the goal of having every child make the grade on state-defined education standards by the end of the 2013–2014 school year. To reach that goal, every state has developed benchmarks to measure progress and to ensure that every child is learning. States are required to separate (or disaggregate) student achievement data, holding schools accountable for subgroups of students so that no child falls through the cracks. A school or school district that does not meet the state's definition of "adequate yearly progress" for two straight years (schoolwide or in any subgroup) is considered to be "in need of improvement."

194. What Is a Highly Qualified Teacher Under NCLB, and Why Is It So Important?

Highly qualified is a specific term defined by NCLB. The law outlines a list of minimum requirements regarding content knowledge and teaching skills that a highly qualified teacher must meet. However, NCLB also recognizes the importance of state and local control of education. Thus, the law provides latitude for each state to develop its definition of highly qualified as long as it is consistent with NCLB standards. The law also allows states to address their own unique needs. The standards for a highly qualified teacher include the following:

- State certification, which may also include alternative certification
- A bachelor's degree
- Demonstrated subject-area competency in core academic areas, which include
  o English
  o Reading or Language Arts
  o Mathematics
  o Science
  o Foreign Language
  o Civics
  o Government
  o Economics
  o Arts
  o History
  o Geography

195. Must Paraprofessionals Meet the Highly Qualified Standard Under NCLB?

Yes, with one exception. Paraprofessionals in Title I programs must acquire a minimum of two years of postsecondary education or an individual with a high school diploma must demonstrate necessary skills on a formal state or local academic assessment. All employees entering Title I programs after January 8, 2002, must have met these requirements, and existing paraprofessionals must have met these requirements by January 2006. However, these requirements do not apply to paraprofessionals used for translation or parental involvement. Otherwise, all paraprofessionals in Title I programs must have earned a high school diploma or its equivalent. The law specifies that paraprofessionals may not provide instructional support services except under the direct supervision of a highly qualified teacher.

196. Are Teachers Required to Meet National Board Certification Standards Under NCLB?

No. National certification is not required under NCLB but is a voluntary certification program designed to improve teaching practices. National Board Certification is an advanced teaching credential presented to teachers meeting rigorous standards involving the specific knowledge and skills that accomplished teachers should possess. It involves a two-phase assessment process that includes the submission of portfolios of instructional materials that demonstrate how the teacher is meeting national board standards. Teachers pursuing National Board Certification must also respond to computer prompts regarding their subject and certain classroom situations based on national standards developed in their fields.

National Board Certification involves at least a one-year process wherein teachers validate their teaching effectiveness through initiating the following activities:

- Documenting student work
- Videotaping their teaching
- Reflecting on their teaching with a view of improving effectiveness

197. Must Charter School Teachers Meet the Highly Qualified Standard Under NCLB?

Yes. All charter school teachers who teach core academic subjects, like other public school teachers, must hold a bachelor's degree and demonstrate competency in the core academic areas in which they teach. They also must have earned full state certification, unless the state's charter school laws specify that such certification is not required for charter school teachers.

198. Must Elementary School Subject Specialists Be Highly Qualified in All Subjects or Simply in the Particular Subject They Teach?

A fully certified, experienced elementary school teacher who teaches only a single subject (e.g., a reading or math specialist) does not necessarily need to demonstrate subject-matter knowledge across the entire elementary curriculum. Rather, a teacher must pass a rigorous state test in the subject area or demonstrate competency in that subject through the state's high, objective, uniform state standard of evaluation (HOUSSE) procedures.

However, all *new* elementary school teachers must pass a rigorous state test in all areas of the elementary school curriculum. Most states currently require new teachers, whether generalists or specialists, to pass a general test before they can obtain full state certification. In these states, teachers who choose to pursue subject-area specializations will have satisfied the requirements for being highly qualified in elementary school. Specialists in noncore academic subjects (e.g., vocational or physical education teachers) are not required to meet the highly qualified teacher requirements.

199. What Is Meant by Alternative Certification Under NCLB?

It can mean at least two things. First, alternative certification programs allow candidates to teach while they are meeting state certification requirements. These programs must provide rigorous, high-quality professional development activities for teachers before they enter the classroom as well as during their teaching experience. Alternative certification programs must also include a mentoring or induction component. Teachers in these programs may teach up to three years while they earn their state certification, provided they have met the bachelor's degree and subject-matter competency requirements.

Second, states may create alternate routes to certification, such as the adoption of a new system supported by the American Board for Certification of Teacher Excellence (ABCTE) that allows teacher candidates to demonstrate their competency through a comprehensive, multifaceted assessment process rather than through coursework in specific education school courses. Teachers who pass the assessment are considered fully certified before they enter the classroom.

200. Are Teachers Who Earn an Emergency Certificate Still Required to Be Highly Qualified?

Yes. New teachers must meet their state's definition of highly qualified in the subjects they are teaching at the time of employment. Full state certification is one of the highly qualified requirements. Experienced teachers instructing under an emergency certificate or temporary permit must have earned full state certification by the 2005–2006 school year. Teachers who are affiliated with an alternative certification program will have already earned a bachelor's degree and have demonstrated subject-matter competency. These teachers meet the definition of highly qualified and are awarded full state certification under the condition that they complete certain certification requirements in three years or less.

Summary of Legal Cases Involving No Child Left Behind

- A U.S. district court in California ruled that a U.S. Department of Education regulation defining teachers in training who are participating in an alternative certification program as "highly qualified" under the NCLB does not conflict with the NCLB requirement that "highly qualified" teachers have "full state certification as a teacher."[5]

- The U.S. Court of Appeals for the Seventh Circuit (Illinois, Indiana, Wisconson) affirmed the dismissal of a lawsuit against the U.S. Department of Education and the Illinois State Board of Education that alleged that the NCLB and the Individuals With Disabilities Education Act (IDEA) are legally incompatible.[6]

- The U.S. Court of Appeals for the Sixth Circuit (Kentucky, Michigan, Ohio, Tennessee) has ruled that a group of school districts from several states, the National Education Association (NEA), and ten NEA-affiliated education associations have stated a valid legal claim that they are not liable for the costs of complying with mandates under the NCLB in excess of the federal funding provided.[7]

- A U.S. district court in Michigan ruled that the NCLB does not authorize providers of supplemental education services (SES) to sue school districts over NCLB's requirement that schools that fail to make adequate yearly progress offer students SES.[8]

- A federal district court in Connecticut has dismissed three of the four claims in Connecticut's lawsuit challenging NCLB. The ruling did not address the merits of any of the claims, only whether the court had jurisdiction to hear the claims.[9]

- A federal district court dismissed the lawsuit of a Kansas special education teacher who sued the U.S. government claiming that NCLB was unconstitutional.[10]

Summary Guides

1. NCLB is the most recent legislation supporting standards-based education reform.

2. The act was legislated to ensure that all children are provided a fair opportunity to obtain a high-quality education, especially students in low-performing schools.

(Continued)

(Continued)

3. There are no national achievement standards established by the act. Standards are set by individual states consistent with the principle of local control of schools.

4. States are provided the latitude to develop their own assessment plan regarding basic skills to be measured in selected grades.

5. The measures required by the act are controversial due to the differential quality standards among the states and a view that some states may lower achievement goals and have teachers teach to the adopted test.

6. Funding is a major issue based on a view that NCLB requires considerably more funding to achieve desired outcomes.

7. Advocates of the act argue that local government has not met students' needs, which has necessitated governmental intervention and increased accountability for student outcomes.

8. The highly qualified requirement has affected schools who engaged teachers to teach outside their areas of certification and teachers who failed to earn credentials in their designated teaching areas.

9. There have been and continues to be significant legal challenges to NCLB covering a range of issues from assessment, deficient funding, adequate yearly progress, students with disabilities, and the constitutionality of the act itself.

NOTES

1. No Child Left Behind Act of 2001, P.L. 07-110.

2. www.ed.gov/legislation/ESEA02/pg1.html.

3. *Coachella Valley Unified School District v. California No. 05-505334* (Cal. Super. Ct. May 25, 2007).

4. *Fresh Start Academy v. Toledo Board of Education*, 2005 WL 757026 (N.D. Ohio Apr. 4, 2005).

5. *Renee v. Spellings*, No. 07-4299 (N.D. Cal. Jun. 17, 2008).

6. *Board of Educ. of Ottawa Twp. High Sch. Dist. 140 v. U.S. Dept. of Educ.*, No. 07-2008 (7th Cir. Feb. 11, 2008).

7. *School Dist. of the City of Pontiac v. Spellings*, No. 05-2708 (6th Cir. Jan. 7, 2008).

8. *Alliance for Children Inc. v. City of Detroit Public Schools*, No. 06-15021 (E.D. Mich. Feb. 15, 2007).

9. *Connecticut v. Spellings*, No. 05, 1330 (D. Conn. Sept. 27, 2006).

10. *Kegerreis v. United States of America*, No. Civ.A.03-2232-KHV (D. Kan. Oct. 9, 2003).

Resource A

Selected Federal Statutes

DISCRIMINATION BASED ON SEX, TITLE IX (SELECTED PARTS)

20 U.S.C.A. § 1681

Prohibition Against Discrimination; Exceptions

No person in the United States shall, on the basis of sex, be excluded from participation in, be denied the benefits of, or be subjected to discrimination under any education program or activity receiving federal financial assistance. The act prohibits sex discrimination in recruiting and admission, financial aid, athletics, textbooks and curriculum, housing facilities, career counseling, inservice and health care, single sex programs, employment, and extracurricular activities.

Affects

Educational institutions receiving federal financial assistance.

Areas Covered

1. Admissions: Discrimination in admissions is prohibited only in vocational institutions (including high schools), graduate and professional schools, and public undergraduate coeducational institutions.

2. Once admitted, female and male students at all educational institutions receiving federal financial assistance must be treated without discrimination.

Remedy

Complaint investigation and attempt to resolve complaint. If not resolved, an administrative hearing follows. The Office of Civil Rights may suspend funds and refer the complaint to the Justice Department for court action.

FAMILY RIGHTS AND PRIVACY ACT (BUCKLEY AMENDMENT) (SELECTED PARTS)

20 U.S.C.A. § 1232G

Covers conditions for availability of funds to educational agencies or institutions, inspection and review of educational records, the specific information to be made available, the procedure for access to educational records, reasonableness of time for such access, hearings, written explanations by parents.

Affects

Educational institutions receiving federal financial assistance.

Areas Covered

Procedures for student recordkeeping, as follows: A parent or student has the right to inspect student records. If it appears that they contain inaccurate material, a hearing must be held before an impartial hearing officer to present the student's side of the story within a reasonable time. An explanation can be placed into the file by the student or parent. Written permission must be secured from the parent or student before information contained in the file is released to others.

If the student is eighteen years of age or older, or is attending a postsecondary institution, these rights are afforded to the student only. An exception may be permitted by the institution for a parent who claims a student as a dependent for income tax purposes.

Parents and students must be notified under the act of their rights to access, challenge, consent, and notice.

Remedy

Investigation by the Department of Education. Possible termination of federal funding. Due process hearing and court action if necessary.

CIVIL RIGHTS ACTS OF 1866, 1870

42 U.S.C. § 1981

Section 1981 provides that *"all persons* within the jurisdiction of the United States shall have the same right . . . *to make and enforce contracts,* to sue, be parties, give evidence, and to the full and equal benefit of all laws and proceedings for the security of persons and property as is enjoyed by white citizens, and shall be subject to like punishments, pains, penalties, taxes, licenses, and exactions of every kind, and to no other."

Affects

Private individuals or private or public institutions, associations, unions, and agencies.

Areas Covered

Admissions, employment, sales, services, leases, loans, etc.

Remedy

Suits for damages or equitable relief in either federal or state courts. Personal liability is possible. No prior administrative procedures are required.

CIVIL RIGHTS ACT OF 1871

42 U.S.C. § 1983

Section 1983 provides that "every person who, under color of any statute, ordinance, regulation, custom or usage, of any State or Territory, subjects, or causes to be subjected, any citizen of the United States or other person within the jurisdiction thereof to the *deprivation of any rights,* privileges or immunities *secured by the Constitution and laws,* shall be liable to the party injured in an action at law, suit in equity, or other proper proceeding for redress."

Affects

Public officials, such as educational institutions, administrators, school districts, and board members.

Areas Covered

Almost all functions and activities occurring at public educational institutions.

Remedy

Lawsuits in either federal or state courts, personal liability, compensatory and punitive damages, and declaratory relief.

42 U.S.C. § 1985 and § 1986

Section 1985(3) provides in part: "If two or more persons in any State or Territory conspire . . . for the purpose of depriving . . . any person or class of persons of the *equal protection of the laws*, or of equal privileges and immunities under the laws: or . . . of preventing or hindering the constituted authorities of any State . . . from . . . securing to all persons within such State . . . the equal protection of the laws . . . the party so injured . . . may have an action for the recovery of damages . . . against any one or more of the conspirators."

Section 1986 provides in part: "Every person who, having knowledge that any of the wrongs conspired to be done . . . [under Section 1985] and having the power to prevent . . . the . . . same, neglects or refuses so to do . . . shall be liable to the party injured . . . for all damages caused by such wrongful act."

Affects

Two or more individuals, public officials.

Areas Covered

Most functions and activities in educational institutions.

Remedy

Lawsuits in either federal or state court, personal liability for damages with a right to a jury trial.

CIVIL RIGHTS ACT OF 1964, TITLE VI (SELECTED PARTS)

42 U.S.C.A. §§ 2000D–D-1

No person in the United States shall, on the ground of race, color, or national origin, be excluded from participation in, be denied the benefits of, or be subjected to discrimination under any program or activity receiving federal financial assistance.

Public Law 88-352, Title VI, § 601, July 2, 1964, 78 Stat. 252

Affects

Public officials, institutions responsible for ensuring that students are provided an equal opportunity to learn.

Areas Covered

Most functions and activities that occur in educational institutions.

Remedy

Lawsuit in either federal or state court, personal liability for damages with a right to a jury trial.

CIVIL RIGHTS ACT OF 1964, TITLE VII (SELECTED PARTS)

42 U.S.C.A. §§ 2000E–E-2

It shall be an unlawful employment practice for an employment agency to fail or refuse to refer for employment, or otherwise to discriminate against, any individual because of his or her race, color, religion, sex, or national origin, or to classify or refer for employment any individual on the basis of his or her race, color, religion, sex, or national origin.

Affects

An employer with fifteen or more employees.

Areas Covered

All employment practices such as hiring, dismissal, classifications, promotions, references for employment based on race, color, religion, sex, or national origin.

Remedy

Complaints filed against institutions or officials; individual or class-action suits should seek administrative remedy prior to filing a lawsuit. The Equal Employment Opportunity Commission (EEOC) handles complaints and has the authority to issue a right-to-sue letter to claimants.

Injunctive awards are possible, back pay, damages, and awards; punitive awards are not available. There is a 180-day timetable to file a complaint with the EEOC, or 300 days if the complaint has been filed with a local or state civil rights agency.

INDIVIDUALS WITH DISABILITIES EDUCATION ACT (SELECTED PARTS)

20 U.S.C. §§ 1400–1485

It is the purpose of this chapter to assure that all children with disabilities have available to them, within the time periods specified in section 1412(2)(B) of this title, a free appropriate public education which emphasizes special education and related services designed to meet their unique needs, to assure that the rights of children with disabilities and their parents or guardians are protected, to assist States and localities to provide for the education of all children with disabilities, and to assess and assure the effectiveness of efforts to educate children with disabilities.

Affects

Public educational institutions.

Areas Covered

Free public education, related services, private education options, readmittance facilities, twelve-month facilities, transitional services, assistive technology support.

Remedy

Due process hearings, impartial hearings with hearing officials, injunctive relief by courts, declaratory relief, alternative placements, attorney fees if suit is successful and nonfrivolous.

AGE DISCRIMINATION ACT

29 U.S.C. § 621 (§ 623)

This section reads as follows:

a. It shall be unlawful for an employer
   1. to fail or refuse to hire or to discharge any individual or otherwise discriminate against any individual with respect to his

compensation, terms, conditions, or privileges of employment, because of such individual's age.

. . . .

c. It shall be unlawful for a labor organization

   1. to exclude or to expel from its membership, or otherwise to discriminate against, any individual because of his age.

   . . . .

   3. to cause or attempt to cause an employer to discriminate against an individual in violation of this section.

   . . . .

f. It shall not be unlawful for an employer, employment agency, or labor organization

   1. to take any action otherwise prohibited under subsections (a), (b), (c), or (e) of this section where age is a bona fide occupational qualification reasonably necessary to the normal operation of the particular business, or where the differentiation is based on reasonable factors other than age.

   . . . .

   3. to discharge or otherwise discipline an individual for good cause.

Affects

Employers of twenty or more individuals, labor unions, and employment agencies.

Areas Covered

Hiring, promotion, compensation, retirement.

Remedy

Suit for damages by the secretary of labor (EEOC); suits for damages by individual claimant, who must provide a sixty-day notice to the secretary of labor of his or her intent to file suit. If the secretary of labor initiates a suit, the private suit is eliminated. There is a two-year statute of limitations.

REHABILITATION ACT OF 1973

29 U.S.C. § 794 (§ 504)

The act provides in part: "No otherwise qualified handicapped individual . . . shall, solely by reason of his handicap, be excluded from the participation in, be denied the benefits of, or be subjected to discrimination under any program or activity receiving Federal financial assistance."

Affects

All institutions that receive federal funds, including elementary, secondary, and postsecondary institutions.

Areas Covered

Facility modification and accessibility, modifying academic requirements, working conditions.

Remedy

The Office of Civil Rights conducts an investigation of complaints and seeks voluntary compliance; financial assistance may be suspended, terminated, or not granted.

PREGNANCY DISCRIMINATION ACT OF 1978

Public Law 95-555

Be it enacted by the Senate and House of Representatives of the United States of America in Congress assembled, That section 701 of the Civil Rights Act of 1964 is amended by adding at the end thereof the following new subsection:

k. The Terms "because of sex" or "on the basis of sex" include, but are not limited to, because of or on the basis of pregnancy, childbirth, or related medical conditions; and women affected by pregnancy, childbirth, or related medical conditions shall be treated the same for all employment-related purposes, including the receipt of benefits under fringe benefit programs, as other persons not so affected but similar in their ability or inability to work, and nothing in section 703(h) of this title shall be interpreted to permit otherwise. This subsection shall not require an employer to pay for health insurance benefits for abortion, except where the life of the mother would be endangered if the fetus were carried to term, or except where medical complications have arisen from an abortion: *Provided,* That nothing herein shall preclude an employer from providing abortion benefits or otherwise affect bargaining agreements in regard to abortion.

Affects

Employers with fifteen or more employees, unions with twenty-five members, employment agencies, federal, state and local governments.

Areas Covered

Employment discrimination, pregnancy, childbirth, or related medical conditions.

Remedy

EEOC files a discrimination complaint within 180 days of alleged discriminatory act. If a complaint is to be filed with an administrative state agency, there is a 300-day period in which to file a charge. EEOC may issue a right-to-sue letter. Claimant may seek relief in a court of law.

Resource B

*The Constitution of
the United States of America*

THE PREAMBLE

We the people of the United States, in order to form a more perfect union, establish justice, insure domestic tranquility, provide for the common defense, promote the general welfare, and secure the blessings of liberty to ourselves and our posterity, do ordain and establish this Constitution for the United States of America.

THE AMENDMENTS

The following are the Amendments to the Constitution. The first ten Amendments collectively are commonly known as the Bill of Rights.

Amendment I: Freedom of Religion, Press, Expression (Ratified 12/15/1791)

Congress shall make no law respecting an establishment of religion, or prohibiting the free exercise thereof; or abridging the freedom of speech, or of the press; or the right of the people peaceably to assemble, and to petition the Government for a redress of grievances.

Amendment II: Right to Bear Arms (Ratified 12/15/1791)

A well regulated Militia, being necessary to the security of a free State, the right of the people to keep and bear Arms, shall not be infringed.

Amendment III: Quartering of Soldiers (Ratified 12/15/1791)

No Soldier shall, in time of peace be quartered in any house, without the consent of the Owner, nor in time of war, but in a manner to be prescribed by law.

Amendment IV: Search and Seizure (Ratified 12/15/1791)

The right of the people to be secure in their persons, houses, papers, and effects, against unreasonable searches and seizures, shall not be violated, and no Warrants shall issue, but upon probable cause, supported by Oath or affirmation, and particularly describing the place to be searched, and the persons or things to be seized.

Amendment V: Trial and Punishment, Compensation for Takings (Ratified 12/15/1791)

No person shall be held to answer for a capital, or otherwise infamous crime, unless on a presentment or indictment of a Grand Jury, except in cases arising in the land or naval forces, or in the Militia, when in actual service in time of War or public danger; nor shall any person be subject for the same offense to be twice put in jeopardy of life or limb; nor shall be compelled in any criminal case to be a witness against himself, nor be deprived of life, liberty, or property, without due process of law; nor shall private property be taken for public use, without just compensation.

Amendment VI: Right to Speedy Trial, Confrontation of Witnesses (Ratified 12/15/1791)

In all criminal prosecutions, the accused shall enjoy the right to a speedy and public trial, by an impartial jury of the State and district wherein the crime shall have been committed, which district shall have been previously ascertained by law, and to be informed of the nature and cause of the accusation; to be confronted with the witnesses against him; to have compulsory process for obtaining witnesses in his favor, and to have the Assistance of Counsel for his defense.

Amendment VII: Trial by Jury in Civil Cases (Ratified 12/15/1791)

In Suits at common law, where the value in controversy shall exceed twenty dollars, the right of trial by jury shall be preserved, and no fact tried by a jury, shall be otherwise re-examined in any Court of the United States, than according to the rules of the common law.

Amendment VIII: Cruel and Unusual Punishment (Ratified 12/15/1791)

Excessive bail shall not be required, nor excessive fines imposed, nor cruel and unusual punishments inflicted.

Amendment IX: Construction of Constitution (Ratified 12/15/1791)

The enumeration in the Constitution, of certain rights, shall not be construed to deny or disparage others retained by the people.

Amendment X: Powers of the States and People (Ratified 12/15/1791)

The powers not delegated to the United States by the Constitution, nor prohibited by it to the States, are reserved to the States respectively, or to the people.

Amendment XI: Judicial Limits (Ratified 2/7/1795)

The Judicial power of the United States shall not be construed to extend to any suit in law or equity, commenced or prosecuted against one of the United States by Citizens of another State, or by Citizens or Subjects of any Foreign State.

Amendment XII: Choosing the President, Vice-President (Ratified 6/15/1804)

The Electors shall meet in their respective states, and vote by ballot for President and Vice-President, one of whom, at least, shall not be an inhabitant of the same state with themselves; they shall name in their ballots the person voted for as President, and in distinct ballots the person voted for as Vice-President, and they shall make distinct lists of all persons voted for as President, and of all persons voted for as Vice-President and of the number of votes for each, which lists they shall sign and certify, and transmit sealed to the seat of the government of the United States, directed to the President of the Senate.

The President of the Senate shall, in the presence of the Senate and House of Representatives, open all the certificates and the votes shall then be counted.

The person having the greatest Number of votes for President, shall be the President, if such number be a majority of the whole number of Electors appointed; and if no person have such majority, then from the persons having the highest numbers not exceeding three on the list of those voted for as President, the House of Representatives shall choose immediately, by ballot, the President. But in choosing the President, the votes shall be taken by states, the representation from each state having one vote; a quorum for this purpose shall consist of a member or members from two-thirds of the states, and a majority of all the states shall be necessary to a choice. And if the House of Representatives shall not choose a President whenever the right of choice shall devolve upon them, before the fourth day of March next following, then the Vice-President shall act as President, as in the case of the death or other constitutional disability of the President.

The person having the greatest number of votes as Vice-President, shall be the Vice-President, if such number be a majority of the whole number of Electors appointed, and if no person have a majority, then from the two highest numbers on the list, the Senate shall choose the Vice-President; a quorum for the purpose shall consist of two-thirds of the whole number of Senators, and a majority of the whole number shall be necessary to a choice. But no person constitutionally ineligible to the office of President shall be eligible to that of Vice-President of the United States.

Amendment XIII: Slavery Abolished (Ratified 12/6/1865)

1. Neither slavery nor involuntary servitude, except as a punishment for crime whereof the party shall have been duly convicted, shall exist within the United States, or any place subject to their jurisdiction.

2. Congress shall have power to enforce this article by appropriate legislation.

Amendment XIV: Citizenship Rights (Ratified 7/9/1868)

1. All persons born or naturalized in the United States, and subject to the jurisdiction thereof, are citizens of the United States and of the State wherein they reside. No State shall make or enforce any law which shall abridge the privileges or immunities of citizens of the United States; nor shall any State deprive any person of life, liberty, or property, without due process of law; nor deny to any person within its jurisdiction the equal protection of the laws.

2. Representatives shall be apportioned among the several States according to their respective numbers, counting the whole number of persons in each State, excluding Indians not taxed. But when the right

to vote at any election for the choice of electors for President and Vice-President of the United States, Representatives in Congress, the Executive and Judicial officers of a State, or the members of the Legislature thereof, is denied to any of the male inhabitants of such State, being twenty-one years of age, and citizens of the United States, or in any way abridged, except for participation in rebellion, or other crime, the basis of representation therein shall be reduced in the proportion which the number of such male citizens shall bear to the whole number of male citizens twenty-one years of age in such State.

3. No person shall be a Senator or Representative in Congress, or elector of President and Vice-President, or hold any office, civil or military, under the United States, or under any State, who, having previously taken an oath, as a member of Congress, or as an officer of the United States, or as a member of any State legislature, or as an executive or judicial officer of any State, to support the Constitution of the United States, shall have engaged in insurrection or rebellion against the same, or given aid or comfort to the enemies thereof. But Congress may by a vote of two-thirds of each House, remove such disability.

4. The validity of the public debt of the United States, authorized by law, including debts incurred for payment of pensions and bounties for services in suppressing insurrection or rebellion, shall not be questioned. But neither the United States nor any State shall assume or pay any debt or obligation incurred in aid of insurrection or rebellion against the United States, or any claim for the loss or emancipation of any slave; but all such debts, obligations and claims shall be held illegal and void.

5. The Congress shall have power to enforce, by appropriate legislation, the provisions of this article.

Amendment XV: Race No Bar to Vote (Ratified 2/3/1870)

1. The right of citizens of the United States to vote shall not be denied or abridged by the United States or by any State on account of race, color, or previous condition of servitude.

2. The Congress shall have power to enforce this article by appropriate legislation.

Amendment XVI: Income Taxes Authorized (Ratified 2/3/1913)

The Congress shall have power to lay and collect taxes on incomes, from whatever source derived, without apportionment among the several States, and without regard to any census or enumeration.

Amendment XVII: Senators Elected by Popular Vote (Ratified 4/8/1913)

The Senate of the United States shall be composed of two Senators from each State, elected by the people thereof, for six years; and each Senator shall have one vote. The electors in each State shall have the qualifications requisite for electors of the most numerous branch of the State legislatures.

When vacancies happen in the representation of any State in the Senate, the executive authority of such State shall issue writs of election to fill such vacancies: Provided, That the legislature of any State may empower the executive thereof to make temporary appointments until the people fill the vacancies by election as the legislature may direct.

This amendment shall not be so construed as to affect the election or term of any Senator chosen before it becomes valid as part of the Constitution.

Amendment XVIII: Liquor Abolished (Ratified 1/16/1919. Repealed by Amendment XXI, 12/5/1933)

1. After one year from the ratification of this article the manufacture, sale, or transportation of intoxicating liquors within, the importation thereof into, or the exportation thereof from the United States and all territory subject to the jurisdiction thereof for beverage purposes is hereby prohibited.

2. The Congress and the several States shall have concurrent power to enforce this article by appropriate legislation.

3. This article shall be inoperative unless it shall have been ratified as an amendment to the Constitution by the legislatures of the several States, as provided in the Constitution, within seven years from the date of the submission hereof to the States by the Congress.

Amendment XIX: Women's Suffrage (Ratified 8/18/1920)

The right of citizens of the United States to vote shall not be denied or abridged by the United States or by any State on account of sex.

Congress shall have power to enforce this article by appropriate legislation.

Amendment XX: Presidential, Congressional Terms (Ratified 1/23/1933)

1. The terms of the President and Vice President shall end at noon on the 20th day of January, and the terms of Senators and Representatives at noon on the 3d day of January, of the years in which such terms

would have ended if this article had not been ratified; and the terms of their successors shall then begin.

2. The Congress shall assemble at least once in every year, and such meeting shall begin at noon on the 3d day of January, unless they shall by law appoint a different day.

3. If, at the time fixed for the beginning of the term of the President, the President elect shall have died, the Vice President elect shall become President. If a President shall not have been chosen before the time fixed for the beginning of his term, or if the President elect shall have failed to qualify, then the Vice President elect shall act as President until a President shall have qualified; and the Congress may by law provide for the case wherein neither a President elect nor a Vice President elect shall have qualified, declaring who shall then act as President, or the manner in which one who is to act shall be selected, and such person shall act accordingly until a President or Vice President shall have qualified.

4. The Congress may by law provide for the case of the death of any of the persons from whom the House of Representatives may choose a President whenever the right of choice shall have devolved upon them, and for the case of the death of any of the persons from whom the Senate may choose a Vice President whenever the right of choice shall have devolved upon them.

5. Sections 1 and 2 shall take effect on the 15th day of October following the ratification of this article.

6. This article shall be inoperative unless it shall have been ratified as an amendment to the Constitution by the legislatures of three-fourths of the several States within seven years from the date of its submission.

Amendment XXI: Amendment XVIII
Repealed (Ratified 12/5/1933)

1. The eighteenth article of amendment to the Constitution of the United States is hereby repealed.

2. The transportation or importation into any State, Territory, or possession of the United States for delivery or use therein of intoxicating liquors, in violation of the laws thereof, is hereby prohibited.

3. The article shall be inoperative unless it shall have been ratified as an amendment to the Constitution by conventions in the several States, as provided in the Constitution, within seven years from the date of the submission hereof to the States by the Congress.

Amendment XXII: Presidential Term Limits (Ratified 2/27/1951)

1. No person shall be elected to the office of the President more than twice, and no person who has held the office of President, or acted as President, for more than two years of a term to which some other person was elected President shall be elected to the office of the President more than once. But this Article shall not apply to any person holding the office of President, when this Article was proposed by the Congress, and shall not prevent any person who may be holding the office of President, or acting as President, during the term within which this Article becomes operative from holding the office of President or acting as President during the remainder of such term.

2. This article shall be inoperative unless it shall have been ratified as an amendment to the Constitution by the legislatures of three-fourths of the several States within seven years from the date of its submission to the States by the Congress.

Amendment XXIII: Presidential Vote for District of Columbia (Ratified 3/29/1961)

1. The District constituting the seat of Government of the United States shall appoint in such manner as the Congress may direct: A number of electors of President and Vice President equal to the whole number of Senators and Representatives in Congress to which the District would be entitled if it were a State, but in no event more than the least populous State; they shall be in addition to those appointed by the States, but they shall be considered, for the purposes of the election of President and Vice President, to be electors appointed by a State; and they shall meet in the District and perform such duties as provided by the twelfth article of amendment.

2. The Congress shall have power to enforce this article by appropriate legislation.

Amendment XXIV: Poll Tax Barred (Ratified 1/23/1964)

1. The right of citizens of the United States to vote in any primary or other election for President or Vice President, for electors for President or Vice President, or for Senator or Representative in Congress, shall not be denied or abridged by the United States or any State by reason of failure to pay any poll tax or other tax.

2. The Congress shall have power to enforce this article by appropriate legislation.

Amendment XXV: Presidential Disability and Succession (Ratified 2/10/1967)

1. In case of the removal of the President from office or of his death or resignation, the Vice President shall become President.

2. Whenever there is a vacancy in the office of the Vice President, the President shall nominate a Vice President who shall take office upon confirmation by a majority vote of both Houses of Congress.

3. Whenever the President transmits to the President pro tempore of the Senate and the Speaker of the House of Representatives his written declaration that he is unable to discharge the powers and duties of his office, and until he transmits to them a written declaration to the contrary, such powers and duties shall be discharged by the Vice President as Acting President.

4. Whenever the Vice President and a majority of either the principal officers of the executive departments or of such other body as Congress may by law provide, transmit to the President pro tempore of the Senate and the Speaker of the House of Representatives their written declaration that the President is unable to discharge the powers and duties of his office, the Vice President shall immediately assume the powers and duties of the office as Acting President.

   Thereafter, when the President transmits to the President pro tempore of the Senate and the Speaker of the House of Representatives his written declaration that no inability exists, he shall resume the powers and duties of his office unless the Vice President and a majority of either the principal officers of the executive department or of such other body as Congress may by law provide, transmit within four days to the President pro tempore of the Senate and the Speaker of the House of Representatives their written declaration that the President is unable to discharge the powers and duties of his office. Thereupon Congress shall decide the issue, assembling within forty eight hours for that purpose if not in session. If the Congress, within twenty one days after receipt of the latter written declaration, or, if Congress is not in session, within twenty one days after Congress is required to assemble, determines by two thirds vote of both Houses that the President is unable to discharge the powers and duties of his office, the Vice President shall continue to discharge the same as Acting President; otherwise, the President shall resume the powers and duties of his office.

Amendment XXVI: Voting Age Set to Eighteen Years (Ratified 7/1/1971)

1. The right of citizens of the United States, who are eighteen years of age or older, to vote shall not be denied or abridged by the United States or by any State on account of age.

2. The Congress shall have power to enforce this article by appropriate legislation.

Amendment XXVII: Congressional Pay Increases (Ratified 5/7/1992)

No law, varying the compensation for the services of the Senators and Representatives, shall take effect, until an election of Representatives shall have intervened.

Resource C

Glossary of Relevant Legal Terms

Action—An action proceeding in a court of law.

Affirm—To approve a lower court decision.

Allegation—A statement in the pleadings of a case which is expected to be proven.

Appeal—A petition to a higher court to amend or rectify a lower court decision.

Appellant—One who carries an appeal to a higher court.

Appellee—The party against whom an appeal is executed.

Arbitrary—Action taken without a defensible cause.

Assault—An offer to use force in a hostile manner.

Case law—A body of law that emanates from court decisions.

Civil action—An action to redress an infringement on personal rights.

Compensatory damages—Compensation awarded to an injured party to restore him or her to the status occupied prior to his or her injury.

Concurring opinion—An opinion issued by a judge expressing the will of the majority.

Defamation—False statements that injure a personal name or reputation.

Defendant—The person or party against whom a suit is brought.

De facto—Separation of races not sanctioned by law.

De jure—Segregation sanctioned by law.

Deposition—Statement of a witness taken under oath.

Discretionary—The exercise of judgment in deciding a course of action.

Dissenting opinion—A statement of disagreement with the majority opinion.

Enjoin—To require an individual by legal writ of injunction to perform or refrain from a certain act.

En banc—By all judges on the bench.

Et al.—And other unidentified parties.

Et seq.—And those following.

Ex parte—A proceeding for the benefit of one party.

Fact finding—A third-party investigation in collective negotiations when an impasse is reached.

Felony—A crime that is punishable by imprisonment or death.

Fiduciary—A special relationship between individuals characterized by trust where one acts on behalf of another.

Finding—The conclusion reached by the court in a case.

Funding disparity—Unequal funding of schools based on distribution of funds to support schools.

Governmental function—One that is required by an agency to protect the welfare of the general public.

Hearing—An examination of a legal issue in a court of law.

Holding—A decision reached by a court.

Impasse—A point in collective negotiations when no further progress is made being due to the inability of parties to reach an agreement.

Injunction—A court order prohibiting the commission of an act that may injure another person.

In loco parentis—In place of parents.

Invitee—A person who occupies property based on invitation.

Judgment—A decision or conclusion reached by a court.

Liable—Obligated by law.

Litigation—A formal challenge involving a dispute in a court of law.

Malfeasance—Commission of an unlawful act.

Malice—A wrongful act committed against a person.

Mandate—A legal command issued by a court.

Material—Important or significant to a case.

Ministerial act—An act that does not involve discretion.

Negligence—Failure to execute a prescribed duty that results in injury to another person.

Parens patriae—The state's guardianship over those incapable of conducting their affairs such as minors.

Per curiam—An opinion written by the entire court rather than by any of several justices.

Plenary power—Full power.

Police powers—The powers of the government to impose restrictions necessary to protect the health, safety, and welfare of citizens.

Precedent—A decision by the court that serves as an authority for later cases involving similar subject matter.

Prima facie—At first view; facts presumed to be true.

Probable cause—Reasonable grounds supported by evidence to lead a reasonable person to believe that another person has committed an illegal act.

Proprietary act—A function not normally required by state statute.

Punitive damages—Monetary award intended to punish an individual for an unacceptable act.

Quid pro quo—Giving one valuable thing in exchange for another.

Remand—To send back to the original court for additional deliberations.

Remedy—A court's enforcement of a right upon the violation of such right.

Respondent superior—The responsibility for the master/employer for the actions of his servants/employees.

Slander—Oral defamation.

Sovereign immunity—A doctrine providing immunity for a governmental body from a lawsuit without its expressed consent.

Stare decisis—Let the decision stand; to stand by the court's decision.

Statute—An act of the state or federal legislative body; a law.

Statute of limitation—An established timeframe beyond which legal action cannot be executed.

Substantive law—The proper law of rights and duties.

Suit—A proceeding in a court of law initiated by the plaintiff.

Summary judgment—A court's decision to settle a legal dispute or dispose of a case expeditiously without conducting full legal proceedings.

Tort—An action or wrong committed against a person independent of contractual considerations.

Trespass—The unauthorized entry upon the property of another without consent.

Ultra vires—Outside the legal powers of an individual or body.

Vacate—To rescind a court decision.

Vested—Fixed; not subject to any contingency.

Vicarious liability—A form of liability in which school districts are held liable for negligent or intentional wrongdoing by their employees when the act is committed within the scope of the district employment position, even though the district may not be directly at fault.

Waive—To forego or relinquish a legal right.

Warrant—A written order of the court; arrest order.

Writ of certiori—A judicial process whereby a case is moved from a lower court to a higher one for review. The record of all proceedings at the lower court is sent to the higher court.

Writ of mandamus—A command from a court directing a court, officer, or body to perform a certain act.

Resource D

Selected Professional Associations
for Teachers and Administrators

AMERICAN ARBITRATION ASSOCIATION

335 Madison Avenue, Floor 10
New York, NY 10017-4605
Phone: 1-800-778-7879
Fax: 212-716-5907
Internet: www.adr.org/

Purpose: The American Arbitration Association (AAA) is available to resolve a wide range of disputes through mediation, arbitration, elections, and other out-of-court settlement procedures. The history, mission, and not-for-profit status of the AAA are unique in the field of alternative dispute resolution (ADR). It is, however, the association's ADR resources—its panels, rules, administration, and education and training services—that provide cost-effective and tangible value to counsel, businesses, industry professionals and their employees, customers, and business partners.

AMERICAN ASSOCIATION OF SCHOOL ADMINISTRATORS

801 N. Quincy Street, Suite 700
Arlington, VA 22203-1730
Phone: 703-528-0700
Fax: 703-841-1543
Internet: www.aasa.org/

Purpose: The mission of the American Association of School Administrators is to support and develop effective school system leaders who are dedicated to the highest-quality public education for all children.

AMERICAN CIVIL LIBERTIES UNION

125 Broad Street, 18th Floor
New York, NY 10004
Phone: 212-549-2500
Internet: www.aclu.org/

Purpose: The American Civil Liberties Union (ACLU) is the nation's guardian of liberty. It works daily in courts, legislatures, and communities to defend and preserve the individual rights and liberties guaranteed to every person in this country by the Constitution and laws of the United States. Its job is to conserve America's original civic values—the Constitution and the Bill of Rights.

The American system of government is founded on two counterbalancing principles:

- The majority of the people govern, through democratically elected representatives.
- The power even of a democratic majority must be limited to ensure individual rights.

AMERICAN FEDERATION OF TEACHERS

555 New Jersey Avenue, NW
Washington, D.C. 20001
Phone: 202-879-4400
Internet: www.aft.org/

Purpose: The mission of the American Federation of Teachers, AFL-CIO, is to improve the lives of its members and their families; to give voice to their legitimate professional, economic, and social aspirations; to strengthen the institutions in which they work; to improve the quality of the services provided; to bring together all members to assist and support one another; and to promote democracy, human rights, and freedom in the union, the nation, and throughout the world.

ASSOCIATION FOR CHILDHOOD EDUCATION INTERNATIONAL

17904 Georgia Avenue, Suite 215
Olney, MD 20832

Phone: 301-570-2111 or 800-423-3563
Fax: 301-570-2212
Email: headquarters@acei.org
Internet: www.acei.org/

Purpose: The mission of the Association for Childhood Education International (ACEI) is to promote and support in the global community the optimal education and development of children, from birth through early adolescence, and to influence the professional growth of educators and the efforts of others committed to the needs of children in a changing society.

ASSOCIATION FOR EDUCATIONAL COMMUNICATIONS AND TECHNOLOGY

1800 N. Stonelake Drive, Suite 2
Bloomington, IN 47404
Phone: 877-677-AECT or 812-335-7675
Email: aect@aect.org
Internet: www.aect.org

Purpose: The mission of the Association for Educational Communications and Technology is to provide international leadership by promoting scholarship and best practices in the creation, use, and management of technologies for effective teaching and learning in a wide range of settings.

ASSOCIATION FOR SUPERVISION AND CURRICULUM DEVELOPMENT

1703 N. Beauregard Street
Alexandria, VA 22311
Phone: 800-933-2723, press 2
Fax: 703-575-5400
Internet: www.ascd.org/

Purpose: Founded in 1943, the Association for Supervision and Curriculum Development (ASCD) is an international nonprofit and nonpartisan organization that represents 160,000 education professionals from more than 135 countries and more than 60 affiliates. Membership spans the entire profession of educators—superintendents, supervisors, principals, teachers, professors of education, and school board members. This diverse community of educators forges covenants in teaching and learning for the success of all learners.

The organization addresses all aspects of effective teaching and learning—such as professional development, educational leadership, and capacity building. The ASCD offers broad, multiple perspectives—across all education professions—in reporting key policies and practices. Because it represents all educators, it is able to focus solely on professional practice within the context of "Is it good for the children?" rather than what is reflective of a specific educator role. In short, ASCD reflects the conscience and content of education.

COUNCIL FOR EXCEPTIONAL CHILDREN

1110 North Glebe Road, Suite 300
Arlington, VA 22201
Voice phone: 703-620-3660
TTY: 866-915-5000
Fax: 703-264-9494
Email: service@cec.sped.org
Internet: www.cec.sped.org/

Purpose: The Council for Exceptional Children (CEC) is the largest international professional organization dedicated to improving educational outcomes for individuals with exceptionalities, students with disabilities, and/or the gifted. CEC advocates for appropriate governmental policies, sets professional standards, provides continual professional development, advocates for newly and historically underserved individuals with exceptionalities, and helps professionals obtain conditions and resources necessary for effective professional practice.

NATIONAL ALLIANCE OF BLACK SCHOOL EDUCATORS

310 Pennsylvania Avenue SE
Washington, D.C. 20003
Phone: 202-608-6310 or 800-221-2654
Fax: 202-608-6319
Internet: www.nabse.org/

Purpose:

- To promote and facilitate the education of all students, with a particular focus on African American students
- To establish a coalition of African American educators, administrators, and other professionals directly and indirectly involved in the educational process
- To create a forum for the exchange of ideas and strategies to improve opportunities for African American educators and students

- To identify and develop African American professionals who will assume leadership positions in education and influence public policy concerning the education of African Americans

NATIONAL ASSOCIATION OF BIOLOGY TEACHERS

12030 Sunrise Valley, Drive Suite 110
Reston, VA 20191
Phone: 703-264-9696 or 800-406-0775
Fax: 703-264-7778
Email: office@nabt.org
Internet: www.nabt.org/

Purpose: The National Association of Biology Teachers (NABT) empowers educators to provide the best possible biology and life science education for all students.

NATIONAL ASSOCIATION OF ELEMENTARY SCHOOL PRINCIPALS

1615 Duke Street
Alexandria, VA 22314
Phone: 800-386-2377 or 703-684-3345
Fax: 800-396-2377
Internet: www.naesp.org/

Purpose: The mission of the National Association of Elementary School Principals is to lead in the advocacy and support of elementary- and middle-level principals and other education leaders in their commitment to all children.

NATIONAL ASSOCIATION OF SECONDARY SCHOOL PRINCIPALS

1904 Association Drive
Reston, VA 20191-1537
Phone: 703-860-0200
Internet: www.nassp.org/

Purpose: In existence since 1916, the National Association of Secondary School Principals (NASSP) is the preeminent organization of and national voice for middle school and high school principals, assistant principals, and aspiring school leaders from across the United States and more than forty-five countries around the world. The mission of NASSP is to promote excellence in school leadership.

NATIONAL BOARD FOR PROFESSIONAL TEACHING STANDARDS

National Office
1525 Wilson Blvd., Suite 500
Arlington, VA 22209
Phone: 703-465-2700
Internet: www.nbpts.org/

Purpose: The National Board for Professional Teaching Standards (NBPTS) is an independent, nonprofit, and nonpartisan organization governed by a board of directors, the majority of whom are classroom teachers. Other members include school administrators, school board leaders, governors and state legislators, higher education officials, teacher union leaders, and business and community leaders. It is rooted in the belief that the single most important action this country can take to improve schools and student learning is to strengthen teaching.

The NBPTS is leading the way in making teaching a profession dedicated to student learning and to upholding high standards for professional performance. It has raised the standards for teachers, strengthened their educational preparation through the standards, and created performance-based assessments that demonstrate accomplished application of the standards. The mission is to advance the quality of teaching and learning by

- maintaining high and rigorous standards for what accomplished teachers should know and be able to do,
- providing a national voluntary system certifying teachers who meet these standards, and
- advocating related education reforms to integrate National Board Certification in American education and to capitalize on the expertise of National Board Certified Teachers.

THE NATIONAL COUNCIL OF TEACHERS OF ENGLISH

1111 W. Kenyon Road
Urbana, IL 61801-1096
Phone: 217-328-3870 or 877-369-6283
Internet: www.ncte.org/

Purpose: The National Council of Teachers of English (NCTE) is devoted to improving the teaching and learning of English and the language arts at all levels of education. Since 1911, NCTE has provided a forum for the profession, an array of opportunities for teachers to continue their professional growth throughout their careers, and a framework for cooperation to deal with issues that affect the teaching of English.

NATIONAL COUNCIL OF TEACHERS OF MATHEMATICS

1906 Association Drive
Reston, VA 20191-1502
Phone: 703-620-9840
Fax: 703-476-2970
Internet: www.nctm.org/

Purpose: The National Council of Teachers of Mathematics is a public voice of mathematics education, providing vision, leadership, and professional development to support teachers in ensuring equitable mathematics learning of the highest quality for all students.

NATIONAL COUNCIL ON DISABILITY

1331 F Street, NW, Suite 850
Washington, D.C. 20004
Phone: 202-272-2004
TTY: 202-272-2074
Fax: 202-272-2022
Internet: www.ncd.gov/brochure.htm

Purpose: The National Council on Disability (NCD) was initially established in 1978 as an advisory board within the Department of Education. The council is composed of fifteen members appointed by the president of the United States and confirmed by the U.S. Senate. The Rehabilitation Act Amendments of 1984 transformed NCD into an independent agency.

The overall purpose of the agency is to promote policies, programs, practices, and procedures that guarantee equal opportunity for all people with disabilities, regardless of the nature or severity of the disability, and to empower them to achieve economic self-sufficiency, independent living, and inclusion and integration into all aspects of society.

NATIONAL EDUCATION ASSOCIATION

1201 16th Street, NW
Washington, D.C. 20036-3290

Phone: 202-833-4000
Fax: 202-822-7974
Internet: www.nea.org/

Purpose: To fulfill the promise of a democratic society, the National Education Association will promote the cause of quality public education and advance the profession of education; expand the rights and further the interests of educational employees; and advocate human, civil, and economic rights for all.

NATIONAL MIDDLE SCHOOL ASSOCIATION

4151 Executive Parkway, Suite 300
Westerville, OH 43081
Phone: 800-528-6672 or 614-895-4730
Fax: 614-895-4750
Email: info@nmsa.org
Internet: www.nmsa.org/

Purpose: Since its inception in 1973, the National Middle School Association (NMSA) has been a voice for those committed to the educational and developmental needs of young adolescents. NMSA is the only national education association dedicated exclusively to those in the middle-level grades.

NATIONAL SCHOOL BOARDS ASSOCIATION

1680 Duke Street
Alexandria, VA 22314
Phone: 703-838-6722
Fax: 703-683-7590
Email: info@nsba.org
Internet: www.nsba.org/site/index.asp/

Purpose: The National School Boards Association (NSBA) is a not-for-profit federation of state associations of school boards across the United States. Its mission is to foster excellence and equity in public education through school board leadership. To do so, the organization represents the school board perspective before federal government agencies and with national organizations that affect education and provides vital information and services to state associations of school boards and local school boards throughout the nation.

NATIONAL SCIENCE TEACHERS ASSOCIATION

1840 Wilson Boulevard
Arlington, VA 22201

Phone: 703-243-7100
Fax: 703-243-7177
Internet: www.nsta.org/

Purpose: The National Science Teachers Association's (NSTA) mission is to promote excellence and innovation in science teaching and learning for all.

NORTH AMERICAN MONTESSORI TEACHERS' ASSOCIATION

13693 Butternut Road
Burton, OH 44021
Phone: 440-834-4011
Fax: 440-834-4016
Email: staff@montessori-namta.org
Internet: www.montessori-namta.org/

Purpose: The North American Montessori Teachers' Association (NAMTA) provides a medium for study, interpretation, and improvement of Montessori education through its publications, audiovisual collection, electronic communications, conferences, and research and service projects throughout North America and the world.

NAMTA endeavors to provide real services in response to the needs of teachers, schools, and parents.

U.S. DEPARTMENT OF EDUCATION

400 Maryland Avenue, SW
Washington, D.C. 20202
Phone: 800-USA-LEARN (1-800-872-5327)
TTY: 1-800-437-0833
Fax: 202-401-0689
Email: customerservice@inet.ed.gov
Internet: www.ed.gov/index.jhtml/

Purpose: Congress established the U.S. Department of Education (DOE) on May 4, 1980, in the Department of Education Organization Act (Public Law 96-88 of October 1979). Under this law, the DOE's mission is to

- strengthen the federal commitment to ensuring access to equal educational opportunity for every individual;
- supplement and complement the efforts of states, the local school systems and other instrumentalities of the states, the private sector, public and private nonprofit educational research institutions,

community-based organizations, parents, and students to improve the quality of education;
- encourage the increased involvement of the public, parents, and students in federal education programs;
- promote improvements in the quality and usefulness of education through federally supported research, evaluation, and sharing of information;
- improve the coordination of federal education programs;
- improve the management of federal education activities; and
- increase the accountability of federal education programs to the president, the Congress, and the public.

U.S. DEPARTMENT OF EDUCATION, NO CHILD LEFT BEHIND ACT

400 Maryland Avenue, SW
Washington, D.C. 20202
Phone: 888-814-NCLB (888-814-6252)
TTY: 800-437-0833
Fax: 202-401-0689
Email: NoChildLeftBehind@ed.gov
Internet: www.ed.gov/nclb/landing.jhtml?src=pb/

Purpose: The No Child Left Behind (NCLB) Act of 2001 is a landmark in education reform designed to improve student achievement and change the culture of America's schools. President George W. Bush described this law as the "cornerstone of my administration." Clearly, our children are our future, and, as President Bush expressed, "Too many of our neediest children are being left behind."

Resource E

List of Cases

Index

CORWIN

A SAGE Company

The Corwin logo—a raven striding across an open book—represents the union of courage and learning. Corwin is committed to improving education for all learners by publishing books and other professional development resources for those serving the field of PreK–12 education. By providing practical, hands-on materials, Corwin continues to carry out the promise of its motto: **"Helping Educators Do Their Work Better."**